Issues, Debates and Approaches in Psychology

AIM HIGHER WITH *MACMILLAN INSIGHTS PSYCHOLOGY*

Also available in this series:

978-0-230-24986-8

978-0-230-27222-4

978-0-230-30150-4

978-0-230-24988-2

978-0-230-24941-7

978-0-230-25265-3

978-0-230-29537-7

978-0-230-24944-8

978-0-230-24987-5

978-0-230-24942-4

978-0-230-29640-4

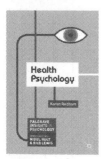
978-0-230-24945-5

978-0-230-29536-0

978-0-230-30273-0

To find out more visit **www.macmillanihe.com/companion/insights**

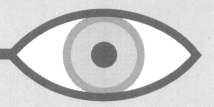

Issues, Debates and Approaches in Psychology

Ian Fairholm

MACMILLAN INSIGHTS IN PSYCHOLOGY

SERIES EDITORS:
**NIGEL HOLT
& ROB LEWIS**

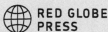

First published 2012 by
RED GLOBE PRESS

Red Globe Press in the UK is an imprint of Springer Nature Limited,
registered in England, company number 785998, of 4 Crinan Street,
London, N1 9XW.

Red Globe Press® is a registered trademark in the United States,
the United Kingdom, Europe and other countries.

ISBN 978–0–230–29537–7   ISBN 978–0–230–36368–7 (eBook)

A catalogue record for this book is available from the British Library.

A catalog record for this book is available from the Library of Congress.

This book is for my parents, for my wife, Rebsie, and for every student who ever asked me a good question.

Contents

Acknowledgements

I've had a lot of help with this book and I hope I've not forgotten to thank anyone. I'd like to thank Nigel Holt, who suggested I could write it in the first place and answered a lot of my queries, and Rob Lewis, who made a crucial recommendation at an early stage about what sort of things it might cover.

I'd also like to thank Karen Rodham and Adrian Scott, who wrote books in the same series – their advice and support proved invaluable.

Thanks are also due to the reviewers, who made some important suggestions and gave me confidence that what I was writing had merit.

Important thanks too go to the very talented Martin Kennedy, who came up with some wonderful cartoons for the book that were unfortunately never used.

And finally, I'd like to thank everyone at Palgrave Macmillan for being extremely helpful, supportive and patient throughout the whole process.

Note from series editors

Knowing where we come from is an important part of understanding where we are now and how we might develop further. How psychology has developed and how this history formed the issues and approaches within our subject is something that Ian Fairholm is perfectly placed to write about.

Ian's professional focus is on the design and delivery of university-level courses. He knows exactly what students need from learning materials and has brought his experience to the development of this book. His interests in psychology are wide, which perhaps explains his fluency with so many different approaches. One of these interests is the history and philosophy of psychology, an area about which he writes with enthusiasm and clarity, as you will see.

- *This book may form part of your pre-university preparation.* If this is the case you will be preparing to take a place to study psychology. You will find that the issues and debates that permeate the subject provide us with a language with which we can talk about and develop our ideas, and structure our learning. As such, this is a perfect book to read before embarking on your university career.
- *This book may form part of your university reading list.* If this is the case it may be for undergraduate or postgraduate study, and it may be part of an introductory course, or a specialized, historical issues course. Ian has chosen material that is perfect for both.
- *You may be using this book while studying for a pre-university course, such as an A-level.* Ian followed the guidelines we gave him very carefully to ensure the coverage would be ideal for students at this

level. Some of the information here will feature in your textbooks, but certainly not all of it, and definitely not in this level of detail. In this volume you will find information that will allow you to outshine other students and make you a strong candidate for the highest possible grades. You'll find a table in the Reading Guide, which will direct you to places in the book that you'll find most useful.

The *Macmillan Insights in Psychology series* is unique in the way it is constructed. The publishers gave us guidelines but realize that the real experts in the area are the academics and examiners who work with students day in, day out. We've been allowed to ask the very best people to write these books, and Ian Fairholm is no exception. He has produced an excellent and academically literate and learned book that we feel sure you will find both interesting and exceptionally readable. We are proud to include it in our series.

Nigel Holt and Rob Lewis
Series Editors

Chapter 1

Introduction and Overview

◁◉▷ Introduction

As a general rule, issues, debates and approaches are not considered to be the most exciting aspects of psychology. For some people, issues and debates are purely abstract – the sort of thing that stuffy academics waffle on and argue about ad infinitum, with no hope of resolution and with absolutely no application to the real world.

Similarly, it is sometimes easy to imagine that different approaches in psychology, such as the school of behaviourism originally developed in America by John Watson, and the psychodynamic school that began with Sigmund Freud, are merely distant historical ideas with no direct relevance to students studying the subject today, or for people trying to live and improve their lives in the modern world.

Part of the aim of this book is to question those ideas, to show that issues and debates may have been around for a long time (in some cases for thousands of years) but that they still have direct relevance today, both to students and to the everyday man or woman in the street. The book will also try to establish that, although the various schools of psychology have somewhat distant origins (to varying extents), this does not mean that achieving an understanding of them is a pointless exercise. Far from it in fact: by understanding where psychology came from and how it has developed readers of this book should gain a richer understanding of the subject as a whole and what implications there might be for the future.

But it would be unwise to launch into this endeavour without first doing something that anyone studying a subject with any degree of seriousness should do and that is defining one's terms.

What are issues, debates and approaches in psychology?

By psychology I mean the science of mind, brain and behaviour, which is generally accepted to be the modern definition of the word. I will not discuss here what is meant by terms such as 'mind' or 'behaviour' because that will come up at various points later in the book, but I will use the two terms frequently throughout this introductory section and I will present working definitions of them below.

It is also worth saying that the science of psychology is relatively new – just over 130 years old – but the discussion of psychological issues, such as the mental processes and behaviours of human and non-human animals, goes back as far as the ancient civilisations of Egypt, Greece, China, India and Persia. I mention these ancient civilisations not to indicate just how old interest in psychology is, but rather to stress that psychology and psychological issues have always been popular and 'hot' topics – that people have always been fascinated by the mind, have always wanted to understand it and have been driven to solve problems such as mental illness, conflict between different people, dealing with troublesome behaviour, managing and motivating people so as to get the best out of them and so on.

One problem with psychology, which is perhaps less true for many other sciences and academic disciplines, is that we all feel that we are experts at it even if we have never received any formal academic, scientific or vocational training within the subject. It is a relatively uncontroversial thing to state that everyone reading this paragraph will have a 'mind' (a collective term for what goes on within our heads – thoughts, perceptions, memories, emotions and so on) and will display some form of behaviour, and that most if not all of the humans and animals you meet today will also have minds (of some form or another – they will demonstrate evidence of having emotions, perceptions and memories of some description) and will also display various forms of behaviour. Therefore we all consider ourselves experts in psychology because we spend pretty much all our time using our own minds and carrying out behaviour, and engaging with the behaviour of others. We may not always do it intentionally but we are constantly collecting data: about our own thoughts and behaviours and about the behaviours of all the people we see and interact with.

In fact, many social psychologists, starting with the influential work of Austrian psychologist Fritz Heider (Heider, 1958), argue that all human beings act like scientists, in that they are constantly forming hypotheses, or attributions, about why people do what they do. This enables us to know what people are like, based on what we attribute their past behaviour to (i.e., what kind of person we think they are), but much more crucially it also enables us to better predict their future behaviour (if this is what they did in the past, then they are likely to do something similar again).

Or at least we might like to think that this is the case – we all like to think that we are good judges of character and that we are able to correctly identify the causes or reasons for a person's behaviour. However, Heider and other social psychologists have argued that although we act like scientists, by constantly making and revising hypotheses based on behavioural data, we tend not to be very good scientists. For example, we only take in a limited amount of data about a particular person or situation; we tend to focus on some details more than others due to preconceived notions or biases; we do not take written notes in the way that good scientists do so; we are purely reliant on our fallible memory system; and so on. The gist here is that we are all psychologists, because we all seek to know why people and animals carry out the behaviour they do, but the equipment we use to collect data for this purpose – our perceptual and memory systems – is biased due to past experience and can lead to various kinds of errors.

But what does this have to do with issues and debates in psychology? Clearly the problem when we make attributions about our own behaviour and the behaviour of others is that we bring personal biases to the data; for example if we have had a bad experience with someone in the past, then this may colour our future encounters with them; we will always see the worst in their behaviour even when their intentions are genuinely neutral or positive. Under circumstances like these, we are viewing the person's behaviour – the behavioural data – primarily in a biased or subjective way.

In science, on the other hand, there is a notion that data should and can be treated in an entirely objective way. This notion is based on the idea that science is fundamentally value-free: that it reflects a truth or reality that is beyond mere opinion; that it relies on a method – the scientific method – that ensures objectivity rather than subjectivity. The data in science, and the way that they are viewed, can be differentiated from opinion because anyone who looks at them carefully, regardless of their **sex**, cultural, political or religious background, should come to the same conclusions. This often leads people to make a distinction between opinions: the subjective attitudes we form in everyday life that are based on our own limited and biased viewpoint, and facts: information collected via the objective methods of science that has been verified by other scientists (or is at the very least verifiable) and that reveals some 'truths' about the real world.

Or at least that's the idea. It has become increasingly questionable whether science can be viewed so simplistically – whether this view, sometimes referred to as the **positivist-realist position**, can be accepted wholeheartedly and uncritically. The argument that people bring personal biases and subjectivity to their everyday personal encounters with others, whilst scientists are able to divorce themselves from such subjective baggage by focusing solely on carrying out the objective methods of science, is rather a weak one. At the very least, scientists bring some values to their research, even if they are only their theoretical background and training, although in some cases it may be much more than this.

It is not the aim of this book to argue that science does have a subjective element to it (this has been argued eloquently elsewhere, and if you're interested in learning more I refer you to, for example, Chalmers, 1999; Collins & Pinch, 1998). However, the fact that we can argue that even scientists bring some degree of personal bias, opinion and subjectivity to their work goes some way to explaining what the issues and debates are in psychology and why they are so important.

◉ Psychology as a science

As I suggested earlier, issues, debates and approaches have perhaps more of an impact for psychology than they do for some of the older sciences – those often referred to as natural or physical sciences (e.g., physics and chemistry). This is not because there are no issues, debates and approaches within those sciences, but rather for two reasons that I referred to earlier: psychology is a young science (certainly when compared with physics and chemistry), and it is a science where what is being studied is also the thing doing the studying – human minds studying the human mind.

The philosopher of science Thomas Kuhn argued that to understand science in general, or particular sciences, we must have an understanding of the theoretical frameworks in which the activity of science takes place. Following a historical study of various sciences, Kuhn (1962) argued that what established sciences such as physics and chemistry have in common is that they have a single paradigm: a set of practices and rules that define that science at a particular time. **Scientific paradigms**, or exemplars, determine what sorts of questions are asked, what sorts of things are studied, how they are studied and how the results of scientific investigations are presented and interpreted.

So, according to Kuhn, all established sciences have a single paradigm, and although having a paradigm does not mean there are no issues or debates in such sciences, it does mean that there is little or no disagreement about the fundamental laws, elements and theoretical assumptions in a particular science. Also, there are clear indications as to what form any ongoing research should take; that is, what theoretical puzzles need to be solved and what methods might be used to try and solve them. There may come a time when difficulties and problems emerge within a paradigm that become insurmountable – what Kuhn termed a crisis state. This crisis state finally ends when a new paradigm emerges that successfully deals with the problems of the old paradigm. The new paradigm attracts the support of more and more scientists whilst the old paradigm is eventually abandoned, and the cycle continues until the next crisis state emerges, although this may take decades or even hundreds of years to occur.

The sort of timeframe that we're talking about here is important: sciences such as physics and chemistry have been around for hundreds of years and in that time there have been long periods of scientific research within particular paradigms, followed by a crisis state, the abandonment of one paradigm and the acceptance of a new one, and this is a process that may have repeated itself many times over. But what of a subject like psychology, where it has only been recognised as a science rather than as a branch of philosophy for a little over 100 years?

Newer sciences – what we might call fledgling, proto or even 'wannabe' sciences – might be considered to be examples of Kuhn's model in action. Physics and chemistry are well established now, but even these sciences had stages when they consisted merely of a loose collection of research, ideas, speculation and theories. This stage of scientific development is referred to as **pre-science or pre-paradigmatic** within Kuhn's framework and not surprisingly refers to any science that lacks a paradigm. Most commonly, when such labels are currently used they are applied to so-called social sciences; that is, sciences that explore aspects of human society, for example sociology, economics, political science and anthropology. However, social science is often used as an umbrella term, which broadly describes sciences that have emerged over the past 100 years or so that cannot be defined as natural sciences.

The complex history of psychology and its diverse subject matter (i.e., it doesn't focus solely on human society and many psychologists never do any work that directly relates to this topic) means that it does not fit entirely comfortably into the social science category either. However, psychology is nevertheless often frequently regarded as having more in common with the social sciences than with natural sciences, partly because natural sciences tend to be older and have paradigms, whilst social sciences are younger and do not.

Different psychologists have applied Kuhn's ideas about scientific development to psychology in an assortment of different ways (e.g., see Lambie, 1991) but, as you might have guessed from some of my earlier comments, the most common way to interpret psychology within a Kuhnian framework is that it is in the pre-paradigmatic stage. Put another way, psychology has no universally accepted way of deciding or conceptualising exactly what should be studied or how it should be studied. This interpretation is easily supported if one thinks about the huge variety of different approaches currently adopted within psychology. Within this book we'll be focusing on only five key approaches – the biological, the behaviourist, the cognitive, the psychodynamic and the humanist – but, as we'll see, there is so much diversity, debate and disagreement because of the contrasting positions of each of these approaches that it's hard to see how psychology could easily become unified by a single paradigm. In Chapter 2, we'll discuss the fundamental principles of each of these five approaches and how exactly they differ from each other.

Some psychologists have taken a rather different stance, agreeing that psychology does not currently have a single paradigm, but suggesting instead that in fact it has many paradigms. But when such psychologists identify these supposed paradigms they usually refer to a list not dissimilar from the one I presented above – the biological, the behaviourist and so on. Therefore, in these cases the term 'paradigm' is not being used in a strictly Kuhnian sense, where by default there can only ever be one dominant paradigm at a time. Two paradigms may compete for a short period of time if there are serious problems and anomalies within the current paradigm, leading eventually to a crisis state in the science, which may be resolved by the emergence of a new and very different paradigm which successfully addresses the problems and anomalies of its failing predecessor. But this is far from what is often described by some psychologists, where the science of psychology seems to be one that has been wrestling with three or more different paradigms for the best part of 100 years.

What seems to be happening in these cases is that authors are using the word 'paradigm', which has a very specific meaning within Kuhn's framework of scientific development, to mean or be synonymous with words such as 'approach', 'school of thought' or 'theory' (Lambie, 1991). Whilst it's certainly not wrong to suggest that there are multiple approaches within psychology, to state there are multiple paradigms suggests a fundamental misunderstanding of what Kuhn meant by the word.

So it seems that to best understand psychology within a Kuhnian interpretation, it should be viewed as a pre-paradigmatic science – and indeed that was the view held by Kuhn himself (Kuhn, 1970). There's no doubt that during the history of psychology some of its approaches or schools of thought might have been considered as prospective paradigms by key advocates of those approaches. For some examples, see the 'In focus box 1'.

In focus box 1

At various points in the history of psychology assorted individuals have suggested that their take on the discipline might create a unified science of mind and/or behaviour. For example, Wilhelm Wundt, arguably the founder of modern psychology, would probably have thought that he was synthesising and unifying various aspects of philosophy and the natural sciences to create a new science of consciousness that emulated the established sciences of the day, such as physics and physiology.

Sigmund Freud (1917) proposed that there had been three great shocks to the collective human **ego** – the Copernican discovery that the Earth was not at the centre of the universe but just one of many planets revolving around the Sun; the Darwinian demonstration that humans are not unique and separate but merely evolved from 'lower' animal species; and Freud's own suggestion that our apparently rational selves are in fact strongly influenced by unconscious forces of which we are unaware and have little control over. This grand proposal from Freud puts his 'science' of **psychoanalysis** up there with two of the most important scientific discoveries in human history, particularly in terms of their impact on how humans view themselves; therefore it's easy to imagine that Freud would have argued that psychoanalysis was a paradigm, had the Kuhnian sense of the term been around in his lifetime. In addition, Freud believed that psychoanalysis was the only method that could successfully treat various psychopathologies in the long term because of its unique focus on the unconscious mind, and therefore set up psychoanalysis as a potential paradigm for clinical psychology.

The final example of a prospective paradigm that I'll offer here is John Watson's behaviourism, which was his attempt, in the early twentieth century, to call for a new form of entirely scientific psychology, focusing solely on the purely objective study, prediction and control of behaviour, without reference to supposedly unverifiable concepts such as 'mind' and 'consciousness'. His strict definition of psychology as the scientific study of behaviour (but not mind) and the standardised terminology and methodologies that he introduced could be seen as an attempt to create something akin to what Kuhn would later call a paradigm.

The fact that not all psychologists agreed with the fundamental elements and theoretical assumptions of the prospective paradigms laid down by Wundt, Freud and Watson – both at the time and now – suggests that they were not successful as paradigms for psychology in a Kuhnian sense. Whether these past failures indicate that a Kuhnian paradigm in psychology is impossible, misconceived or undesirable is something that is still very much open for debate.

Psychology: A fragmented science?

So at various stages in its history, psychology has had potential or would-be paradigms, although as yet none have successfully unified, defined and dominated the field in the way that is required by the

Kuhnian framework. In fact this has led some to claim that the history of psychology has largely consisted of a 'sequence of failed paradigms' (Sternberg & Grigorenko, 2001, p. 1075), and that the current state of the subject is apparently more fragmented and confused than ever before due to a proliferation of schools of thought, all with their own theories, methods and jargon.

As I noted before, issues, debates and even different approaches are by no means unique to pre-paradigmatic sciences. However, there is no doubt that without a unifying paradigm various approaches in psychology that might otherwise either have been entirely rejected or otherwise integrated into a paradigm instead just carry on as they are, unable or unwilling to communicate with other approaches, and so the cycle continues with new approaches emerging from time to time to join the existing ones. Because each different approach becomes increasingly separate and isolated from the others, it can mean that issues and debates sometimes fail to be resolved.

This idea is actually contrary to a long-held idea of how humans should pursue truth and acquire knowledge. The ancient Greek philosopher Plato introduced the term dialectic to describe a method of argument whereby two or more people with different views could seek the truth by ultimately aiming to agree with each other. In a traditional debate people with differing views seek to persuade or prove the other person wrong, but using a **dialectic method** requires both parties to consider the weaknesses of their extreme positions. The end result of such a process might mean that one of the two extreme positions is ultimately rejected or refuted, but more commonly the aim is to achieve a synthesis or combination of the two positions, or at least to encourage the two parties to consider each other's positions.

This approach is sometimes summarised as having three stages: thesis (the original proposition), antithesis (the opposite of, or reaction to, the original proposition) and synthesis (the resolution of the conflict via identifying the valid elements of both propositions and reconciling them by creating a new proposition that takes the best of both). The idea is that the dialectic method resolves disagreement and achieves clarification by careful definition, rational discussion and argument and counter-argument.

As you'll see, some (though not all) of the debates covered in this book follow the dialectic pattern. In particular, within psychology, the nature and nurture debate (Chapter 5) and the **free will** and **determinism** debate (Chapter 8) have often been defined by their extreme positions, but more recently there have been attempts made to achieve some degree of synthesis or resolution on these matters. That doesn't mean that these debates have been entirely resolved, but considerable progress has been made and some of the issues have been successfully clarified. Such progress and clarification may allow these debates to be resolved at some point in the future.

The debates just referred to are often considered to be internal in nature, in the sense that they involve different psychologists, often from different perspectives or schools of thought, arguing and debating about data and ideas. However, psychology's development has not just been affected by internal conflict and the influences of different theoretical approaches. Many of the other issues and debates addressed in this book – such as ethical issues or questions surrounding the extent and effects of **gender** and **cultural bias** – show how psychology is embedded within a wider social, cultural, moral, political and historical context. The prevailing ideas in science and **culture** of the time have often also had a considerable impact on psychology and will almost certainly continue to do so.

Since Wundt founded psychology as a modern science in the 1870s the subject has been largely dominated by white middle-class men from Europe and North America. In addition, much of the research has been carried out on animals and university undergraduate students in psychology laboratories. This does not mean that there haven't been any important researchers or teachers in psychology who have been women, or who have had different ethnic origins, or have come from different parts of the world. The reason for this dominance is partly the way that all sciences have tended to be dominated by white middle-class men from Europe and America over the past 150 years or so. This doesn't reflect the superiority of this group but rather shows how cultural tendencies and discrimination by race, religion and gender can, and indeed have, affected the make-up and history of various scientific disciplines.

These problems are potentially even more serious because, not only have the demographics of who studies and becomes prominent within psychology been affected by cultural and historical trends, the groups of people that have been studied and the way the research has been carried out can be said to have been affected by cultural and historical trends too. So for example, psychologists in Western cultures (i.e., Western Europe and North America) often tended to assume that psychological processes were universal. However, this may not in fact be the case – a problem that is further compounded if psychologists from these cultures don't carry out research in other cultures to confirm their findings/ conclusions or, if on the occasions that they do, they use culturally biased tools that fail to pick up on subtle cultural differences. I'll discuss more of these problems and how psychology has attempted to address them, through fields such as **cultural and cross-cultural psychology**, in Chapter 7.

Already I hope it is becoming obvious that issues, debates and approaches in psychology are not simply dry and theoretical but have had in the past, and will continue to have, serious implications for animals and people. I'll expand upon this point further in the next section.

 ## Why are issues, debates and approaches in psychology important?

Hopefully in the previous section you will have developed a greater appreciation of exactly what is meant by issues, debate and approaches in psychology. At certain points I referred to philosophers, ancient history and questions of whether psychology is a science or not. Some students wonder whether philosophical questions from the distant past or abstract debates about psychology's status as a science really matter. What have Plato's views on how best to resolve an argument got to do with the problems of someone who is suffering with schizophrenia? What does it matter if psychology is accepted as fitting in with Kuhn's framework of science or otherwise – does it make any difference to psychologists who are trying to solve everyday applied problems in the real world?

The links between theoretical issues and debates and problems in the real world, such as the ones referred to above, are not always automatically obvious. But if you look at the history of mental illness, for example, you will see that at different points in time the prevailing trends amongst people who were trying to help or cure those labelled mentally ill tended to favour either largely situational accounts of mental health problems (mental illnesses are really just problems in living), or somatic accounts of those problems (mental illnesses are really diseases or afflictions of the brain or nervous system). There were various reasons for those different positions being adopted at different times, but often there was very little consideration by proponents of one position about the merits of the opposite position. As Plato himself might have predicted, this led to the continual propagation of these two rather extreme positions throughout much of the twentieth century, but very few attempts were made in this time to reconcile the positions or resolve the controversy, and therefore a middle way, or compromise, which identified the strengths and limitations of both approaches to mental illness, was a long time coming.

Arguably the dialectic method was finally employed in relation to mental illness within the twentieth century by an American psychiatrist, George Engel (Engel, 1977), when he formulated what is now known as the **biopsychosocial model**. This model stresses that sociology, psychology and biology are all factors in illness (both physical and mental), thereby taking on elements from both traditional biomedical models (e.g., concepts of disease, illness and injury) and sociocultural theories (e.g., stressing the importance of economic and cultural factors in illness and health), and integrating them into a new framework that considers the role of the three types of factors, not only independently but also the ways in which they interact. This model has subsequently been applied to a wide range of mental and physical illnesses, stressing the need to consider a number of factors when looking at a person's health. It has been argued that the biopsychosocial model is not strictly a model at all in a scientific sense (McLaren, 1998, 2010), in that it doesn't propose what the precise individual contributions of biological, psychological and sociological factors are for individual illnesses in a way that can be scientifically tested. However, it can at least be viewed as a framework that considers an individual's problems in a context wider than merely addressing their biology or their environment in isolation of the other, as was often the case for much of the twentieth century. Therefore, adopting a dialectic approach, which considers the merits and possible integration of different positions, can have fruitful implications for practical areas such as mental health and clinical psychology.

Similarly, although we might question whether it really matters to psychologists as they go about their daily work if psychology is classified as a science or not, the fact is that science is a powerful enterprise that enables the acquisition, organisation and development of knowledge within particular areas. Psychology has become an extremely popular subject since it was founded by Wundt and its diverse subject matter (interpersonal relationships, emotion, mental illness, consciousness) guarantees that people will continue to be fascinated by it. But arguably, despite its many successes, psychology has yet to solve many of the problems it initially identified and this could, at least in part, be because of the continued disunity created by the presence of so many different approaches within the subject.

It's not the mere presence of multiple perspectives, approaches or theories in a science that are the problem, and indeed as I discuss the five key approaches throughout this book you will see that they all have much to offer. The difficulty is more when these different approaches are unable to agree on various things, such as: what are the core principles of psychology; what terminology should be used and what does the terminology mean; what problems need to be solved and what questions need to be answered; and what methods should be used to solve these problems and answer these questions? You will also see that the different approaches within psychology have yet to agree on most of these points, and it is often these disagreements that will form the basis for our discussion of the issues and debates in this book.

These disagreements between the different approaches, and how we feel about and engage with them, are amongst the things that make psychology such an interesting subject to study. But Kuhn would probably have argued that they are also the main reason why psychology has so far failed to develop into a fully fledged science, and also why it has failed to resolve some of its major debates. Of course it's possible that Kuhn could be wrong about the development of science, or that psychology may develop in a different way from other sciences. On the other hand, if Kuhn is only partially right, it's possible that the lack of a unified paradigm in psychology is to some extent responsible for the slow progress in solving various problems in the subject. Many of these problems may seem to be merely theoretical, but psychology aims to solve practical problems via the application of theory, so failures to solve theoretical problems may have very real consequences for areas as diverse as the legal system, schools, the health service, international relations, business and even our local supermarket. Whether psychology is a science or not (or indeed whether it could become one), and what kind of science it is (or could be), may have extremely large and very real consequences for all of us.

The importance of the issues and debates discussed in this book

Each of the issues and debates discussed in this book are important, with implications that reach beyond purely philosophical or theoretical levels. Ethical issues in psychology have a considerable impact on what psychologists can and cannot do and also aim to keep participants and subjects as safe from harm and discomfort as possible. Ethical issues can therefore partly determine the speed at which psychology develops and have a big impact on what sort of knowledge can be acquired and how psychologists can go about acquiring it.

I have already made some reference to the nature and nurture debate, and this debate has long been considered at the heart of many of the issues in psychology. It's an important debate not just because it takes in all manner of psychological issues, such as personality, intelligence, morality, sexuality, mental illness and violence but also because it may tell us how people can achieve their potential and be the best person they can be, or reduce their chances of becoming a criminal, suffering from mental illness or even of getting divorced (to provide just three examples). As suggested by my earlier discussion of the biopsychosocial framework, this debate has become more complicated in recent years, but I'll go into more detail about it in Chapter 5.

The nature and nurture debate also has some implications for other issues and debates that I will be discussing in later chapters, for example **gender bias**, cultural bias and determinism and free will. So we all have a gender and we all have some form of cultural background, but is gender primarily determined by biology or by culture? And how do our gender and culture affect and bias our experiences of the world? And perhaps most importantly, if the history and development of psychology has largely been dominated by white middle-class men from Europe and America, is that a problem? Well, if we accept the notion that I discussed earlier in this chapter that science is fundamentally value-free and relies on a method that ensures objectivity rather than subjectivity, then in principle the subject of psychology should not have been affected by the gender and cultural background of the psychologists who carried out the research, developed the theories and wrote the papers. We'll question that notion again later, but even if it's true there is still the possibility that gender and cultural biases arise, not because of who carries out the research but because of who participates in it and under what circumstances. So does psychology produce general laws that apply equally well to all human beings regardless of their gender or cultural background, or do psychologists need to think very carefully about how to test and study people of different genders and cultures to avoid missing out on subtle (and even not so subtle) differences in their mental activity and behaviour? If psychologists assume the former when the latter is true, then their work may produce a very distorted picture of the truth and this explains why they need to at least consider the dangers of and ways to combat gender and cultural biases.

The debate about determinism and free will is another that is sometimes thought to be purely philosophical in nature, perhaps partly because most human beings just seem to take for granted that they have free will and find it difficult to imagine the alternative. But in some ways this debate has greater implications for the real world than some of the other debates so far discussed.

For example, the nature and nurture debate is about how different factors – some inherited and some acquired through learning, experience and the environment – can impact on our mental lives and behaviour. The nature and nurture debate is about what those factors are, how much each contributes to mental activity and behaviour, and how they interact, but identifying those factors doesn't necessarily tell us how much control they have over our lives, or how free we are to act despite their involvement.

So theories that emphasise the nature side of things may stress that genes have a role in our tendency towards aggressive behaviour, for example, whilst arguments favouring the nurture side might stress that patterns of rewards and punishments and the influence of role models influence our tendency to behave in an aggressive manner. But neither approach necessarily suggests that genes or learning strongly determine our aggressive behaviour; just that they contribute to it. So some psychologists might argue that even if you inherit a particular gene that increases the likelihood of aggressive behaviour in adulthood and you are also brought up by parents who often resort to violence and reward aggressive behaviour in their children, you may still not grow up to be a particularly aggressive or violent person later in life.

The suggestion here then is that although genes and experience can shape or contribute to our behaviour, that doesn't mean that they are entirely responsible for how we behave or what kind of people we turn out to be. Theoretical positions that emphasise free will suggest that, despite numerous factors impinging on our lives, we still have a strong degree of personal choice and responsibility. I'll address this debate about free will and determinism more fully in Chapter 8, but hopefully it should be obvious that the issues raised can have serious practical implications that go beyond mere philosophical concerns. If psychologists establish that humans have no sense of free will, and that their mental lives and behaviours are heavily determined by genetic and/or environmental factors, then this may have serious consequences for how we define concepts such as responsibility and also for legal issues – if a person's behaviour can be said to be determined by factors beyond their control, then is it possible, for example, to apportion blame or guilt?

Psychology may not have all the answers to questions that relate to the issues of free will and determinism, partly because different perspectives within psychology have different views about the debate, partly because we don't yet have a full understanding about the way the various different variables – including genes and environment – interact, and partly because of the problems with defining such complex concepts as 'free will' in the first place. But the key point for now is to stress that this is another debate where clarifying the issues may help us to further understand aspects of the human condition, and in turn this may have an impact on real-world issues such as legal and moral responsibility, and whether people are free to choose what they do in later life or whether they are likely to be limited to a small range of options in terms of what jobs they do, how successful they relationships will be, whether they will be good parents or not, and so on.

Each of the issues and debates selected for this book has been chosen for three reasons. The first is that they all have lengthy histories in psychology and, in some cases, these histories predate the development of modern psychology, so there is lots to discuss; also, the issues have yet to be fully resolved so they are still a part of modern psychology as it continues to develop and move forward into the twenty-first century. The second reason is that by discussing these issues and debates it is possible to gain a richer and deeper understanding of the positions taken by the different approaches within psychology by looking at where each approach stands on each of the issues. The third and final reason is that all of the issues and debates have some important implications, for both the subject of psychology and for the way that real people go about living their lives. I'll say much more about exactly how these issues and debates continue to have relevance for our lives within the chapters themselves. And that leads me nicely onto the final part of this chapter . . .

What will the book cover?

So now that you know a little more about what the issues and debates in psychology are and why they are so important, I should now give you a few details about what exactly this book will do and how it will do it.

Chapter 2 will focus on the five approaches covered in this book – their fundamental principles and the key differences between them. From then onwards, each chapter centres on a particular issue, with details provided about its nature, its history and any practical issues connected with it. I described above the reasons for choosing each of these issues/debates, and there will be one chapter on each of the following: ethical issues in human and animal psychology, the nature and nurture debate, gender bias, cultural bias, determinism and free will, and finally **reductionism**. Do not worry too much about all the terminology at this point – I have already referred to most of these issues and debates in the sections above, but all should become clear within the chapters themselves.

As I also mentioned above, some of these issues/debates, as well as being interesting or important in their own right, are also useful because it is possible to use them to demonstrate where different approaches in psychology stand on different issues. This should help you to understand the issues and debates themselves, but should also provide you with a deeper understanding of the theoretical underpinnings and practical standpoints of the different psychological approaches, which I'll be outlining in Chapter 2.

After the six different issues have been covered in their own separate chapters the book will end, naturally enough, with a concluding chapter. One of the problems with concluding chapters is the need to say something conclusive, and if anything is apparent so far in this book, it is probably that psychology still seems to be a long way from being able to say many conclusive things. However, in the concluding chapter I will aim to give an overview of psychology's current status and standing, based on the five psychological approaches and the six issues and debates discussed, and also consider where psychology might go next based on its past outcomes and current position. But that is all in the future, and we have plenty of material to address before we get there.

Further reading

Chalmers, A. F. (1999). *What is this thing called science?* (3rd Edition). Buckingham: Open University Press.

Lambie, J. (1991). The misuse of Kuhn in psychology. *The Psychologist*, *4*(1), 6–11.

Chapter 2

Approaches in Psychology

◉ Introduction

The main aim of this chapter is to introduce you to the five approaches that will be discussed and referred to throughout the rest of the book. The five different approaches in psychology that have been selected represent important developments in the history of the discipline, but they are also dominant theoretical approaches in contemporary understandings of mind and behaviour, and they are all used in applied areas too. All five approaches will be presented shortly (in alphabetical order), each with a brief description of its theoretical angle and an indication of how this is applied to practical problems. But before that it is necessary to identify an important distinction within psychology that is highly relevant to the different approaches we'll be discussing.

◉ Nomothetic versus idiographic approaches

A very important question that has driven and continues to drive psychologists to adopt or put forward a particular approach is whether they are more interested in the uniqueness of individuals, or whether they are most concerned with discovering universal rules.

The more traditional natural science approach we identified in Chapter 1 usually tends to adopt what is often referred to as a **nomothetic** approach to its subject matter. Nomothetic comes from the Greek word *nomos*, which means 'law', and this is appropriate because in psychology it refers to any approach or method that seeks to establish or identify general patterns or laws of mental activity or behaviour that should apply equally well to all individuals.

In stark contrast are **idiographic** approaches. The term idiographic also has Greek origins – the Greek word *idios* means 'own' or 'private' – and refers to approaches in psychology that are particularly concerned with the individual, that are more interested in private and internal mental experiences or choose to focus on what makes animals and/or people unique.

These two broad approaches are not simply philosophical or theoretical – it's not just a question of what a psychologist chooses to believe is most appropriate. Whether a psychologist adopts a nomothetic or idiographic approach will be reflected in the questions they attempt to answer, the research they carry out and the methods they use.

Nomothetic approaches in psychology are traditionally associated with and favour experimental and other **quantitative methodologies**, where numerical data are gathered from a sample in an attempt to establish the common forms of mental and behavioural functioning common to all members of a population or species.

Idiographic approaches, on the other hand, tend to focus on more **qualitative methodologies**, where the aim is not to collect lots of data from large samples and transform it into numbers to identify what is shared by most or all, but rather to carry out more in-depth analyses of individuals or very small groups, and to tease out personal meanings and the impact of specific contexts. Idiographic researchers are likely to use methods such as case studies, informal interviews and unstructured observations, focusing specifically on a person's expressions within particular contexts.

Four of the five psychological approaches introduced in this chapter can be considered to adopt either a broadly nomothetic or idiographic stance, though as we'll see the remaining approach is difficult to place as it has elements of both. Often the origins of the approach explain why a particular stance is taken: those psychological approaches that broadly attempt to follow the natural science approach, seeking to collect data experimentally to learn about general laws, tend to adopt a nomothetic stance. The ultimate aim of these approaches is usually prediction and explanation that will apply to most or all people. On the other hand, those approaches that are based more on one-to-one therapeutic relationships, individual needs, internal mental conflicts, specific events in a person's past development, or personal goals for their future development, are inevitably likely to draw on the idiographic stance to at least some extent. The ultimate aim of these approaches is usually to provide individuals with greater self-knowledge and to help them become psychologically healthier, so the focus is more on the individual's needs and what is right for them, rather than what rules might apply to everyone. The Section 'The five approaches' will briefly summarise each of the five approaches, including whether they are broadly nomothetic or idiographic in nature.

The five approaches

The behaviourist approach

This was a dominant and influential form of psychology throughout much of the twentieth century and was particularly interested in how human beings and animals learn and are affected by the environments they operate within. Even today this approach plays an important part in theories and applications for areas such education, animal training and mental health. It is an approach that focuses specifically on the measurement, study and causes and effects of observable behaviour and has traditionally been less interested in non-observable mental events, often either assuming that they do not really exist or aren't important for the science of psychology.

The limited focus and subject matter of this approach has often been criticised; however, more recent versions or developments of the **behaviourist approach**, such as **social cognitive theory** (Bandura, 1989), have considered the various roles that thoughts and cognitions play in psychology.

In terms of methodology the behaviourist approach tends to favour experimental studies, carried out on both human participants and animal subjects (both are assumed to share the same principles of learning). One of the key strengths of this approach is often argued to be its tendency to define psychological concepts using standardised, objectively defined terminology. Because of its focus on experimental methods, observable and measurable behaviour and laws of learning that apply to both animals and humans, this approach within psychology not surprisingly adopts a nomothetic stance.

The biological approach

This approach focuses on how the functions and structures of the brain and nervous system create, influence and interact with our psychological states. At a very practical level the approach is interested in the biological origins of, and possible treatments for, assorted psychological problems that affect individuals and societies, including addiction, dementia and mental illness. More broadly, it considers the roles of genetic, physio-logical and neurobiological factors and processes in behaviour, emotion, thinking and consciousness.

One of the key strengths of this approach is that it links psycholog-ical concepts to those of the more well-established science of biology, although some critics question whether instead of psychological concepts being explained in biological terminology they are in fact being explained away (something that we'll address in more detail in Chapter 9).

It shares many similarities with the behaviourist approach in terms of preferred methodology and assumptions about the relationship between animals and humans. It too favours experimental methods and studies the similarities and differences between animals and humans, sometimes using the similarities as a justification for studying the former to learn more about the latter (there will be much more about this in Chapter 3). However, whilst the behaviourist approach is primarily interested in behaviour and learning, the **biological approach** is more interested in the relationships between behaviour and biological functioning. This approach also occasionally relies on data obtained from case studies, but data from unusual cases (e.g., patients with brain damage where the dam-age has led to unusual patterns of behaviour or psychological functioning) are usually used to supplement, refine or challenge theories about general mental functioning. So again, with this focus on experimental methods and generalised laws it should come as no surprise that the biological approach is a nomothetic one.

The cognitive approach

This approach represented both a development from the behaviourist movement and a reaction to its limited scope and subject matter, by moving beyond the emphasis on learning and environmental influences to focus much more on the role of individuals and internal processes involved in thinking, problem-solving, reasoning, memory, perception and attention. It crucially defines the human mind as a type of information processor, similar to a computer, but cognitive psychologists have also spent several decades establishing the many ways in which human brains differ from computers (e.g., although we can establish the capacity of any given computer the exact capacity of the human brain is far from clear).

This approach is perhaps the most dominant and successful within modern psychology and has been influential in answering assorted questions, such as why people forget things, why visual illusions occur, why people make bad decisions and why eyewitnesses to crimes are often inaccurate in their testimonies. The range of mental processes and behaviours that can be studied via the **cognitive approach** is considerable, though this approach is sometimes criticised for its focus on cognition at the expense of other aspects of the human mind (e.g., how does cognition interact with emotion?).

There are key differences between the cognitive and behaviourist approaches. For example, the former focuses more on individual differences in cognitive abilities and less on the idea of discovering generalised laws that explain the way all minds work. Also, the cognitive approach is more interested in unobservable mental processes, whereas the behaviourist approach has often wanted to remove them from psychology. However, despite these differences the cognitive approach still primarily relies on experiments to gather data (though unlike the behaviourist and biological approaches, it largely relies on human participants because the human cognitive system is considered to be very different from the cognitive systems of even our closest animal cousins) and rarely uses qualitative methodologies or carries out in-depth analyses of individuals. Therefore the cognitive approach is still a broadly nomothetic one.

The humanist approach

This approach represented another reaction to the behaviourist movement and to other seemingly pessimistic and dehumanising branches of psychology, stressing instead the innate goodness, uniqueness and potential of human beings. This approach was arguably at its peak when the extreme behaviourist approach it was protesting against was still dominant within psychology (the middle of the twentieth century). It still acts as an important voice in stressing that mental health and social problems can arise when human beings are denied their fundamental rights to dignity, personal growth and freedom, and continues to make important contributions to psychotherapy, education, healthcare and ethics.

This approach emphasises the importance of subjective experience, particularly a person's subjective experience of the present. Because subjective experience is something private and unique to each individual, it is something traditional scientific/nomothetic methods have difficulties with. Therefore the **humanist approach** favours methods that focus on the individual's attempts to explore their true nature (e.g., case studies – in-depth qualitative engagements with an individual and their present experience). Psychologists who adopt this approach are not interested in predicting what an individual's potential and ultimate destiny might be based on past work with others, because each individual and their experiences are unique, but they do aim to help people explore and achieve their potential and to encourage them to experience the world in a way that is consistent with who they really are. Not surprisingly the humanist approach finds the nomothetic stance to be extremely restrictive and instead favours an idiographic stance.

The humanistic approach tends to be praised within certain quarters for its refusal to restrict itself to nomothetic and dehumanising aspects of psychology, but it also receives criticism from those psychologists who value the traditional scientific approach and question the merits of a branch of psychology that is unable or unwilling to make testable predictions, and which doesn't produce replicable or even easily measurable outcomes.

The psychodynamic approach

This approach emphasises the role that drives and unconscious forces play in human thought, personality and behaviour. It is also a therapeutic approach that seeks to help people with a variety of psychological disorders or personal problems. According to this approach, all individuals experience conflict and have their personalities shaped by the opposing demands of different unconscious forces.

There are similarities here with the humanist approach in the sense that both are largely therapeutic. But whilst humanist psychologists emphasise that people have great potential and a fundamental right to freedom, **psychodynamic approaches** tend to be less positive for they assume people have less control over their own psyche and that unresolved conflicts are a key part of personality development.

Much of the evidence for psychodynamic approaches comes from case studies of individuals with psychological problems and the attempts made to find the unconscious source of those problems, to bring them into consciousness so that the individual might resolve them. Each individual has unique childhood experiences and will have developed particular **defence mechanisms** – unconscious strategies that are designed to help the conscious mind deal with unresolved conflicts. In both these senses, the psychodynamic approach is appropriately described as idiographic in nature. However, psychodynamic theorists often argue that all humans share the same basic psychological apparatus, plus there have been various attempts to test hypotheses that derive from psychodynamic approaches, to establish if it's possible to use quantitative methods to provide evidence in support of the theories. In both these senses, then, there are nomothetic aspects to the psychodynamic approach.

Final comments on the approaches

It is important to stress that, by their very nature, the five psychological approaches do not necessarily have a particularly or equally strong stance on every one of the issues and debates discussed in this book, so each chapter will only include material on a particular approach when that approach has a significant stance on the issue/debate in question. For example, the psychodynamic and cognitive approaches have particular stances on the determinism and free will debate, but do not have as much to contribute to the subject of ethical issues in psychology (see Chapter 3). By comparison, I think it is fair to say that all the other approaches have something to say or have made important contributions to both of these issues/debates.

It is also important to stress that although I've referred to five distinct approaches, there is considerable variety amongst theorists, researchers and therapists within each of the approaches, so two psychologists based within the same approach may have quite different positions on a particular issue or debate. Similarly, contemporary psychology is as diverse and eclectic as ever, and many psychologists seek to combine or take elements from more than one approach. Therefore, when I write about these different psychological approaches and where they position themselves on a particular issue or debate, I am obviously referring to general trends and skimming over individual differences that might exist within a given approach.

Bearing all of that in mind, you'll find a summary of the five approaches in the 'In summary box 1'.

In summary box 1

Behaviourist approach:

- Focus on learning and observable behaviour and how this is shaped by the environment
- Main strengths: defines psychological concepts using standardised, objectively defined terminology
- Main weaknesses: limited scope and subject matter; more interested in behaviour than the mind
- Favoured method(s) of study: experiments with animals and humans
- Nomothetic approach

Biological approach:

- Focus on how the functions and structures of the brain and nervous system create, influence and interact with our psychological states
- Main strengths: links psychological concepts to those of the more well-established science of biology
- Main weaknesses: danger that psychological concepts are reduced to the level of biological ones (see Chapter 8)
- Favoured method(s) of study: experiments with animals and humans, some cases studies
- Nomothetic approach

Cognitive approach:

- Focus on internal processes involved in thinking, problem-solving, reasoning, memory, perception and attention; defines human mind as a type of information processor, similar to a computer

- Main strengths: a very wide range of mental processes and behaviours can be studied via this approach
- Main weaknesses: focus on cognition at the expense of other aspects of the human mind (e.g., how does cognition interact with emotion?)
- Favoured method(s) of study: experiments with humans, some use of computer simulations
- Nomothetic approach

Humanist approach:

- Focus on innate goodness, uniqueness and potential of human beings
- Main strengths: emphasises the importance of subjective experience, the uniqueness of individuals and the distinctly 'human' and positive aspects of psychology
- Main weaknesses: unwilling or unable to make testable predictions and doesn't produce replicable or easily measurable outcomes
- Favoured method(s) of study: cases studies, one-to-one therapy
- Idiographic approach

Psychodynamic approach:

- Focus on the role that drives and unconscious forces play in human thought, personality and behaviour
- Main strengths: emphasises the uniqueness and importance of childhood experiences for later personality and mental health
- Main weaknesses: difficult to test and find evidence for, partly because of the focus on unconscious aspects of mental functioning, and partly because the approach is largely based on clinical case studies
- Favoured method(s) of study: case studies, one-to-one therapy, some attempts at experimental work but mixed views on the value of such work
- Has elements of both idiographic and nomothetic approaches

Further reading

The rest of this book – each of the approaches will be discussed further throughout the remaining eight chapters, and their relevance to the issues and debates will be addressed.

Chapter 3

Ethical Issues in Psychology 1

👁 Introduction

In Chapter 2, I summarised the key features of the five psychological approaches we'll be focusing on in this book. In this chapter, we start addressing the first of the key debates, which asks questions about who is studied in psychology, why and, most importantly, how they are treated and kept safe. A number of the approaches discussed in Chapter 2 have made important contributions to the discussion of ethical issues in psychology. In this chapter we'll introduce and define some of the key issues in this area and focus on the issue of animal ethics in psychology. We'll then move onto human ethics in the next chapter.

I suspect that very few people go into psychology specifically because they are interested in ethical issues. That's not to say that there are no psychologists who are interested in human ethical capacity, how we acquire it and how it develops, but that is not quite what I mean by ethical issues. Instead I'm referring to the idea of how psychology and psychologists are regulated and advised so that they behave ethically and treat their participants and subjects (I will explain this distinction shortly) respectfully, competently and responsibly.

Ethics are now considered to be an essential part of psychological research. There are governmental regulations that psychologists must adhere to, so that the rights of their participants are maintained and protected. In addition, national psychological organisations, such as the British Psychological Society (BPS) and the American Psychological

Association (APA), have clear guidelines that are regularly revised to ensure that they are clear, appropriate, current and relevant.

The currency and relevance of ethical guidelines have always been important issues but are particularly important now as the technologies used in psychological research are regularly changing. The use of the Internet, for example, as both a research object and a medium for data collection, has developed significantly since the 1990s, and in a relatively short space of time the range of methodologies used and topics addressed by Internet-based research has increased greatly (Bell & Kennedy, 1999). Internet-based research is just one example of how psychological research can change dramatically over time and can throw up new ethical issues and challenges that might not even have been contemplated in earlier times.

◉ Definition of ethics

Of course ethical issues are not unique to psychology. The term 'ethics' refers to a very broad range of topics and areas but can basically be considered to refer to a series of rules and guidelines that are useful and important when carrying out interactions with people and animals.

As with most issues and debates within psychology, the origins of the consideration of ethical issues can be found within philosophy. Philosophers have considered, over the course of many centuries, concepts such as good and evil, right and wrong, equality and justice, and they have also sought answers to questions such as 'What does it mean to live a good life?' Many of these concepts and questions are not really directly appropriate to the field of psychology, but ethical issues are not just a series of philosophical quandaries – applied ethics is a discipline within philosophy that is specifically interested in how theoretical ethical issues apply to real-life situations.

Psychology is involved with a number of real-life situations that raise ethical issues, and these mainly relate to the duty of care that psychologists have, whether to patients or clients in the case of clinical psychologists or psychotherapists, or to participants or subjects in the case of psychological research. Fundamentally, the basic ethical issues raised in psychology are not surprising, nor are they particularly different from those found in other occupations or sciences, though one distinction that psychology shares with some other sciences is that it studies both animals and human beings.

Not surprisingly, the ethical issues for animals and human beings are not exactly the same, something that is reflected in animals and humans having two separate chapters in this book. It's also reflected in the terms often used to describe animal and human involvement in psychological research. For more than 100 years the term *subjects* was used to describe individuals taking part in psychology experiments, whether they were humans or animals. However, more recently a distinction has been made between *subjects* and *participants*, with the former commonly referring to animals and the latter referring to human beings.

I will explain later why the single term of subjects came to be used for both animals and humans throughout much of the twentieth century, and why more recently a distinction has been made between the two via the introduction of the term 'participants', but it's not essential to know this just yet.

The key thing to appreciate here is that although psychological associations, and other such professional bodies from around the world, may have slightly different ethical rules, the fundamental ethical standards they follow are very similar. Psychologists are expected to act in honest, just and non-discriminatory ways towards human beings, to treat all people and animals in a respectful, responsible, competent and professional manner, and to protect participants and subjects and, wherever possible, keep them from harm.

This might sound like a tall order for the individual psychologist who has to follow strict ethical regulations and maintain high moral standards but fortunately psychologists do not operate alone. Not only can every psychologist refer to the guidelines set down by his or her professional body, and gain advice from colleagues within the same institution, it is also now commonplace at most academic and research institutions for there to be some form of special committee that reviews research proposals and considers the ethical issues raised by them.

Traditionally such committees consist of several psychologists (and sometimes, depending on the nature of the research, the proposal or the institution, non-psychologists too) who will scrutinise the research proposal for ethical problems or areas of ambiguity and, where necessary/appropriate, make suggestions about how such problems might be solved or what clarifications might be needed. Often such committees have the final say as to whether a particular piece of research goes ahead or not (at least within the institution the committee and researcher are a part of). In addition, a distinction is often made between research that can be carried out immediately without any changes or clarifications, research that could be carried out if specified changes were made and/or if significant points were clarified, and research that needs to be completely re-thought because it does not meet the requirements of the committee.

Different committees work in different ways, with some requiring a unanimous decision from all members, whilst others discuss the proposals but leave the final decision up the chair of the committee. Either way, different psychologists can and frequently do disagree about what constitutes an ethically sound study. This latter point stresses that ethical issues in psychology are rarely straightforward, as we'll further explore throughout the rest of this chapter and into the next one.

Animals

When I studied psychology at college, one of the most controversial issues in my particular classroom related to the use of animals in research. There were certain students in my class who felt extremely strongly that animals should not be studied at all in psychology, or at least not unless there was some obvious benefit for the individual animal or the species that the animal belonged to.

There was a feeling amongst these students that over the years psychologists had carried out numerous experiments on animals and that often these experiments were cruel and caused unnecessary suffering. This suffering was considered unnecessary in large part because although the studies were carried out on animals this was largely because the studies could not realistically be carried out on human beings for ethical reasons.

The logic behind these studies seemed to be that psychological knowledge about various topics, such as drug addiction, depression and maternal deprivation, was important and needed to be obtained, but the kinds of experiments that were needed to show clear causal relationships between variables were unethical if they were carried out on humans. It was judged morally acceptable, however, to carry out these experiments on animals such monkeys, dogs and rats, which are considered to be similar enough to humans in terms of their brains and nervous systems that results from the former can be applied to the latter.

So, by carrying out well-controlled experiments on animals, psychologists were able to acquire important data without putting humans into situations that would be considered unethical. What was clear at the time was just how much of a contentious and emotional issue this was for many people.

In some senses things have not changed much since my college days. The basic arguments against using animals in psychology experiments, put forward by my classmates, are still used today. Similarly, some psychological research still uses animal subjects even in the twenty-first century. It is worth stressing that only a minority of experiments in psychology are now carried out on animals. According to Passer *et al.* (2009), of these animal experiments around 90 per cent involve rodents and birds, and another 5 per cent use nonhuman primates.

There are likely to be different motivations for using animals in these experiments, and it can be argued that there are three main reasons for studying animals in psychology. Some psychologists study animals specifically to learn more about the behaviour of those particular animals. As suggested earlier, other psychologists study animals because it is one way to uncover principles and find out more about human behaviour, and therefore it is important to choose animals where meaningful comparisons with humans are possible. The third main type of animal research in psychology, and certainly the most controversial, is the one that shares a similarity with the use of animals in medical research: animals are exposed to stimuli or put in environments that would be considered too dangerous for human beings.

Not all psychological experiments involving animals are necessarily cruel or involve inflicting physical or mental harm but clearly some are and do. Some critics argue that humans should not carry out experimental research on animals at all and that any such research is automatically unethical because the animal is being forced to do something that it would not naturally do and has no way to offer consent or choose not to be involved.

This is an extreme position and it is not one that is very commonly adopted – it is much more common for critics to argue that animal experiments are justifiable when the animals face minimal levels of physical or psychological distress, and then only when the experiments will either directly benefit the animals involved or their species. This latter position is often adopted by anti-vivisectionists who stress that animal experimentation is only justifiable when the animals themselves benefit from the research. However, many psychologists would disagree with such strict restrictions, arguing that hard-and-fast rules about the use of animals are not appropriate because the benefits of research are not always foreseeable.

For example, a single experiment involving a relatively small number of animals may provide considerable insights into understanding the causes or treatment of a particular psychological disorder in humans; therefore in cases like these, it is argued that the needs of the many will far outweigh the needs of the few.

Critics of animal experimentation may counter-argue that here the many are humans and the few are animals, but again it is worth remembering that research that has positive benefits for humans may also turn out to have benefits for animals. Limiting animal experimentation only to cases where it is definitely known that animals will benefit from the research reduces the chances that any unexpected benefits may occur. One thing that is clear from the histories of science, medicine and psychology is that unexpected benefits are often found at some later point and these may benefit animals as well as humans.

◉ Some of the complexities of animal ethics

What is quite interesting about a statistic like the one reported earlier from Passer *et al.* (2009) – that the majority of animal experiments are carried out on rodents and birds, but only a small minority are carried out on non-human primates – is that many people will find it vaguely comforting. This is because humans view different animals in different ways: although most humans do not seem to like the idea of animals being subjected to cruelty, they find the idea of certain types of animals being subjected to cruelty more distressing than they do others. They may not like the idea of birds or rats being treated cruelly, but they might consider this to be a lesser evil than experiments being carried out on monkeys or apes. This may well be because non-human primates can easily be viewed as more similar to humans than birds or rats are, and the more similar to us animals appear to be the more sympathy we are likely to have for them.

In one sense, the way humans view different animals might seem a little odd but Hal Herzog, a psychologist and **anthrozoologist** who specialises in the study of human–animal interactions (or, more accurately, interactions between human and non-human animals), argues that there is nothing logical or consistent about the way humans treat, think and feel about animals. Herzog (2010) further argues that our complex and some-times contradictory relationships with different animals reflect different processes and operating systems in our brains.

For example, most humans have 'theory of mind', a term that refers to our beliefs about the 'minds' of others and also our ability to imagine and appreciate the mental states of other humans and animals, to consider what they might be thinking and feeling. It is this that seems to underlie our ability to predict what others will do and to try to work out what their intentions are, but it also seems to account for our ability to empathise with others – often referred to as our ability to put ourselves in the shoes of someone else or to see the world through someone else's eyes.

Empathy is obviously a desirable trait to have in many circumstances, but it can actually make the performance of certain behaviours more dif-ficult. For example, a psychologist who works with animals may need to have a good understanding of the animals' intentions and be able to predict their behaviour, but that same empathy might be problematic if the psychologist has to do anything negative or unpleasant to the animal. Herzog argues that this is at the heart of the moral ambiguity we often face when dealing with animals. They are both similar to and different from humans and by appreciating their similarities we are able to empathise with them more, but some of the ways in which they are different can conflict with human goals and can also lead to or be used to justify them being treated less well by humans.

Our mental representations of different animals can also partly explain other contradictions, such as the fact that Great Britain considers itself to be a nation of animal lovers and yet meat consumption in Britain occurs at a very high level and commonly, as part of this, animals are raised in poor conditions and have to be transported over long distances before being slaughtered. How can such a contradiction be accounted for? Herzog points out that in urbanised western cultures such as Britain animals that are commonly eaten are rarely seen as living creatures in their natural environments and this enables detachment from the killing process.

It is possible then that Herzog's arguments can be applied equally well to attitudes to animal experimentation. Most people are not directly involved in or aware of what happens to animals in psychology exper-iments. If they were, they might not always be comfortable with what happens to the animals; on the other hand, if the experiments are con-sidered important and necessary, then most people would probably rather that they were carried out on animals rather than humans and, if given the choice, they would rather that they were carried out on animals with fewer similarities to human beings. It may well be that our human tendency towards empathy creates a hierarchy, with humans and the animals that share certain physical and/or mental traits with us positioned at the top, and animals that share fewer of those traits positioned much lower down.

It is worth stressing that this empathic hierarchy is not the only basis for selecting which animals are studied in psychology experiments. As noted before, a key reason for studying animals is to learn more about psychological traits and principles that are also found in human beings. The challenge here is not just ethical as there are also important questions about the validity of such comparisons. If a psychologist wants to learn something about human mental processes or behaviour, then, not surprisingly, the most valid way to do this is nearly always to study humans. But, as noted before, there are practical and ethical limits to what types of experiments can be carried out on humans (the ethical limits will be addressed in more detail later on in this and Chapter 4). To put it bluntly, there is research that can be carried out on animals that could or would not be carried out on humans.

For example, no psychology experiment would involve a human child being permanently deprived of its mother. Many psychological case studies and cross-sectional studies have been carried out on children who have grown up without their mothers but animal experiments on the same topic would involve the psychologist actively intervening by separating a randomly selected mother animal from her child. This hypothetical experiment (though based on real experiments that have been carried out in the past) would most likely involve monkeys or some other non-human primates as the subjects, based on the argument that if you want to apply the results of maternal deprivation studies carried out on animals to equivalent human behaviour, then you need to choose animals that are as similar in terms of physiology, anatomy and behaviour as possible.

The problem with this is that because of the aforementioned hierarchy those animals that are most like humans in those terms are also the ones we are most likely to feel empathy for. So the animals most likely to provide valid comparisons in psychological research are also the ones most likely to have intelligence, experience emotional pain and so on, and this raises the ethical question of whether it's any more appropriate to put them through such emotional rigours.

However, one of the five psychological approaches focused on in this book, the behaviourist approach, might arguably have attempted to resolve this ethical dilemma throughout parts of the twentieth century, albeit rather indirectly. But to get to the behaviourist approach and how it relates to the ethics of both animal and human experimentation, we first have to take yet another historical detour.

◉ A historical detour

The history of animal versus human experimentation is rather complex. If we go back to Europe in the seventeenth century, a time of great progress in the development of scientific thought and discovery, it's perhaps surprising to learn that the Christian church still had a powerful influence on scientific research and methodology. One example of this is that the established church dogma of the time stressed that there was a fundamental difference between humans and animals and that difference was that humans had souls whilst animals did not (Schultz & Schultz, 2004).

The scientific spirit of the time was driven by the idea that the physical universe was a giant, predictable, precise and measurable mechanical machine, and it was thought that the scientific method might reveal that the bodies of humans and animals were also machines of some form. I'll come back to this idea of predictability in Chapter 6 when I talk about determinism, but for now it's important to understand how, in the seventeenth century, the scientific method was optimistically thought to be able to uncover the organised nature of the universe and the biological machines that operated within it.

The influence of the church, however, required a place in this mechanical universe for the human soul, but the theological division between humans and animals stressed that the former were unique in their possession of souls. The soul was thought to underlie all higher states of human psychological functioning, including feelings such as pain. Accordingly animals not only lacked souls, they also did not feel pain and this meant that it was perfectly justifiable for scientists of the time, in the days before anaesthetics, to cut up and examine their bodies. Any noises the animals produced during this process were not evidence of pain but were thought to be akin to the noises that any working machine might make whilst being prodded or dismantled.

The falsehood that no animals feel pain was convenient for both the Christian church, which was trying to maintain the uniqueness of the human soul, and for scientists who wanted to learn more about animals without having to worry about them experiencing discomfort. So there are two elements here that are relevant to the ethics of animal experimentation: the first suggests that animals cannot feel pain, the second relates to the idea that humans and animals are fundamentally different and completely distinct from each other. I'll address each of these points in turn.

◉ Do animals feel pain?

The whole question of whether animals can feel pain is a controversial and complex one. Part of the problem is that pain can be considered to have (at least) two components (Sneddon, n.d.): physical pain or discomfort caused by some form of damage to, or irritation of, the body, and emotional suffering. There is very little doubt amongst the scientific community today that many animals can experience pain, at least according to a definition based on the first component. It is worth stressing that apparent similarities between animals and humans must be treated with caution, but three types of evidence (looking at mechanisms, brain areas and behaviour) can be cited which support the idea that at least some animals do experience physical pain.

First, many animals have similar mechanisms of pain detection to humans (Sneddon, n.d.). This process is called **nociception** and technically should be distinguished from pain because what it actually refers to is a mere detection of the occurrence of damage or the presence of a noxious stimulus, which then leads to a reflexive withdrawal response. It is nociceptive nerves that are responsible for this process and these have been found in a variety of animals, including invertebrates, such as leeches and sea slugs.

Scientists distinguish nociception from pain because it's possible, as in the cases of the aforementioned invertebrates, to have the stimulus–response reaction but to lack the necessary brains areas or systems to have a *feeling* of pain. As we'll see later, the behaviourist approach attempted to reduce all human and non-human animal behaviour to the level of stimulus–response reactions without reference to any accompanying feeling.

What generally distinguishes **vertebrates** from invertebrates in this regard is that the former have their nociceptive messages collated together in the brain, allowing pain signals to be sent around the nervous system and for the intensity of the pain to be varied (Sneddon, n.d.), therefore providing vertebrates with greater flexibility in the regulation of pain. Vertebrates all share the same brain areas for dealing with nociceptive information – the medulla, thalamus and limbic system – but it seems that another part of the brain that is found in all vertebrates might also be important for pain perception, namely the cortex.

The relative size of the cortex varies across different vertebrate species, with the proportion of cortical tissue seemingly related to how high up the evolutionary ladder the animal is. So humans have the greatest proportion of cortical tissue, with approximately 80 per cent of human brain tissue found in the cortex (Simon, 2007). Then there are increasingly smaller proportions for primates (such as monkeys), non-primate mammals (such as dogs), birds, reptiles (such as snakes), amphibia (such as frogs) and finally fish, which have a very basic cortex (Sneddon, n.d.).

The cortex, then, seems to be an important part of the experience of pain as far as humans know it, and it's not clear that animals without a cortex are able to *feel* pain at all. The larger the cortical area in the brains of non-human animals, the more confident we can be that they are not merely responding in a stimulus–response way when they come into contact with a noxious stimulus and that they are in fact feeling pain. For those vertebrates with relatively minimal cortical tissue, it's not entirely clear whether they experience pain or not.

For example, the cortex in fish seems to be primarily involved in sensory reception (particularly sense of smell) and, as mentioned earlier, in modulating nociceptive information, but otherwise it doesn't seem that fish need their cortex to make normal responses to noxious stimuli (Rose, 2002). In fact, if a fish has its cortex removed its behaviour is not greatly affected; the most serious deficit the fish suffers is the loss of its sense of smell, so most behavioural changes seem to be a result of that rather than the loss of an ability to feel pain. But even if a relatively limited amount of cortical tissue doesn't necessarily lead to an experience of pain, there are many other species with relatively more cortex that are very likely to experience something analogous to the human experience of pain, even if it may turn out to be qualitatively and quantitatively different.

Research looking at mechanisms and brain areas can be quite complex to carry out and difficult to interpret, so the third type of evidence is a little more straightforward in the sense that it's how we make judgements about whether other humans are likely to be feeling pain or not.

When humans are in pain their behaviour and physiology change in fairly predictable ways, for example they may eat less food, their social behaviour may be suppressed, they may emit cries of distress, their body and face are likely to tense up, and they are likely to experience changes in their respiration and cardiovascular activity. These changes are particularly useful when trying to identify if a human child who has yet to acquire language is in pain, and therefore they are also useful indicators for detecting pain in animals.

Research has shown that many animals do display these different behaviours and physiological changes, and because they represent a series of complex and coordinated responses it's likely that they are not merely stimulus–response reflexes to a noxious stimulus but are modulated by the brain (Sneddon, n.d.). For example, although fish may lack the necessary cortical tissue to feel pain in the way that humans do, they do show a number of predictable and complex behaviours after receiving damage, such as increased respiration and a failure to respond to external stimuli, which suggests that they respond in much the same way that more sophisticated animals do (Sneddon).

Based on these different types of evidence there is fairly strong support for the idea that many different types of animal experience physical hurt or discomfort. But what about that second type of pain that humans experience: emotional suffering? This can be defined as a physical sensation of pain but without any physical damage, such as the pain we feel during a period of bereavement, following the break-up of a relationship or when we see someone else suffering. It seems much more difficult to establish whether animals experience this kind of pain, partly because of the problems with defining the precise nature of emotional suffering.

Some scientists have linked the ability to experience emotional pain with specific brain areas, such as the neocortex, which is only found in mammals (Sneddon, n.d.), whilst others (such as Rose, 2002) have suggested that it is only found in animals that have consciousness. At the core of the latter argument is essentially the idea that for an animal to feel emotional pain it needs to have some sense of 'I', a notion that it exists as a distinct entity, that things happen to it and that those things make it feel in particular ways. Unfortunately, using consciousness as a criterion for experiencing emotional pain doesn't really help us because defining, assessing and establishing animal consciousness is another conundrum that scientists have been wrestling with for centuries.

Part of the problem with trying to establish whether animals experience emotional pain relates to Herzog's (2010) point about empathy that was raised earlier. We tend to empathise with some animals more than others and it's easy to identify what we think are examples of emotional suffering in certain animals, but it's not always possible to show that they are actually experiencing the feelings attributed to them (either because the animals are simply unable to experience those feelings, or because we don't currently have the means to show that they can). This represents the potential dangers of **anthropomorphism**, the tendency to attribute human feelings or qualities to things that are not human. Anthropomorphism isn't automatically a bad thing in science, but there are dangers in reading too much into an animal's behaviour based on our tendency to see parallels with our own. As you'll see later in the chapter, anthropomorphism was one of the things that the behaviourist approach attempted to remove from psychology.

As you can see, there are numerous complications and difficulties when it comes to deciding whether animals feel pain or not. It is currently impossible to know for certain if animals definitely feel pain, particularly emotional pain, in the way that humans do. This is partly because we are unable to know what it feels like for the animal when it is presented with a noxious stimulus or an emotionally distressing event. As the philosopher Thomas Nagel (1974) has noted, even if we have a thorough description of an animal's behaviour and a good scientific understanding of its brain and nervous system, it's extremely difficult, if not impossible, for us to know what it feels like for the animal to be that animal and to have its experiences.

However, even if we are forever denied access to their subjective states there is already considerable evidence to suggest that many animals share with humans the necessary biological apparatus to detect and respond to noxious stimuli, display behaviour that suggests they are feeling pain in an analogous way to humans, and possess some of the same brain structures that provide human beings with their experience of pain. Clearly this doesn't answer all the questions we might have about animals and pain, and it may well be that what animals experience as pain is something very different from what humans experience, though we may never have sufficient information to know this for certain. However, the body of evidence we do now have is sufficient to suggest that the position adopted by many scientists and the Christian church in the seventeenth century was wrong. Humans are not the only animals to experience pain and therefore psychologists have an ethical responsibility to keep this in mind when designing and running experiments involving non-human animals.

◉ Are humans and animals are fundamentally different?

Although we've addressed the question of whether animals feel pain you might still be wondering what it was that led the scientific community to reconsider the whole idea of there being a fundamental difference between humans and animals in the first place. Well, it was a major turning point, not only for science but also, as Freud (1917) referred to it, a great shock to the collective human ego: Darwin's demonstration that humans are not unique and separate but merely evolved from 'lower' animal species.

Darwin's pivotal work, in which he set down his own particular theory of evolution, was *On the Origin of Species by Means of Natural Selection* (1859). This book would be highly influential, highlighting the struggle for survival for all organisms, in which some species adapted or adjusted to their environments and others that could not adapt did not survive. The book focuses primarily on how the principles of natural selection affect populations of animals and how the accumulation of heritable adaptive traits over time leads to the formation of new species. Darwin didn't spend much time considering human origins in the book, no doubt because this would have been an extremely controversial topic (at the time and, to some extent, even now), though because he suggests that all living things are descended from a common ancestor via the same process, the implication is that humans are not excluded from this.

Following the success of *On the Origin of Species* Darwin wrote a second major work on evolution: *The Descent of Man* (1871). Here he did take the steps that he had apparently been unwilling to take in 1859, by presenting evidence that suggested humans had evolved from 'lower' life forms and by emphasising the similarities in human and animal mental functioning, though it's worth noting that much of the evidence reported here was anecdotal and less rigorous than that of his earlier work (Greenwood, 2009). He continued in this comparative vein with a third work, *The Expression of the Emotions in Man and Animals* (1872), in which he stressed the similarities between the physical manifestations of emotional states in the two groups, again suggesting a shared ancestry and denying the idea that human emotions were entirely unique.

Darwin's work has many implications, but some of the most significant, at least as far as this chapter is concerned, relate to animal psychology and ethics. As noted earlier, in times past animals had been studied because they provided a means of studying the biological machinery they share with human beings, with the added advantage of not having to inflict pain on sentient beings in the process. Darwin's evidence in the late nineteenth century pointed to the conclusion that as well as the physical similarities no sharp distinction existed between human and animal minds either, suggesting instead a continuity between the two. Darwin himself wrote: 'There is no fundamental difference between man & the higher mammals in their mental faculties' (1871, p. 66).

This was an important breakthrough in our psychological conception of animals, suggesting that the study of animal behaviour and mental functioning could be as important for psychology as the study of animal bodies was for biology, and therefore this provided the foundation for comparative psychology (Schultz & Schultz, 2004). But it also raised the sorts of ethical questions we have been considering throughout much of this chapter.

However, it's also worth saying that although Darwin was a pre-eminent scientist he was perhaps also prone to anthropomorphism and, as noted earlier, in his later comparative work sometimes relied on anecdote and intuition rather than hard evidence. He suggested that the lower animals experienced a range of sensations and emotions, had vivid dreams and even displayed some form of imagination, with even worms being attributed with sexual passion and sociability (Schultz & Schultz, 2004). It's not necessarily a question of whether Darwin was accurate when making these claims, but rather it's difficult to see how he could have been certain about any of these conclusions based solely on the data he collected or received second-hand, particularly when contemporary scientists are still not sure to what extent various different animals can be considered to have complex mental processes and emotions.

As Greenwood (2009) has noted, at times Darwin's arguments that animals possess certain higher mental functions seem to be based on little more than assumptions driven by anecdote, for example his readers are encouraged to accept that animals are able to reason since they 'may constantly be seen to pause, deliberate and resolve' (Darwin, 1871, p. 46). Nevertheless, spurred on by Darwin's work and enthusiasm, a new phase of research began in the latter half of the nineteenth century as psychologists, other scientists and the general public sought evidence for signs of intelligence, consciousness and other higher level human mental traits in the animal kingdom.

The quality and rigour of the research that made up this new phase was unfortunately extremely variable, often relying solely on anecdotal reports or narratives from uncritical and untrained observers. There was often a tendency during this period for even well-trained observers and researchers to attribute higher levels of intelligence or more impressive levels of mental functioning than was justified by the behavioural displays offered by the animals.

A formal identification of the dangers of these anecdotal and anthropomorphic studies was finally made in 1894 by a British psychologist, Conwy Lloyd Morgan. Morgan noted many cases of animal behaviour that could be construed as involving higher mental processes but which nevertheless were easily explainable by much simpler or more basic principles of learning, such as trial and error (what behaviourists would later call **operant conditioning**). For example, Morgan observed the occasion of his fox terrier, Toby, opening a garden gate – behaviour that one could easily view as a case of insight, with the dog suddenly gaining a rational understanding into the workings of the gate. However, Morgan had watched and recorded the series of steps that the dog had taken over time (a period of nearly three weeks) which had enabled it to slowly learn the action of the gate via a series of successes and failures.

Morgan agreed with his fellow researchers that subjective observation was a necessary means of studying the behaviour and mental processes of animals, but warned of the problems with relying on anecdotal accounts based on a limited number of observations and of potentially taking behaviour out of context. Morgan was also aware that with poor data and/or a tendency to anthropomorphise there was always the danger of giving the animal too much credit, or of ascribing to it mental abilities that it didn't possess or wasn't necessarily displaying. He proposed a law of parsimony, also called Lloyd Morgan's Canon, which states that: 'In no case is an animal activity to be interpreted in terms of higher psychological processes, if it can be fairly interpreted in terms of processes which stand lower in the scale of psychological evolution and development' (Morgan, 1903, p. 59). Morgan believed that by applying this law it was possible to avoid some of the pitfalls of subjective observation.

It's important to stress that Morgan did not seem to want to exclude anthropomorphism or empathy entirely from studies of animal behaviour but rather to minimise the chances that higher mental capacities would be wrongly attributed when simpler ones might be more appropriate. Morgan's proposal was that principles could be introduced to naturalistic observation that would bring a greater degree of scientific objectivity to both the methods and the theoretical interpretation of the results (Greenwood, 2009). However, Morgan's efforts represented the first steps in a general move away from anthropomorphism, towards a more objective, positivist-realist position in comparative psychology, and indeed psychology as a whole, particularly in the US where the behaviourist approach would become dominant. As you'll see shortly, this had an impact on the ethics of both animal and human experimentation.

Morgan's call for a more scientific approach in comparative psychology was not unique, and in fact by the early twentieth century psychology as a whole was under some pressure, both from many psychologists within and from other scientists outside of the discipline, to focus its attention on objectively observable and verifiable phenomena that could be tested and measured as part of well-controlled and replicable experiments. The science of psychology, as developed by Wundt, had consciousness as its primary subject matter, and even many of the studies carried out within comparative psychology had focused on the idea of trying to establish the nature and extent of animal consciousness (or other mental capacities that at the time were equally difficult to measure objectively).

Darwin's suggestion of a continuity between humans and animals raised the definite possibility that animals had some form of conscious mind but such suppositions were difficult to test. As Morgan had noted, a combination of enthusiasm and anthropomorphism on behalf of scientists and the general public, and the use of anecdotal data formed from isolated observations of animal behaviour, tended to lead to more complex explanations when much simpler ones might suffice. Morgan had arguably challenged psychologists to explain behaviour without necessarily referring to concepts such as consciousness and cognition, but if the scientific legitimacy of using these mentalistic terms for animals was in question, then didn't this also apply to humans as well?

The rise and fall of animal experimentation in psychology

As it would turn out, the most influential figure to consider this question was American psychologist John Watson, who would initially argue that the psychological study of animals should be limited to the observation of stimulus–response connections in their behaviour (Watson, 1909), therefore avoiding all talk of higher level mental processes. Only a few years later Watson (1913) extended the same argument to research on humans and in doing so effectively set down his manifesto for a new kind of psychology, which he called behaviourism (the beginnings of the behaviourist approach I introduced in Chapter 2).

The central ideas of Watson's approach to psychology were not entirely new; they brought together a number of elements that had been widely discussed by psychologists since the presentation of Lloyd Morgan's Canon. Watson wanted to move psychology away from being the science of consciousness and instead make it the science of behaviour, which in turn meant it was possible to make it more objective and experimental. As part of this, experiments would be carried out on both humans and animals and the results would be described in clearly measurable terms, such as stimulus and response, rather than terms that Watson considered dangerously elusive, such as consciousness, mind and mental states.

Morgan had warned of the potential dangers of anthropomorphism when studying animals, but Watson was in a sense warning psychologists that these dangers could apply just as well to the study of humans. It was possible to attribute poorly defined higher mental traits to humans when in fact their behaviour could be more accurately explained in terms of simpler processes, and there was even the possibility that these higher traits might not even exist at all.

Watson (1913), like Darwin before him, recognised 'no dividing line between man and brute' (p. 158), but whilst Darwin had used this lack of a clear distinction to argue for the possibility that animals might share some of the higher mental traits of human beings, Watson tended to focus more on the other direction – an attempt to identify the laws and mechanisms of lower levels of learning that applied to the behaviours of both humans and animals.

This view of animals and humans as learning machines rather than conscious thinking creatures, to be studied purely as subjects under well-controlled experimental conditions, which was already around before

Watson's 1913 paper but which nevertheless became particularly success-ful through his advocacy, had both advantages and disadvantages.

Its advantages, which I'm not going to dwell on here, made psychology more scientifically respectable and gave it a solid experimental founda-tion. Arguably one of the disadvantages was that it devalued the abilities, needs and ethical rights of animals and humans, reducing them all to exactly the same level: that of objects to be prodded and poked within a laboratory, if that's what the research required. That's not to say that subjects in psychology experiments were necessarily treated badly, but it is probably true to say that not enough attention was given to the ethics of psychological experimentation throughout the first half of the twentieth century. I'll say more about how this manifested itself in research carried out on humans in Chapter 4, but I'll continue to focus on animals for the time being.

Animal rights groups first formally emerged in the nineteenth cen-tury, with the Society for the Prevention of Cruelty to Animals officially forming in England in 1824, and a counterpart organisation founded in the US in 1866 (Schultz & Schultz, 2004). Initially groups such as these targeted physiology and biology departments in universities and medical schools (there were initially no psychology laboratories studying animals for these groups to protest against). But as comparative psychology devel-oped and flourished these groups also began to condemn research in this area. Animal rights activists were particularly critical of vivisection, which was not especially common in psychology at the time, at least when compared with work in other scientific areas, but nevertheless some psy-chologists, as would-be defenders of scientific progress, did get involved in the debate.

For example, Ivan Pavlov, who most famously studied processes of learning in dogs, treated his laboratory animals in a humane manner, but also argued that vivisection and other surgical procedures were essential because they provided the only means of studying various physiological functions. Such outspoken support was widely condemned by support-ers of animal rights but, perhaps not surprisingly, it was Watson and the followers of his behaviourist approach who faced even stronger criticisms from those groups opposed to the use of animal experimentation.

For example, probably Watson's most controversial animal experi-ments, published in 1907, involved him investigating whether rats were still able to learn their way around a maze if their sensory abilities were impaired (Schultz & Schultz, 2004). Although this is certainly an interesting scientific question, the methods he employed, which included using surgical procedures to selectively remove the eyes, hearing organs, olfactory sense organs and whiskers of the animals, and anesthetising the soles of their feet, were justifiably criticised. Although Watson didn't continue with these experiments (he moved on to study emotions and conditioning in humans children instead, which you can read more about in the next chapter), other researchers using animals continued to come under pressure and the APA eventually addressed the controversy by setting up the Committee on Precautions in Animal Experimentation. The two key steps taken by the committee were to adopt guidelines already set down by the American Medical Association, which specified how research animals should be treated, and to discourage editors of journals from publishing articles where researchers appeared not to strictly adhere to these guidelines.

The guidelines certainly represented a move in the right direction and addressed some of the ethical concerns raised by animal research in psychology at the time. However, this was not the end of the debate, and many critics of animal experimentation in psychology will point to the fact that some of the most controversial examples of psychological research using animals were not carried out before the establishment of the Committee on Precautions in Animal Experimentation but much more recently. Earlier in this chapter I referred to three topics in psychology – drug addiction, depression and maternal deprivation – that have been studied via experimentation on animals. I didn't choose those three topics randomly but for a very specific reason: some of the animal experiments used to investigate those topics have been identified as amongst the most controversial and ethically questionable in the history of the subject. You can read more about these infamous experiments in the three 'In focus' boxes 2–4.

In focus box 2

Harry Harlow carried out a series of experiments on rhesus monkeys to study how the quality of maternal care can impact on infant development, with a particular focus on the importance of physical contact between mother and infant. These experiments crucially involved baby rhesus monkeys being separated from their mothers.

In one experiment Harlow (1958) raised baby monkeys in a cage following their maternal separation and gave them a choice of two surrogate mothers, both of which consisted of a wire cylinder very loosely made to represent an adult female monkey. At the top of each cylinder was an artificial head and underneath that head was either a feeding bottle, approximately where the monkeys would have suckled their mother's breast, or nothing. The surrogate mother without a feeding bottle was covered in a soft cloth, which meant that one of the surrogates provided food but no physical comfort whilst the other provided comfort but no food.

Despite the monkeys' obvious physical need for food it was the cloth rather than the wire mother that they ran and clung to when exposed to stressful situations and they often sought to maintain contact with the cloth mother even when taking food from the wire mother. Monkeys that were raised in a cage with just a wire mother and no cloth mother at all tended to have greater difficulties digesting the milk and suffered with more diarrhoea, which Harlow interpreted as signs of psychological distress resulting from a lack of physical contact. Harlow therefore showed that bodily contact with something physically comforting was just as, if not more, important for the monkeys than acquiring physical nourishment, and monkeys without any physical comfort were affected negatively, both psychologically and physically.

Having established the importance of physical comfort for rhesus monkeys, Harlow followed up on these experiments by testing this point to its logical extreme – that is, what happens to monkeys deprived of *any* social contact for long periods of time? Harlow, Dodsworth and Harlow (1965) studied the effects of total social isolation by taking monkeys a few hours after birth and placing them into stainless-steel chambers for three, six or twelve months. During these periods the monkeys were provided with food, light and opportunities for exploration and play but were totally denied any social interaction with monkeys, humans or any other animals. Perhaps not surprisingly the monkeys involved in these experiments became severely psychologically disturbed and the longer the period of isolation, the more serious and long-lasting the effects on their behaviour.

In focus box 3

In another series of experiments looking at how psychological distress affects animals, Seligman and Maier (1967) investigated a concept that the authors would call **learned helplessness**. The studies involved dogs either being placed in harnesses for a period of time without any harm being done to them, being placed in harnesses and subjected to painful electric shocks, which the dogs themselves could stop by pressing a lever, or being placed in harnesses and subjected to the same intensity of electric shock but where the pressing of the lever did not cause the shocks to stop. For the third group of dogs the shocks apparently began and ended purely randomly and they were not able to do anything about them happening.

All the dogs were later put into another environment where they could learn to escape electric shocks easily if they jumped over a barrier within ten seconds of a warning signal. Dogs from the first two groups learned this avoidance behaviour very quickly, but a large majority (though not all) of the third group seemed unable to do so, instead showing apparent resignation to the shocks, for example by lying down and whining. Even if a dog from this group did avoid the shock on one occasion, it often failed to do so again. These dogs were interpreted as having learnt from the first part of the experiment that nothing they did could stop the shocks so they simply did nothing, even though it was possible to avoid the shocks quite easily in the second part.

In focus box 4

Another groups of experiments (Deneau, Yanagita & Seevers, 1969) studied drug addiction in animals by developing a method that permitted rhesus monkeys to self-administer drug solutions at will. Psychological dependence on a drug was defined strictly in terms of whether a monkey that had previously had no exposure to that drug later initiated and continued to carry out self-administration of it.

Monkeys in the study were shown to develop a psychological dependence on a number of the drugs, including morphine, codeine, cocaine, amphetamine, ethanol and caffeine, and dependence on all of these drugs, except for caffeine, had **psychotoxic effects** on the animals (i.e., negative effects on their personality and/or behaviour), either directly or following abrupt withdrawal from the drug. This study therefore suggests the addictive properties of various drugs and their possible negative side effects, but under controlled conditions that are rarely if ever possible in cases of human drug abuse.

The Harlow experiments looking at attachment and deprivation in baby monkeys, the Seligman and Maier studies on learned helplessness in dogs, and the Deneau *et al.* experiments studying psychoactive substance dependence in monkeys all reported above are obviously different in many ways but they also have a number of things in common.

To begin with they are typical of the kinds of psychological experiments that are often pointed to by critics as being unnecessarily cruel and of questionable value. The main arguments for the latter of those two points often relate to questions of whether the behaviour of the animals can be directly compared with that of humans. If not then such studies have limited scientific validity and therefore they are even less ethically appropriate because it cannot be argued that the ends justify the means. As we'll see shortly, however, the results of these studies generally are considered to have been successfully applied to humans and are argued to have formed an important foundation for research and development in both animal and human mental health.

Not unconnected to the questions of cruelty and scientific value is the fact that if all three of these groups of experiments were submitted for ethical approval now using the current ethical guidelines they would almost certainly not be allowed to take place, or at least not in the form reported above.

If we're speculating about the idea of a psychologist being allowed to *replicate* these studies now, this would most likely be deemed entirely unnecessary as the results from the studies are well established and therefore putting more animals through the same conditions would simply not be justifiable. But even if the experiments were being proposed in the twenty-first century for the first time, with the researchers claiming that they would offer important insights into the topics of maternal deprivation, depression and drug addiction, it's highly unlikely that the particular methodologies would be considered acceptable, and the numbers and types of animals used in all three experiments (either non-human primates or other mammals) would be other likely issues of contention. It might also be argued that the more extreme aspects of studies like these, involving animals that humans tend to have a strong empathy with, highlighted the emotional stresses that such animals were regularly being put through during the 1960s and 1970s, and also that this strengthened the resolve of animal rights protestors of the time.

There is certainly no doubt that animal rights groups (including some that have emerged from within psychology itself) have continued to put pressure on governments and universities over the past few decades to reduce the amount of animal research that takes place, apparently with some success. The number of research animals and procedures has declined considerably over that period, with some estimates suggesting that the drop could be as much as 50 per cent (Schultz & Schultz, 2004). In that same period the number of UK and US psychology departments with animal research laboratories has also dropped.

On the other hand, despite the fact that the studies I've highlighted here are considered ethically controversial and would not be given the go-ahead using today's ethical guidelines, another thing that they all have in common, and that I mentioned before, is their importance for the development of psychological theory and practice in applied areas.

Harlow's work was crucially important for understanding the importance of maternal care, physical contact and social interaction in the healthy physical and psychological development of young animals and humans, and therefore has had an immeasurable impact on developmental psychology and therapeutic interventions for various species.

The experiments carried out by Seligman and Maier were foundational not only for the concept of learned helplessness, which has subsequently been shown to occur in other animal species including humans (Miller & Seligman, 1975), but also for developing an improved understanding of clinical depression, which within the learned helplessness framework can be viewed as being related to having a perceived lack of control over the outcome of various situations (Seligman, 1975). In fact over time learned helplessness has been seen as a useful way of approaching and potentially treating a range of physical and psychological health problems where a key component is motivation or where the required life changes involved in treating the condition can seem unachievable to the sufferer.

And the experiments looking at psychoactive substance dependence in monkeys were extremely important at the time in establishing just how addictive each of the investigated drugs were and what their impact was likely to be on human mental processes and behaviour. Due to the difficulties in finding participants willing to be involved in experiments studying the effects of illegal drug use in humans, as well as the numerous extraneous variables that cannot be controlled for when looking at drug-taking behaviour in the real world, well-controlled laboratory experiments using rhesus monkeys almost certainly represented the best way at the time to validly assess the dangers of these psychoactive substances.

So, even with these particularly disturbing and emotive examples of animal research in psychology you can hopefully see why it was considered necessary for animals to be tested on in these and similar cases. In each case the study of 'lower' animals would not have provided the same degree of insight into human psychology, whilst depriving human children of social contact for months at a time, subjecting humans to electric shocks in an attempt to induce feelings of helplessness and depression, and giving people psychoactive substances in an attempt to see if they will get addicted would not have been ethical alternatives.

It should also be acknowledged that these experiments have gone on to represent landmarks in the history of psychology, in part because humans, and in some cases animals too, have benefited greatly from their findings, and in part because the ethical treatment of the animal subjects in each case has been openly questioned, considered and discussed by psychologists and animal activists alike, and such discussions have since led to revisions in ethical guidelines and improvements in the ways that animals are treated in psychology research. An important point to stress here then is that even experiments that cannot now be ethically condoned may nevertheless produce important data that adds to our understanding of psychology and may also better educate us about ethical issues within the subject.

◁◉▷ Contemporary animal ethics in psychology

The nature of research on animals in psychology has changed considerably since the days of Watson, who arguably discouraged psychologists from thinking too much about the emotional states and psychological difficulties of their subjects, whether animals or humans.

In more recent times the use of animals in psychological experiments has been greatly reduced but nevertheless national psychological organisations in the twenty-first century, including the APA, BPS and the Experimental Psychology Society (EPS – another UK-based organisation, founded in 1946, which focuses on facilitating experimental research and scientific communication among experimental psychologists and those working in related fields), continue to agree on one thing and that is that animal research has been and continues to be an essential part of psychology, particularly in applied areas where both humans and animals may stand to benefit. These organisations stress that psychology is a diverse subject and that research involves a wide variety of methods and techniques, including experiments on humans and computer modelling. However, these organisations also stress that although experiments with animals make up a relatively small part of psychological research, it is nevertheless an essential and unavoidable part.

I mentioned earlier that the APA set up the Committee on Precautions in Animal Experimentation, which devised strict guidelines for psychologists working with animals. Since then, national psychological organisations have continued to revise, expand and clarify such guidelines so that animals are better protected and more humanely treated, psychologists are better informed and advised about animal ethics and what is considered appropriate research, and penalties for psychologists who do not follow such guidelines are now much tougher.

All research in the UK that involves animals, whether psychological or not, is regulated by the Home Office and there is a specific Act of Parliament that governs such research – the Animals (Scientific Procedures) Act 1986. Anyone wanting to carry out animal research in the UK needs a special licence, granted by the Home Secretary, and such licences are only granted according to certain principles, which are designed to ensure that the proposed research can be genuinely described as essential and unavoidable (EPS, n.d.). These principles are sometimes referred to as the 3Rs: replacement, reduction and refinement (EPS).

Replacement refers to the principle that the researcher should be certain that the objectives of the experiment could not be met by replacing the animal subjects with human participants or by using simulation techniques instead, such as computer models. Reduction refers to an assessment of the number of animals required for the research, combined with an assurance that only the minimum number needed to reach a valid conclusion will be used. Refinement refers to the experimenter's commitment to make every possible effort to keep any distress experienced by the animals to an absolute minimum.

In addition to following these principles researchers must also carry out appropriate training that has been approved by the Home Office and apply to a local ethical review panel, which consists of psychology researchers, animal care and welfare officers, and members of the general public without any particular qualifications. As part of the application the researchers must consider the needs and likely experiences of the animals in the experiments, and show 'that the costs to the animals are outweighed by the likely benefits of the proposed programme of work'

(Lea, 2000, p. 556). Furthermore, researchers are expected to obtain their animals from legally recognised sources, to choose their animals wisely, both in terms of the species' natural history and the temperament and experiences of individual animals, and to immediately stop any procedures if the adverse effects to the animal are greater than were originally anticipated (Lea).

As you can hopefully gather, ethical guidelines and procedures for psychologists carrying out experiments on animals are considerably more thorough and stringent now than at any other point in the history of psychology. Legal requirements and legislation are clearly spelt out and taken very seriously, whilst the psychology community as a whole sets down and communicates principles of best practice that aim to encourage individual psychologists to respect and care for the animals used in their research.

If John Watson were alive today, he would probably be surprised, and perhaps disappointed, to find that psychologists are now being asked to regularly consider the likely experiences of the animals involved in their experiments, perhaps arguing that there are no such experiences for animals to have. But many animal experiments have been carried out since the time of Watson, and many of them, including those of Harlow and Seligman, have raised questions about whether it's appropriate to ignore the emotional states of animals (humans and non-humans alike).

Both Harlow's research and that of Seligman suggest that animals experience complex internal mental states, whether as a result of long term social isolation or not being able to change a negative situation they find themselves in, respectively, and so both sets of experiments, though ethically problematic, in turn helped to question the behaviourist notion that all animals were nothing more than biological machines responding in automatic and rather simplistic ways to stimuli. Experiments such as these therefore played an important part in leading to the changes and improvements within animal ethics that have been seen over the past four decades.

It's worth noting before we finish this chapter that there is far more to animal ethics in psychology than just considering the welfare and humane treatment of animals when they are being used in experiments. Although a lot of the high-profile criticism of psychology made by animal rights groups tends to focus on this area, the BPS and other organisations rightly extend their guidelines to cover other less controversial but nevertheless ethically important areas.

Animals are widely used as part of psychological therapeutic practice. For example, spiders and snakes are used in behaviour therapy for the treatment of common animal phobias (Lea, 2000), whilst pets in therapy, or **animal-assisted therapy**, refer to a popular trend of recent times where animals, most commonly cats and dogs, are used to aid or support the therapeutic process in people facing loneliness, bereavement, chronic pain, depression and so on by providing companionship, affection and a focal point in their lives. These are worthwhile ventures, but it's vital that the needs and treatment of the animals are considered, just as they are for experimental work. And indeed the BPS, for example, stresses that the care and well-being of therapeutic animals should be considered in very much the same way as they are for experimental animals, though in fact there are ethical considerations that may be more relevant for therapeutic animals than their experimental counterparts, such as the temperament of the individual animal and the training it receives (Lea).

This raises the point that although animal experimentation is often viewed with suspicion and regarded as cruel and inhumane, and animal-assisted therapy is often judged to be entirely benevolent, there are equally important ethical issues in both areas. Psychologists need to focus on the ethical issues and potential risks to the animals involved, and not just assume that because the intentions behind the work are good there is nothing to worry about.

When it comes to animal ethics much of the pressure on psychology relates to animal experimentation and, based on its history and some of the experiments described, this is perhaps not surprising. However, as I have stressed, animal experimentation is a relatively small part of psychology, its use is in decline, the ethical guidelines and legislation are more comprehensive than ever before, and all psychologists working with animals are actively encouraged to consider their needs and welfare and to consider viable alternatives.

The fundamental bone of contention between many psychologists and animal rights activists is the use of animals at all, with many of the latter group arguing that animals should never be experimented on unless they directly benefit from the research, and that if the research is being used to learn more about humans, then it's only appropriate to study humans or simulations.

Many psychologists and psychological organisations, however, would argue that to rule out the use of animals in experimentation altogether would in itself be unethical, as it would stall progress in research on topics such as mental health and neurological disorders, which would therefore prolong human suffering, plus it would also prevent the possibility of any unforeseen benefits to animals. As we noted earlier, science does not always develop in the ways researchers expect and, sometimes, unexpected effects can be hugely beneficial to both humans and animals. Without any experiments on animals, some psychologists argue, the frontiers of science are greatly limited to the point that both humans and animals can be greatly disadvantaged.

In the end this debate comes down to two very different perspectives, with most psychologists arguing that the positive benefits of animal experimentation (for both animals and humans) justify the means, at least until a suitable replacement can be found which would mean that animals were no longer needed. Many animal rights protestors, on the other hand, argue that inflicting physical or psychological pain on any living creature is morally wrong unless there are direct benefits to that creature.

With such extremely polarised perspectives a compromise is unlikely to be reached, or at least not until suitable replacements are found, though developing accurate simulations of animals and humans obviously requires that we know more about the creatures being simulated, which takes us back to the question of how we acquire that information. In the meantime, psychologists need to be aware of their responsibilities to the animals they study and maintain the highest of standards, and ethical bodies and organisations need to regularly reconsider and, where appropriate, revise their guidelines in light of new findings and developments. You'll find a summary of the ethical issues associated with animals in 'In summary box 2'.

In summary box 2

The key ethical questions regarding animal experimentation:

- Do animals feel physical pain? Yes, it seems that many different types of animal do experience physical pain of some description
- Do animals experience emotional suffering? This is much harder to answer because we don't have access to their subjective mental experiences

Animal research should be essential, unavoidable and guided by the 3Rs (EPS, n.d.):

- Replacement – the researcher must be certain the objectives of the experiment could not be met by replacing animal subjects with humans or computer simulations
- Reduction – the number of animals required should be assessed and only the minimum number needed to reach a valid conclusion should be used
- Refinement – researchers should make every possible effort to keep distress experienced by animals to an absolute minimum

Other key ethical issues regarding the use of animals in psychology:

- Researchers must receive appropriate training
- Researchers must apply to an ethical review panel
- Researchers must consider the needs and likely experiences of the animals
- The costs to the animals must be outweighed by the likely benefits of the research programme
- Animals must obtained from legally recognised sources
- Animals should be chosen carefully, both according to the natural history of the species and the temperament and experiences of individual animals
- Procedures should be immediately stopped if adverse effects to animals are greater than anticipated
- The issues listed above apply to the care and well-being of animals used as part of therapeutic practice just as much as those used in experiments

In Chapter 4, we'll consider the ethical issues associated with human beings in psychology.

◉ Further reading

Herzog, H. (2010). *Some we love, some we hate, some we eat: Why it's so hard to think straight about animals.* London: HarperCollins.

Lea, S. E. G. (2000). Towards an ethical use of animals. *The Psychologist,* *13*(11), 556–557.

Sneddon, L. U. (n.d.). Can animals feel pain? *Pain: Science, medicine, history, culture.* Retrieved from http://www.wellcome.ac.uk/en/ pain/microsite/culture2.html. Accessed date: 20 December 2010.

Chapter 4

Ethical Issues
in Psychology 2

◉ Introduction

In Chapter 3, we discussed the role of animals in psychology and the ethical issues that this can raise, but a much larger part of psychology deals with humans and therefore obviously their ethical needs also need to be considered.

Critics of animal experimentation in psychology often argue that humans would never be subjected to the kinds of degrading and psychologically harmful conditions that animals have been put through in the history of the subject, but actually that's not entirely true. Just as the history of animal experimentation in psychology has produced its share of controversial and questionable talking points, the history of comparable research with humans provides some shocking examples and interesting quandaries.

Some of the ethical questions that apply to animals apply equally well to humans, such as do the ends justify the means, do the needs of many outweigh the needs of a few, and just how much psychological and physical harm is it acceptable to inflict on someone? But it's generally acknowledged that humans have additional, possibly unique, capacities and faculties, such as language and consciousness, which means that there are additional dimensions that psychologists have to consider when deciding what is ethically appropriate when carrying out experiments with human participants.

However, this distinction was not always entirely obvious or accepted as fact within psychology, something I referred to in Chapter 3. The behaviourist John Watson was very keen on the idea of focusing on the similarities between humans and animals, but less keen on emphasising their differences. Clearly Watson couldn't deny that human beings possessed language, but he was reluctant to use the word consciousness in psychology, believing that it either did not exist or that it was not possible to study it in an objective, scientific manner. Watson's aim was to achieve standardisation across the species, by having psychology treat all animals, human and non-human alike, in exactly the same way, and this meant avoiding speculation and discussion of internal mental states.

Psychology, as Watson saw it from his behaviourist perspective, should consist purely of experimental manipulations, and observations and measurements of behaviour that resulted from those manipulations. It didn't matter for the behaviourist school whether the things that were doing the behaving were rats, pigeons or humans; they were all experimental subjects. The ultimate aim in studying these various different species in very standardised ways was to find the laws of learning that applied to most if not all organisms.

And so it was that in the early part of the twentieth century, particularly in the US, psychology became dominated by the behaviourist approach to psychology, and humans were studied as subjects in well-controlled experiments in much the same way as any other animal. That's obviously an exaggeration, of course – I don't wish you to imagine that human subjects were stripped, put into locked boxes and forced to press buttons if they wanted to obtain food and water, in an effort to assess their ability to learn from reinforcement. But there's little doubt that Watson didn't consider humans to be particularly trustworthy, at least in a scientific sense – you could ask them questions about what they were thinking or feeling when they carried out a task, but you had no idea if they were lying or telling the truth, or if they had any genuine insights in what they were doing and why they were doing it. If the verbal reports of humans – their introspections – were not to be trusted and didn't provide valid, reliable and meaningful data about psychological processes, then why bother with them? You may as well, reasoned Watson, rely on the same methods and data that you have to rely on when studying animals (because of course they have no spoken language) – careful observation of their behaviour within controlled conditions.

Watson was arguably correct and made valid points, at least when stressing the need for objective data to be collected under controlled conditions. He was also justified, I think, in suggesting that it might be possible to compare the behaviour of animals and humans and identify similarities in their learning. But somewhere along the way Watson and the behaviourist movement could perhaps be argued to have degraded human beings as part of this process.

As I suggested Chapter 3, by focusing on the lowest levels of learning shared by most species, Watson tended to downplay the differences and also the importance of higher level traits that might be unique to human beings. Also, the approach that Watson and the behaviourists favoured stresses the need for the experimenter to be in full control of their subjects, which rather limits the power of the subject to assert their ethical rights (Orr, 2010). As I also stated earlier, this doesn't mean that human subjects in psychology experiments around this time had no ethical rights or that they were automatically treated badly, but there was certainly no standardised code of ethics for psychologists in America until 1953, so there was presumably considerable variability in the way in which human subjects were treated in experiments before then.

Little Albert: Origins and ethics

One of the earliest examples of a controversial and unethical experiment carried out on a human (and a vulnerable human at that) came, perhaps not surprisingly, from Watson himself.

As you may recall, Watson had been carrying out experiments on animals that had led to criticisms from animal rights activists of the time. As part of his behaviourist approach Watson stressed that humans and animals were likely to be very similar in their learning mechanisms.

Watson had become inspired by the research that Ivan Pavlov had carried out on the learning processes of dogs. Pavlov had shown that dogs could, over time, learn to associate a new or neutral stimulus, such as the sound of a buzzer or a tone, with a stimulus that produced an automatic, physiological response. For example, dogs automatically salivate when food is put into their mouths, but they don't usually do so when they hear the noise of a buzzer. However, Pavlov found that if the noise of the buzzer was repeatedly and predictably paired with the presentation of the food in the dog's mouth then, over time, the dog would start to salivate at the sound of the buzzer alone (i.e., without the presentation of the food).

Pavlov initially called this learnt association between the previously unrelated noise and the presentation of the food a psychic reflex, but over time he came to feel that this term relied on imagining the animal's subjective mental states (Schultz & Schultz, 2004). Pavlov instead preferred a more objective approach to describing what was happening, in line with the trend started by Lloyd Morgan, and so conditioned reflex became the accepted term for this association or connection between the stimulus and the response.

Pavlov's demonstration of what is now called **classical conditioning** showed psychologists that there was a workable way of measuring what appeared to be quite a complex psychological process under controlled laboratory conditions and without having to imagine the internal mental states of the animal. Watson recognised the value of classical conditioning and sought to investigate the process in humans but also wanted to go beyond investigating the kinds of associations that had been thoroughly researched by Pavlov.

Around that time there was some debate in psychology as to whether emotional tendencies displayed by adult humans were innate, and therefore perhaps inherited. There were also cases of people who suffered from debilitating fears, or phobias, and Sigmund Freud had argued via his psychoanalytic theory (a part of the psychodynamic approach which we'll talk about in more detail in later chapters) that such problems occurred due to unconscious conflicts. Watson's position, following research on newborn human infants that began in 1916, was that there were a limited number of innate, unlearned emotional response patterns (fear, rage and love), but that all other emotional responses developed over time and were acquired via conditioned learning (Schultz & Schultz, 2004).

Watson saw an opportunity to use Pavlov's method to test this position, and if the experiments proved successful this would not only show that the principles of classical conditioning applied equally well to humans, it would also show that emotions could be learnt rather than necessarily being innate. This would provide an alternative account of the acquisition of phobic behaviour that didn't require reference to Freud's non-scientific concept of unconscious conflicts. Watson set up a laboratory specifically for the study of human child development and the end result was arguably his most famous but also his most ethically controversial study. You can read about the details of this study in the 'In focus' box 5.

In focus box 5

The experiment in question was carried out by Watson and his research assistant Rosalie Rayner (Watson & Rayner, 1920). Watson's starting position was that a child is not born with any particular emotional tendencies but rather they simply have a set of overt bodily responses and a series of accompanying internal physiological changes, and it is the co-occurrence of these overt responses and internal changes that forms the basis for the three unlearned emotional response patterns that we label fear, rage and love.

Based on his earlier research Watson concluded that these three emotions occur in all children and that they predictably occur whenever a child is subjected to certain stimulus situations (e.g., a loud, unexpected noise will routinely produce a fear response). However, although these three basic emotions are found in all human infants, Watson proposed that the majority of human emotions, including the wide variety of anxieties and aversions that can be observed in adults, are acquired over the course of a lifetime via the kind of simple learning processes that had been studied by Pavlov. Watson further argued that the three basic emotions became attached to an increasingly large number of new stimuli that previously elicited no emotional response, creating a wide range of emotional compounds. Watson realised that a way to test this theory would be to take a young infant without any fear of a particular object and, via classical conditioning, instil that fear.

The infant selected by Watson and Rayner (1920) for the study was given the pseudonym of Little Albert B and was around nine months old at the time of selection. As for why this particular child was selected, the Watson and Rayner article seems to highlight three main reasons: he was available locally (he was living at the Harriet Lane Home for Invalid Children, a paediatric facility at Johns Hopkins University campus where Watson worked), he had been physically healthy since birth, and he was judged to be stable and largely unemotional. Watson and Rayner use these latter points to mount their ethical defence of the study: surely the experiment they describe could do little harm to such a healthy infant. As we'll see shortly, current ethical principles in psychology research would argue that such a defence rather misses the point.

The experiment involved three stages, the first of which involved Albert, still aged around nine months, being presented with a range of stimuli, including a white rat, a rabbit, a dog, a monkey and a Santa

Claus mask with white whiskers. Crucially, at this stage none of the stimuli produced a fear response in Albert.

Around two months later Watson and Rayner began pairing the presence of the white rat with a loud noise (a steel bar struck with a hammer), which based on Watson's earlier research had been consistently shown to produce a natural fear response in an infant and had also been found to frighten Albert when presented on its own. By repeatedly pairing the presence of the rat with the noise Watson hoped to show that Albert could learn to associate the two stimuli. Indeed, following multiple presentations Albert started to display a fear response when presented with the rat on its own.

The third stage of the experiment investigated whether Albert would transfer his new fear of white rats to other stimuli with similar properties. Albert was again exposed to the full range of stimuli that had previously produced no emotional reaction in him a couple of months earlier. Following the period of learning, however, the infant now displayed fearful reactions to not only the white rat but also, at least on some occasions, to other animals or objects that shared certain properties with the rat, including the rabbit, the dog and the Santa Claus mask (with its fluffy white whiskers).

The experiment was considered successful because it had seemingly shown that Albert, a healthy and stable human infant with apparently few fears other than those common to all children of his age, could nevertheless learn to attach his basic fear responses to a stimulus he was previously ambivalent about (the white rat) when it was repeatedly paired with a naturally fear-inducing stimulus (a loud noise). Furthermore, this fear response could then subsequently be initiated by other similar stimuli (other fluffy objects), something that behaviourists call **generalisation**, the tendency to make the same behavioural response to two similar but different stimuli.

The only downside, the authors note, is that it was not possible to detach or remove the conditioned emotional responses (Watson & Rayner, 1920). It seems that Watson had always envisaged trying to eliminate Albert's newly acquired fears, no doubt because he appreciated the possible practical applications this might have for people suffering with phobias and other emotional problems. The paper even lists several methods that the researchers had identified as possible ways of removing the conditioned emotional response, including 'reconditioning' (repeatedly pairing the feared rat with stimuli that Albert found pleasurable) and repeatedly presenting Albert with the rat, but without the noise, in the hope that there would eventually be some extinction of the fear reflex. It's worth noting that these ideas were purely speculative. Although Watson knew from Pavlov's work with dogs that conditioned behavioural responses tended to abate over time, he could not be certain that this would also be the case with a human infant. He was therefore taking a significant risk by inducing a fear in a healthy child without the certain knowledge that he could later remove it.

What might arguably make Watson's decision to carry out the experiment seem even less ethical is the reason why Watson and Rayner were not able to remove the conditioned emotional responses. It's not that they tried to do so and failed, it's that Albert's mother removed him from the hospital where the conditioning was taking place. It's worth stressing that Watson and Rayner were fully aware in advance that this was going to happen, by their own admission in their research paper. They knew how long they would have to induce the fear and study its effects on Albert, and they were also aware that because of Albert's imminent departure they would not have enough time to carry out the reversal of the process (Harris, 1979; Watson & Rayner, 1920).

It might be argued that even without the opportunity to remove Albert's newly acquired fear, it would have naturally subsided over time anyway without further reinforcement – that is, as long as he regularly encountered white and fluffy objects without being exposed to unpleasant loud noises. The problem here is that Watson couldn't be sure that this had occurred because he never carried out any later follow-ups to check on Albert's well-being. In fact, for a very long time virtually nothing was known about what happened to Albert in later life, leading to much speculation and occasionally spurious claims on the part of various psychologists (Harris, 1979).

Interestingly, Albert's real identity and the story of his later life may only very recently have been uncovered. Beck, Levinson, and Irons (2009) carried out a seven-year search that involved reviewing Watson's work and correspondence, as well as assorted public documents, and they managed to establish the location of Watson and Rayner's original experiment. Via these sources they believe that they were able to identify Albert's mother and, from this, reveal his real name as one Douglas Merritte. There was little evidence available to confirm this, though careful examination of a photograph of Douglas and comparisons with Watson and Rayner's filmed footage of their experiment suggests that he and Albert B were one and the same.

Assuming this is the case, the same lack of evidence means that it's impossible to know whether Albert/Douglas suffered any longer term psychological problems (such as a phobia of animals) as a result of the Watson and Rayner study. What is known, however, is that if Albert was indeed Douglas then his story did not end happily, for he died at the age of six of hydrocephalus, a build-up of fluid in his brain.

As for Watson himself, the study of Albert B would represent his last official academic paper because following a series of scandalous events in his life, completely unrelated to either his research with animals or children, his career in academia came to an end. He did have some involvement a few years later with a study that sought to investigate the one thing he had not had chance to do with Albert: the elimination of a conditioned fear of an animal in a young child, and the experiment, carried out by Mary Cover Jones, did appear to have a successful result (Greenwood, 2009; Schultz & Schultz, 2004), which perhaps in some way vindicates Watson's beliefs about the merits of the Albert B study.

Was the Albert B study unethical?

At the time the study seemingly generated little fuss – perhaps this is because it was very much a product of its time, or perhaps it was overshadowed by the big ethical controversy of the period: the use of animals in experimentation.

Although Watson and Rayner (1920) wrote in their report of the experiment that they didn't believe Albert would come to any harm, it's clear that they themselves had certain doubts about the procedures. They wrote of their considerable hesitation when they came to actually induce the fear experimentally and also commented on the responsibility that doing this placed on them.

Their final justification for inducing the fear conditioning was that Albert had lived a sheltered life up until then (having spent almost the first year of his life at the Harriet Lane Home for Invalid Children) but would in the future encounter frightening situations anyway, whether they carried out the experiment or not, implying that one distressing situation introduced experimentally would not make much difference either way. Perhaps not surprisingly, current ethical guidelines do not agree with such a conclusion.

In fact, if an ethics committee was considering the Albert B study now it's likely that it would be rejected on numerous grounds. One crucial element would be Albert's age – all psychology research that is carried out on children has very strict ethical rules and regulations associated with it, but it's considered that very young children are particularly vulnerable.

In addition, it would be considered highly unethical to expose a human to intentionally frightening stimuli, unless they had given their informed consent and even then they would have to be informed of the likely risks and possible benefits of the research. Of course Albert was not in a position to give his consent and in studies involving participants under the age of eighteen years parents or guardians have to give their consent instead. All of the available evidence suggests that Albert's mother did give consent for the research to take place, though it's unclear how much information she received about exactly what it would involve and whether she was present when the experimental trials took place (current ethical guidelines would suggest that a parent or guardian should be on hand, both to comfort the infant if necessary and to withdraw them if they have any concerns about the research). It's also highly unlikely that Albert's mother was fully informed of the likely risks of the study because it's not clear that Watson and Rayner were in any position to know what those risks were.

It's also now a general principle of experiments in psychology that human participants should not be made to suffer unnecessary distress, and this is especially true for vulnerable groups such as young children. In this case the distress was entirely unnecessary because, by Watson and Rayner's admission, Albert was an emotionally stable and healthy child. He had nothing to gain from experiencing the distress of the experiment, nor from acquiring a conditioned fear of stimuli he previously had no fear of, and Watson and Rayner knew in advance that they would not have an opportunity to reverse the procedure – assuming that they could have done so, which of course was by no means certain.

When evaluating past psychological experiments in terms of their ethical status it is sometimes considered appropriate to suggest that even if a particular experiment doesn't live up to contemporary ethical standards at least we can learn from its results, as this adds to scientific knowledge and also means that future psychologists can consider alternative and more ethical ways of further exploring the area. In fact, we noted that this stance has been taken with the controversial animal experiments reported in Chapter 3. Following this logic, it's sometimes argued that the Watson and Rayner study still represents an influential landmark in psychology despite its ethical failings. However, although there is no doubt that the research with Albert may have inspired later psychologists to further investigate methods to treat fears and phobias in humans, including the aforementioned study by Mary Cover Jones, it's debateable whether the Watson and Rayner study can be considered a clear-cut and valid example of psychological science.

For example, Albert was a single case and therefore it is unwise and unjustifiable to generalise his behaviour to a wider population. Perhaps a reasonable response to this would be to suggest that the trials with Albert merely represented a pilot study; and if Watson had not left academia, we might have seen him replicate and verify the findings with other children. However, subsequent attempts by Watson's contemporaries to replicate his findings proved unsuccessful (Harris, 1979).

Furthermore, Albert's emotional reactions to the different stimuli across different trials were often inconsistent or ambiguous, which suggests that such emotional reactions do not provide easily measurable and verifiable objective data. In fact when reading their article it appears that Watson and Rayner interpreted Albert's emotional states and made somewhat subjective judgements about whether he showed consistent fear behaviour in response to the stimuli he was presented with. Such ambiguous data and subjective interpretations are hardly in keeping with Watson's vision of an objective science of psychology that uses standardised methodologies and measurements. It's also worth stating that Watson's failure to carry out any long-term follow-up study of Albert is not only ethically problematic, it is also another methodological weakness of the experiment (Harris, 1979).

So overall then, the Watson and Rayner study is not only ethically questionable, it is not even possible to refer to it as a well-designed piece of research that set-down a solid and objective methodology and that provided clear results for later psychologists to replicate and build on.

 ## Electric shocks and prison simulations: Later ethical challenges for psychology

So the Albert B study is a classic example of how a lack of standardised ethical guidelines in psychology can lead to dubious treatment of humans as well as animals, even when the psychologists themselves acknowledge that with their research comes a considerable level of responsibility. It's perhaps surprising in a way that it took as long as it did for the APA to decide on the need to develop a code of ethics for its membership (the APA was founded in 1892 but as noted earlier it didn't develop a code of ethics until 1953).

It's also worth stressing, however, that, just as with the ethical issues associated with animal research discussed in Chapter 3, the development of a code of ethics did not mean the end of ethically controversial research with human participants in psychology. A number of particularly controversial experiments were carried out in a period covering the 1960s and 1970s. It's interesting to note that the controversial animal experiments described earlier were carried out during a similar time period, suggesting that this was a highly creative time in the history of psychology, but also a time when psychologists were pushing at the limits in terms of what was considered ethically acceptable for scientific research. I'm not going to go into a great deal of detail here about the following two examples of controversial experiments carried out on humans during this period because each has been covered in considerable detail elsewhere, but nevertheless a very brief summary is required just to highlight the ethical issues involved.

Milgram (1963) carried out two experiments on obedience to authority. Although the experiments were subtly different, both involved deceiving participants into thinking that they had been randomly allocated to the role of a teacher and that they were required to ask another participant, who had been assigned to the role of learner (but was actually a confederate of the experimenter), a series of questions. Participants were told that the research was investigating the impact of punishment on learning and the teachers were required to administer electric shocks to the learner every time he got an answer wrong or refused/failed to answer, with the voltage of the shock apparently increasing each time.

In reality there were no real shocks and the answers from the learner (who was supposedly in the next room), and his later sounds of protest and pain, were all pre-recorded and played on a tape that could be clearly heard by the teacher, as though the learner really was receiving the shocks in the adjacent room. Teachers were encouraged by a pseudo experimenter to continue to administer the shocks even when it was apparent (from the tape) that the learner was in distress and, at later stages of the experiment, unconscious or possibly even dead.

The real participants playing the teacher role clearly found the experience distressing and frequently expressed concern for the learner and questioned whether they should continue with the experiment. Nevertheless all of the teachers administered shocks up to the 300-volt level, and a majority went up to the maximum level of 450 volts before firmly refusing to carry on. The 'generator', which the teachers used to administer the shocks, clearly indicated the danger of the higher voltages and there was little ambiguity as to the apparent effects of the shocks on the learner. Although the teachers obediently carried out the experiment, the stress of doing so clearly took its toll on them – the real participants showed great anguish and exhibited overt signs of intense stress, with some even experiencing seizures.

Whilst the Milgram studies investigated whether participants would inflict harm on another person simply because they were told to by an authority figure, another study carried out by Haney, Banks and Zimbardo (1973) was interested in what would happen when students were randomly allocated to positions of power or weakness.

This field experiment is often referred to as the Stanford prison experiment and involved randomly assigning a group of mentally stable and mature male students to two different roles – each student would either become a guard or a prisoner in a simulated prison environment for a period of two weeks.

Those allocated as prisoners were 'arrested' on the first day of the experiment and taken to the mock prison where they were incarcerated, denied personal belongings and kept under constant surveillance for the rest of the experiment's duration. Those in the guard role were given the task of maintaining a reasonable level of order to ensure the prison could function effectively, though without any specific details of how that might be achieved.

Within a very short period of time the mood in this mock prison environment became distinctly negative, with prisoners becoming extremely passive and several showing signs of intense stress and depression. The experimenters emphasised that they would not accept any physical violence in the prison and the guards kept to this rule but nevertheless commonly displayed less direct aggressive behaviour to the prisoners, including frequent verbal abuse. Indeed a subset of the guards regularly harassed and humiliated the prisoners in increasingly creative and cruel ways, even as it was obvious that prisoner morale was deteriorating. As noted above, the simulation was due to run for two weeks, but because of the intense stress responses of some of the prisoners and the increasing aggression of some of the guards, it was stopped after only six days.

The ethics of the Milgram obedience studies and the Stanford prison experiment

Both of these research studies are legendary and infamous within psychology. There is no doubt that both provided important insights into aspects of human behaviour and experience, particularly those that relate to the use and abuse of power, and both keenly highlight the dangers of such abuses, of how obedience to perceived authority figures can lead to unwise decision-making and harm to others, and how certain environments and social roles can lead us to become tyrants, bullies or victims. But perhaps not surprisingly, both have also raised significant ethical objections.

These objections, some made at the time the studies were published and some since then, have come from various different sources within psychology, but they are particularly linked with one of the approaches discussed in this book, namely the humanist approach. Given that psychologists who adopt this approach tend to oppose dehumanising aspects of psychology, stress the innate goodness of human beings and consider that they have fundamental rights to dignity and freedom, it's perhaps not surprising that they should have something critical to say about experiments such as those carried out by Milgram and Haney *et al*. Of course, one doesn't have to be from the humanist approach to criticise such experiments on ethical grounds. Some psychologists who have outspokenly criticised these experiments over the years would not necessarily consider themselves to be a part of the humanist approach, but nevertheless their line of ethical criticism may still reflect this approach in spirit.

For the experiments on obedience the main areas for ethical concern are that the participants were deceived on a number of levels, which amongst other things violated their full right to be able to choose whether they wanted to be involved in the study or not, and they were also not protected from distress and emotional conflict. Current ethical guidelines suggest that humans should not have to face levels of distress any greater than those they would normally be likely to face in real life, but being put in a position where you are led to believe you have killed another human being is not something that most people face day-to-day. The distress participants experienced during the experiment itself is not the only issue either; the revelation that they could carry out such acts might have had long-term consequences for their self-concept and psychological well-being.

It can also be debated whether Milgram's participants were given the right to withdraw from the experiment, something that is considered fundamental to all psychological research carried out on humans. Although participants did technically have the option of withdrawing from the study at any time, and were informed that the money they had been paid for taking part was theirs regardless of whether they completed it fully or not, one of the study's key features involved the pseudo experimenter issuing a series of standardised prompts whenever the teacher expressed doubts about carrying on with the shocks and the questions, for example 'the experiment requires that you continue', 'it is absolutely essential that you continue' and 'you have no other choice, you must go on' (Milgram, 1963). Although participants did have every right not to carry on, these prompts suggested the exact opposite.

Milgram himself and others have offered strong counter-arguments against these ethical criticisms. On the grounds of deceit and denying participants the right to withdraw, Milgram is clearly guilty, and yet it's difficult to see how the experiments could have been carried out without these two aspects. Without the deception it's impossible to be sure how people would truly act when placed in such a situation – the well-known experimental phenomenon of social desirability suggests that when participants know they are being judged or tested morally they will seek to present their best side, to display more morally acceptable forms of behaviour and to generally act more in the way that society would expect them to, though of course this may be very different from how they would act if they were not aware of their involvement in the experiment (Coolican, 1999).

Participants who knew in advance they were being tested on their willingness to inflict harm on another person under the influence of an authority figure would almost certainly be much more restrained than those who were deceived in Milgram's experiments. This is supported by the fact that whenever students or members of the general public are asked if they think that they, in the same situation, would go up to the 450-volt level, it's very rare to hear someone say that they would. The key point of Milgram's experiments is surely that hardly anyone thinks that they would or could, but nevertheless a surprisingly large proportion of people do. Similarly, it's hard to see how participants who were constantly reminded of their right to withdraw could be meaningfully tested on their tendency to follow orders to such an extreme end.

The use of deception in Milgram's experiments, and the suggestion that participants were denied the right to withdraw, represent fundamental violations of good ethical practice, and yet these studies are unusual in that these very violations are at the heart of what is being investigated – without the violations the validity of the studies is seriously threatened and the benefits of the research are diminished or lost. Although ethical bodies in psychology stress that deception should be avoided at all costs they have also identified possible ways that psychologists who feel they must deceive because of their research topic can do so in as responsible and ethical a way as possible.

One way is to effectively gain permission to deceive (Coolican, 1999) so that volunteers who are signing up to a participant pool or similar are given a number of options about different kinds of research. They are encouraged to only select those types of study that they would be willing and comfortable to participate in, and one of the options could refer to, for example, 'research in which you will be misled about the purpose until afterward' (Coolican, 1999, p. 479). However, there are potential concerns about getting participants to commit to what kinds of studies they would wish to participate in far in advance – they may forget or change their mind – plus there is the practical issue for researchers of needing access to a participant pool of this kind to carry out a particular piece of research. A final concern about presenting potential participants with this kind of information is that it may make them naturally suspicious and wary about any psychological research they are involved in – that is, if they are told that some of the research they might participate in involves being misled they may actively look out for such deception when participating, whether it's there or not.

Another more common method used to address the issues raised by deceiving participants is to ensure that they are given a particularly comprehensive debriefing. All psychological research with humans should involve some form of debriefing, in which the participants are given information about the study, its rationale and background. The true purpose and aims should also be fully explained and, if participants might have good reason to feel anxious, distressed or more negative about themselves afterwards, researchers should seek to offer advice and support to address those concerns. In studies where participants have been deceived, however, particular care must be taken to reassure, explain and advise.

Milgram, for example, went to great lengths to debrief and follow-up on his participants. In addition to debriefing each participant at length immediately following the experiment itself, a few weeks later he sent the ex-participants a questionnaire: 84 per cent said that they had been 'glad' or 'very glad' to take part in the original experiments, with only 1 per cent expressing regret at having taken part. Furthermore, a year later he arranged for an independent psychiatrist to interview a random sample of the former participants, a process that indicated there was no evidence of psychological harm or trauma (Milgram, 1974). Although it's impossible to know for certain how many of the participants were adversely affected by their involvement in the experiments, and to what extent, there is no doubt that Milgram made greater efforts to debrief his participants and follow-up on their psychological well-being than most psychologists have, before or since.

The third and final recommendation made by ethical bodies to researchers considering the use of deception in their experiments is to get independent advice on how its use might affect the participants involved. In fact ethical bodies encourage researchers to consult with disinterested third parties about any aspects of their work that might be considered ethically problematic.

As far as I'm aware, Milgram didn't specifically seek further advice about the use of deception but he did question a number of people before the study, including psychiatrists, academics, university students and middle-class adults, and asked them to indicate how many of the participants they thought would go all the way up to the maximum shock value of 450 volts. The consensus was that virtually no one would – there were estimates that about 1 per cent of the sample might, but it was thought that most would stop around the 150-volt level, which contrasts quite dramatically with the 65 per cent in the study who actually did go up to the maximum. So although many critics argued that Milgram shouldn't have put his participants through that level of stress and internal conflict, it could be argued that no one really expected so many of the participants would find themselves facing the dilemma of whether to go to 450 volts or not, because most were expected to have refused to go on long before that.

Aronson (2003) has argued that it is this very fact that makes people particularly question the ethics of Milgram's experiments. Aronson describes research carried out by Bickman and Zarantonello in 1978 that specifically tests this idea. They asked 100 people to read about what happened in Milgram's experiments. However, whilst some of the people were given the entirely true information that a high proportion of participants had been fully obedient and had delivered the 450 volts, others were informed that hardly anyone had gone all the way up to the maximum level. The former group who had been faced with the uncomfortable and true facts rated the experiment as more harmful and less ethical than did those people who had read the untrue but much more comforting version. This suggests that it's partly because Milgram's results were so at odds with what we would like to think would happen that we find the experiments to be so ethically problematic.

It's worth saying that there are similar issues with the Haney *et al.* prison simulation study. In hindsight this research seems to be a terrible ethical travesty, with participants being put into a horrendous situation that encouraged those cast as guards to become sadistic and which put the prisoners at risk of intense stress, psychological abuse and humiliation. And yet this study received the support and approval of three different organisations before it took place: the American Navy (who sponsored the research), the Psychology Department at Stanford University and the Committee of Human Experimentation at the same institution. None of the organisations suggested at the time that the research should not be carried out or that it was ethically inappropriate.

This is partly because the basic proposal for the study is not in itself ethically problematic: unlike the Milgram study, participants were not deceived, they knew what they were letting themselves in for, they gave their consent to be involved and they were all adults. In fact, as noted earlier, the volunteers were also screened beforehand and those selected had been identified as normal, stable and healthy. And by randomly allocating the students to the two groups there was no question that those with a desire to dominate others volunteered to be guards and those with a tendency towards passivity and meekness chose to be prisoners. So no one perceived there to be any great risks, and because this study had never been carried out before, why should they?

That the study went so sour so quickly came as a great surprise, and it is the intensity of the emotional anguish experienced by some of the prisoners and the cruelty of some of the guards that makes it so shocking. As with the Milgram study, it is partly that the results of the Stanford prison experiment were so unpleasant and surprising, and that no one – neither the volunteers, the researchers or anyone at the various organisations associated with the project – had really foreseen the disastrous consequences or the speed with which they would play out, which makes this such a fascinating and valuable piece of psychological research.

 ## Ethics and partial replication

It's worth stressing that current ethical guidelines and standards mean that neither the Milgram study nor the prison simulation experiment could be replicated today in exactly the same form as they have been reported here. However, as we've noted before, if a finding is considered to be surprising and/or important, then there is often a need for someone else to repeat it so that the results can be verified or possibly reinterpreted. This therefore creates a quandary for psychologists: how does one replicate the results of an ethically questionable study?

The answer seems to lie in **partial replication**, whereby the features of the original experiment are replicated as closely as possible, but where specific elements that are considered unethical today are removed or modified. For example, Burger (2009) was able to gain ethical approval for a partial replication of Milgram's obedience studies, which offered participants greater protection by stopping the experiment at the point where the learner first began his verbal protest (at 150 volts). Stopping at this point was considered an appropriate compromise because 79 per cent of Milgram's original participants who went past this point also went on to the 450-volt level, which meant some reasonable predictions could be made without putting the participants at further risk. Interestingly, Burger found obedience rates only slightly lower than those of Milgram. For another partial replication of the Milgram studies, see 'In focus' box 6.

In focus box 6

Slater *et al.* (2006) carried out a partial replication of the Milgram studies which was made ethically more viable because of one key change to the methodology: the study was carried out in an 'immersive virtual environment' or virtual reality, which meant that in this instance the learner was not a confederate of the experimenter but a virtual human female. The basic procedure was the same but participants were put into one of two possible conditions, one in which they could see and hear the virtual learner, and one in which the virtual learner responded (provided answers or protests) via text.

Obedience rates were consistent with Milgram's findings: in the text-only condition participants were far more likely to administer the maximum number/intensity of shocks (twenty), but in the condition where the virtual learner was both seen and heard most participants still administered nineteen out of the twenty shocks.

It might be argued that such high levels of obedience reflect the fact that the learner was obviously virtual and not a real human being. However, not only is this the key feature of this partial replication that makes it more ethical – the issue of deception is automatically removed because participants know from the start that the learner is virtual and not real – but subjective responses and physiological and behavioural measures suggest that participants responded and interacted as though they thought of the virtual character as 'real' even though they knew that she wasn't, and this was particularly true in the condition where participants could see and hear the learner.

On the positive side this particular study shows one way that technology can be utilised to partially replicate an ethically problematic study, by removing the key ethical issue of deception.

On the negative side, it's worth noting that although deception is removed other ethical issues are not, or at least not entirely. Regarding the tricky issue of the participants having the right to withdraw, Slater et al. (2006) replaced the ethically problematic standardised prompts of Milgram's studies ('the experiment requires that you continue', 'it is absolutely essential that you continue' and 'you have no other choice, you must go on') with more balanced prompts that both remind the participants of their right to withdraw but also strongly encourage them to continue (e.g., 'Although you can stop whenever you want, it is best for the experiment that you continue, but you can stop whenever you want'). So participants are reminded of their rights but are still subtly pressured into not acting on them.

The other ethical issue that is not fully addressed is that of the stress suffered by participants. As noted, participants in this virtual version did show physiological signs of distress. However, the researchers argue that distress in this partial replication was transitory and kept at an absolute minimum. The participant knows from the start that the learner is not real and at the end of the experiment she is shown to be 'alive' and states that nothing really happened and she is fine.

So although this study still raises some ethical questions, its virtual nature provides psychologists with a method that, compared with the original Milgram studies, removes some ethical problems and reduces others, but still produces consistent results. As virtual reality technology continues to improve and is used more widely it may become increasingly adopted by psychologists wanting to study certain phenomena in ways that offer better protection to their participants.

In a similar vein to the partial replications of the Milgram studies presented above, psychologists Alex Haslam and Steve Reicher planned and designed a television series in 2002 that acted as a partial replication of the prison simulation experiment (Reicher & Haslam, 2006). The study had to secure ethical approval from the University of Exeter; plus the BBC, the broadcaster behind the series, insisted on a number of ethical safeguards designed to address and avoid the kinds of problems that had occurred during the original experiment.

These safeguards included participants being screened by clinical psychologists and having to go through medical tests and police background checks before the experiment began. The whole experiment was also monitored around the clock by clinical psychologists and medical and security personnel, and the participants had to complete psychometric and physiological tests on a daily basis. Finally, a special six-person ethics committee was set up that had the power to stop the experiment at any time, particularly if it was felt that any participants were experiencing, or were in danger of experiencing, psychological or physical harm. This power was applied and the experiment was ended two days earlier than planned when some participants talked of creating a tyrannical regime that Reicher and Haslam felt might endanger the participants.

The study produced very different results and interpretations from the original prison simulation experiment (for more details, see Reicher & Haslam, 2006), but crucially for this discussion it arguably protected its participants much more successfully than its predecessor had. Although both experiments were stopped earlier than intended, the original arguably did so when some of the participants had already experienced extreme levels of stress, whilst Reicher and Haslam recognised possible risks and stopped their experiment before serious problems began.

Overview of the ethics of psychological research with humans

In all the three cases discussed above it is certainly unfair to directly compare the original studies with their partial replications, or to suggest that the latter represent better examples of psychological studies, whether ethically or in overall scientific terms.

What can be said is that there is a process here: no code of ethics can predict all potential problems, particularly in new research areas, and in areas where actual behaviour may deviate wildly from the predictions of ethics committees, academics and members of the general public (as in the Milgram and Haney *et al.* cases).

By carrying out research in new areas psychologists may put their participants under new pressures and additional risks. Does this mean that psychologists should not investigate these new areas? Certainly not: Milgram and Haney *et al.* developed creative experimental designs that provided useful insights into human behaviour, but these studies also quite rightly raised ethical issues. What is crucial is that psychology as a whole learns from such examples, and it's worth saying that ethical guidelines, codes and standards for the study of human participants in psychology have arguably become much stricter and more comprehensive since the early 1970s.

On the other hand, it's also worth saying that there are limits to what can be done and there may even be downsides to introducing more stringent ethical rules across the board. As noted earlier, no ethical code can predict all problems and in addition not all research has the potential to be as damaging as the examples discussed in this section. All research in psychology can quite rightly be considered to have some ethical issues connected with it, but a large number of studies can be considered relatively harmless. For example, many questionnaire designs in psychology are uncontroversial as long as respondents are given the right to withdraw from the study (whether that be their personal involvement or their data at some later point), the data are kept anonymous and confidential, and the questions are not insensitive or offensive.

Nevertheless, the process of making applications to ethics committees can greatly slow down the process of research and sometimes codes of conduct demand that participants have to read lengthy documents listing all slight but potential risks, which can result in them getting bored or anxious, potentially leading to reduced response rates, and therefore making it harder to recruit sufficiently large samples in certain cases.

So clearly there is a balance to be maintained here, which rewards innovation on the one hand, but protects participants on the other, and which identifies genuine risks in research but without preventing psychologists from carrying out good work because of unnecessary and/or inflexible bureaucracy. Fortunately, recent examples of research, such as that of Burger (2009), Slater *et al.* (2006) and Reicher and Haslam (2006), indicate that it's still possible to study ethically sensitive issues and keep within current guidelines. For a summary of the main ethical issues, principles and concepts recognised by national psychological organisations, such as the BPS and the APA, and discussed in this chapter, see 'In summary box 3'.

In summary box 3

- Psychologists should always consider the ethical implications and psychological consequences for participants in their research
- Foreseeable threats to physical and psychological health and well-being should be eliminated, which includes potential embarrassment, humiliation and damage to self-esteem. Risks of harm should be no greater than the participant would encounter in their ordinary life
- Participation in research should be voluntary, which includes the right to withdraw personal involvement at the time or data at a later stage – the right to withdraw should be irrespective of whether payment or some inducement has been offered to the participant
- Informed consent should be obtained from participants, which should include permission for results to be published
- If research involves individuals who cannot give consent (such as children or people who have issues with understanding and/or communication), then consent should be obtained from parents or a member of the individual's family
- Deception should be avoided – if deception is an essential part of the research, then participants should be informed of it as soon as possible

- Debriefing should be provided, though this does not justify unethical aspects of an investigation – debriefing information should help the participant understand the nature of the research and minimise negative effects or misconceptions
- A participant's data should be kept confidential and anonymous, unless this is otherwise agreed in advance – this should continue to the publication stage, to prevent the participant being identified or traced
- Psychologists should be professional in all their conduct – this includes identifying and providing appropriate sources of professional advice for participants with concerns, and encouraging colleagues who appear to be carrying out unethical research to re-evaluate what they are doing

Conclusions

It's hopefully clear that there are no straightforward right or wrong decisions that can be taken about most ethical issues in psychology. This is partly because times and ethical standards change, such that what was once considered ethically appropriate may later become regarded as shocking and wholly unacceptable.

Ethical guidelines, rules, regulations and codes of practice are now in place for all psychologists and relate to all of the different fields of psychology, from how clinical psychologists should interact with their patients, through to the ethics of research, which is what I've focused on primarily in this chapter and Chapter 3.

In a sense the assorted issues of ethics in psychology have changed a great deal in the past 100 years or so. In the earliest days of the subject psychologists had no specific set of ethical rules that they were obliged to follow and had to rely on their own conscience and the social conventions of the times; plus there were no national psychological organisations to set down rules or to make decisions.

At present, guidelines are not only in place, they are also regularly amended, updated and revised, and there are now specific guidelines for vulnerable populations (children, pregnant women, people suffering with mental illness or those with physical or intellectual disabilities, prisoners, and those with specific medical conditions, to name but a few). Both human participants and animal subjects are arguably better protected, considered and cared for now than at any other point in the history of psychology. This is all good news, not just because a more ethical psychology is a good thing in its own right, but also because it helps to reassure the general public that psychologists genuinely care and that they pursue their research with integrity and respect for their subjects/participants.

There are also different ethical considerations for different forms of methodology within psychology – I have largely focused on experimental work within this chapter because many of the most serious and common ethical problems arise from such work, but there are also ethical considerations for psychologists carrying out observational research and for those who are giving their participants questionnaires of a sensitive nature. But regardless of the methodology, most ethical issues stay pretty consistent: ultimately the psychologist's job is to minimise harm, risk and distress, to show due care and respect (for both humans and animals), to obtain consent and avoid deception wherever possible, to keep data confidential and anonymous, and to debrief and, in some cases, to offer advice to humans participating in their research.

There are still questions to be asked and answered – for example, does the ethical process sometimes slow down or even impede progress in psychology, and if so does this in itself raise ethical issues; or, on the other hand, is the humanist approach in psychology right to argue that psychologists should continue to prioritise dignity, honesty and humanity over the accumulation of knowledge – but for now at least the debate is over to you . . .

 Further reading

Harris, B. (1979). Whatever happened to little Albert? *American Psychologist, 34*, 151–160.

Chapter 5

The Nature and Nurture Debate

In Chapter 4 we saw how ethical issues have been around since the early days of experimental psychology, but the debate we're going to focus on in this chapter is one of the oldest in the history of psychological thinking. The debate itself started a long time before psychology was officially founded as a science by Wundt in the 1870s. In fact it can be traced back to at least the fifth century BC when philosophers such as Plato and Aristotle became interested in and tried to resolve the debate.

Obviously if a debate is as long lasting as this, it suggests that it must be an incredibly important one, and indeed it is, although part of the reason it has lasted as long as it has is because for a long time scientists were unable to establish exactly what it was that really lay at the heart of the debate. Even as I write this, it has not been completely resolved, and indeed in certain circles there is still controversy and heated discussion of the issues and their apparent implications, but contemporary research is coming closer to telling us the respective contributions of nature and nurture to psychology. But before I go on, I'd better tell you just what this debate actually refers to.

◉ Explanation/definition of the two terms

The nature and nurture debate is fundamentally one about what makes humans (and possibly animals) what they are. Every human being is a unique individual and even identical twins are by no means identical in every aspect of their behaviour, personality and psychological being (in fact if you are friends with identical twins, you will know just how very different they can be). The question is where do these differences come from? Are we born the way we are? Is what makes us the person we are something that exists innately within us? Or are we a product of our personal experiences, the environments we are in and the people we spend time with?

The nature side of the debate adopts the former position, stressing that we are what we are from birth, or possibly even from conception (or even possibly before then, depending on one's views about eternal souls, reincarnation and so on, though as these are spiritual or religious ideas they are rather outside the remit of science).

Exactly how it is that we innately possess certain psychological traits, or at least possess the innate potential to display them, has not always been clear. As suggested earlier, supernatural causes were often put forward to explain individual differences in human beings, but from a rather more scientific perspective it had sometimes been suggested that psychological traits might somehow run in families.

It was not really until the work of Sir Francis Galton that the idea of mental inheritance was seriously considered (Galton, 1869, 1883) and I'll say more about his work later. What was not fully known in Galton's time, however, was the precise biological basis behind inheritance (whether physical or mental), but thanks to advances in the field of genetics we now have a very good idea of the process that underlies the transmission of genes from parents to offspring. So current versions of the nature position in psychology tend to argue that behavioural traits and mental capacities are the result of a genetic contribution.

The nurture side adopts the opposite position, arguing that it is our personal encounters and experiences in the world that create the person we are. The seventeenth-century philosopher John Locke used the Latin term **tabula rasa** (which loosely translates into English as blank slate) to describe the state of a child's mind at birth, suggesting that it has no in-built mental content of any kind. It is the child's experiences then that imprint on the mind, enabling the acquisition of knowledge about the world and shaping or causing the child's personality, behaviour and intelligence.

This position is sometimes referred to as representing a form of extreme environmentalism, which means that the child is considered completely malleable; that is, there is no certainty that the child will become violent or passive, sociable or shy, or that he or she will develop or display any particular psychological trait to any particular extent – it all depends on the environments the child is exposed to or brought up in.

The term nurture used to refer specifically to the type and quality of care the child received from its parents (particularly the mother) and how important this care was in the development of a particular psychological trait, but more recently the meaning of the term has been greatly expanded. It now tends to refer to any environmental (and therefore non-genetic) factor, which obviously includes parental influence but also incorporates stimuli that offspring can experience or be affected by whilst in the mother's womb, plus the impact of extended family members and peers, and influences from the media, schooling and socio-economic status throughout life.

Now you may be thinking, surely most psychological traits are influenced to some extent by elements of both nature and nurture? Of course you'd be right and this is a point I will be expanding upon throughout the chapter. There are reasons why distinctions are often made between nature and nurture when talking about this issue, implying that it's a case of either one or the other. The main reason is a historical one and it relates back to a point I made in the opening chapter: that debates are often defined by their extreme positions.

For much of the twentieth century this debate tended to be dominated by psychologists who favoured one side almost exclusively over the other, though it's probably fair to say that most psychologists actually tended to occupy a position somewhere in between those two extremes. In the last couple of decades progress has slowly been made, in terms of the science used to study the contributions of nature and nurture and also in terms of encouraging both sides to consider if some form of synthesis might be possible. The idea that there is some degree of interaction between nature and nurture is becoming increasingly common, though the debate is now moving towards questions about the precise relationship between the two interacting forces for different psychological variables. Not surprisingly, psychologists who argue that aspects of nature and nurture interact in determining mental capacities and behaviour are referred to as adopting an interactionist position within this debate.

I'll identify where the five key approaches in psychology this book focuses on fit within the nature and nurture debate shortly, but first I'll offer a brief reminder about why this debate is so important.

Just why is the nature and nurture debate so important for psychology?

In Chapter 1, I gave a brief answer to this question. I don't wish to repeat myself too much here, but I do think it is worth going back over some of those earlier points. One reason why it's so important is that it is an extremely comprehensive debate, one that can be considered to address virtually every aspect of psychology and who we are. A full answer to the nature and nurture debate would effectively tell us what makes human beings the way they are and would explain exactly what it is that makes each human being unique.

And in addition to telling us why people are the way they are, it could also be extremely helpful in identifying people's strengths and weaknesses, even at a very early age, predicting in what areas of their life they are likely to fail, succeed or require more encouragement and training, to offer assistance for those who want change or improve their lives in all kinds of different ways, plus it could be extremely helpful in the early diagnosis and treatment of mental illnesses, possibly even preventing them from developing fully in the first place. If we know what aspects of personality, mental health, relationships, quality of life, achievement, success and failure are primarily attributable to genetics and what aspects are largely attributable to features in the environment, then arguably there could be all kinds of benefits to individuals and to societies.

If this sounds like a rather utopian view, it's worth noting two things. First, psychologists are still a long way from having this kind of in-depth and comprehensive knowledge. Second, it's not entirely clear that if psychologists did have this kind of knowledge it would necessarily be a good thing. There are numerous ethical, legal and social issues connected to knowledge of this kind.

For example, if it were possible to produce truly comprehensive information about people's psychological profiles based on their genetic and environmental histories, would everyone be able to gain access to such profiles, or would they only be available to those people wealthy enough to afford them? And who else would have access to this information, how might it be used and how might it affect individuals and society's perceptions of individuals?

Of course these are practical issues to do with the use and application of such knowledge. With any major advances within science there are usually important legal, moral, financial and social issues and concerns that need to be addressed and discussed. This is certainly not a reason to abandon research into identifying the relative contributions of nature and nurture on aspects of human psychology, though it does stress that even if psychologists were able to acquire comprehensive knowledge of this kind, it would not automatically be to everyone's advantage and that the issues are not just about scientific progress – there is an important moral/ethical dimension to be explored too.

In fact some critics, particularly psychologists from the humanist approach, have argued that knowledge of this kind is dangerous not only because it may be misused but also because it may erode vital human notions such as free will, choice and responsibility. The argument goes something like this: if people were able to obtain considerable information about themselves, both about their genetic inheritance and the environments they might likely thrive or fail in, or the behaviours they might be best or least suited for, would this deny them a fundamental right (as argued by the humanist approach) to choose their own path? Some psychologists would argue that there are various important experiential aspects of being human, such as being able to take risks, to go with one's intuition or gut, to explore and question oneself, and even to make and learn from mistakes, all of which might be lost in a world where psychological information about our future lives and opportunities is readily available.

There will be more later about where exactly the humanist approach can be said to stand with regard to the nature and nurture debate, but hopefully it's already clear how the availability and use (or misuse) of information about causes or determinants of psychological capacities is related to another debate that we'll be considering later in the book: free will versus determinism. We'll be fully defining the terminology of that debate in Chapter 8, but hopefully it's already obvious that nature, nurture or possibly some combination of the two could shape or determine the development (whether partially or entirely) of various psychological traits and behaviours.

When I introduced Locke's notion of the blank slate I described it as extreme environmentalism – the idea that we have little or no choice in who/what we become but rather we are at the whim of all the things that happen to us, the environments we are raised in and so on, and that it is these things that determine our intelligence, our personality and the rest of our psychological traits and faculties.

It's interesting to note, however, that in the history of the nature and nurture debate in psychology, since the time of Sir Francis Galton (who arguably introduced the debate for psychology in the first place) it has more often been deterministic aspects of the nature side that have produced the most anxiety and disquiet. Deterministic elements from the nurture side, by comparison, have tended to have a rather easier time of it (Pinker, 2003). This aspect of the debate will be discussed in much greater detail within the Section 'History of the nature and nurture debate', as we look at how the different approaches within psychology got involved.

But the crux of the matter is this: throughout the twentieth century members of the public and some psychologists argued that if human psychology was suggested to be entirely, largely or even somewhat influenced by nature, then this denied the possibility of human free will and morality and placed restrictions on an individual's choices, opportunities and potential.

This idea of our innate biological natures somehow determining or restricting our choices, producing unavoidable and unalterable effects in our lives, is sometimes called **genetic determinism**. Given that most humans believe that they have free will (an idea strongly supported by the humanist approach but not, as we'll see in Chapter 8, by all approaches within psychology), it's perhaps not surprising to find that theoretical positions on human psychology that emphasise the influence of nature have not always been well received, by the general public or by all psychologists.

It is worth stressing, therefore, that this debate does have a life outside of academic psychology: just as with the ethical debate about animal experimentation, and the free will versus determinism debate, the public can have a view on the roles of nature and nurture in psychology, and public opinion can sometimes stall one side of the debate or stimulate the other.

Clearly then, changes and developments within psychology can impact on society, but equally societal attitudes and the **Zeitgeist** (the spirit of the times – the general cultural, intellectual, ethical and/or political mood of a particular time and place) can impact on and contribute to the development and success of certain trends in psychology. One example of this can be seen in the way that the nature and nurture debate has raged in psychology over the past 140 years or so. I will next use the history of this debate to demonstrate where the different approaches in psychology stand in relation to it.

👁 History of the nature and nurture debate

As I've already suggested, this debate actually pre-dates the official founding of the science of psychology by many thousands of years. For example, the ancient Greek philosopher Plato stressed the importance of individual differences in personality and ability, but believed that such dispositions are primarily innate (Hothersall, 2004), largely because they often 'emerge' at such an early age and sometimes seem fully formed, which made it unlikely that they had somehow been acquired through learning or experience.

Plato's explanation for these innate capacities, according to his **theory of recollection** (Greenwood, 2009), was that the soul was immortal and reincarnated after death in a new body, and the apparent emergence of these individual characteristics and knowledge occurred as a child remembered the stored knowledge possessed by the immortal psyche. If this doesn't sound like a very scientific explanation, then it's worth remembering that this was well over 2000 years ago, long before the concept of genetics had even been conceived of.

In stark contrast to Plato's position is that of Aristotle, another major Greek philosopher of the time. He was at one point in his life a devoted student of Plato but nevertheless proposed pretty much the exact opposite view – an early version of Locke's tabula rasa idea. For Aristotle, the mind at birth was blank but had the potential to be filled, but only by the world acting upon it (Hothersall, 2004). The problem with these two completely contrasting views, both at the time Plato and Aristotle originally presented them and for much of the 2000 years that would follow, is that they were extremely difficult to test scientifically – which is not to suggest that no attempts were ever made.

Possibly the earliest reported example, in fact possibly the first psychology experiment to ever be recorded, appears in *The Histories of Herodotus*, a very early example of a history book, completed around 429 BC (Colman, 1988). Herodotus claims that the ancient Egyptian Pharaoh Psammetichus I (or Psamtik I) carried out an experiment to discover whether human beings have an innate capacity for language.

He arranged for two newborn infants to be raised in isolation by a single herdsman who was instructed to care for them but never speak to them or utter a word in their presence. The idea was that if language really was innate, then the children would begin to speak words despite the lack of spoken input in their environment, but if language was acquired, then a lack of exposure to spoken words would prevent them displaying it.

The results of the experiment as reported by Herodotus are rather difficult to interpret, but then the results are not really the point anyway because this was in no way a well-designed piece of research (for a start we have no way of knowing for certain whether the herdsman was a particularly trustworthy experimenter – whether he ever spoke to the infants or kept silent the whole time as he was supposed to). There are even doubts about whether the experiment ever really took place: Herodotus is not regarded as the most trustworthy of historians, the information he presents often appears to have been based on anecdotes and no other historical sources verify this story. But even if no such experiment ever took place the idea still came from somewhere, which suggests that people were thinking about the nature and nurture debate and considering possible ways to investigate it experimentally even back in 429 BC.

However, even if experiments that might conceivably test aspects of the nature and nurture debate were being considered a long time ago, few such experiments were ever actually carried out (from an ethical point of view at least this is surely a good thing). Perhaps because of this the debate continued, off and on, with little real progress for the next 2000 years or so, with the two extreme positions offered by Plato and Aristotle recurring many times during that period.

Darwin's contribution

It was Charles Darwin's pivotal work on natural selection, covered in some detail in Chapter 4, that was particularly important for introducing the debate to the newly emerging psychology in the nineteenth century. Darwin's work emphasised the importance of individual differences because such differences might ultimately enable some members of a species to survive, reproduce and therefore pass those valuable differences onto future generations, and so on.

Darwin was aware that environments changed, sometimes with devastating results to species that lived in them, and species that stayed exactly the same from generation to generation would struggle to adapt to such changes. But if there were variety in members of a species, then that variety might enable some members of the species to survive and reproduce more successfully than others. Those animals possessing traits better suited to survive in the new environment would be the ones more likely to have more offspring, and those offspring would be likely to inherit those traits, whilst animals without those traits would slowly die out over time.

In addition, there is also variation within offspring, meaning that some will possess more useful traits, or show more of a particular useful trait, than others. Again, those with the traits best suited to survive will be more likely to do so. Via the processes of variation and transmission Darwin had apparently explained the differences within and between the various species found in the world today. But as noted in Chapter 4, Darwin's work had many implications, and just as he explained how important physical differences within and between species were for biology, it also raised an interesting idea: that perhaps individual differences in mental capacities might be just as important for psychology, and that these differences might be transmitted from one generation to the next in similar ways.

Darwin's work, therefore, was a crucial starting point for the development of the biological approach within psychology, for it stressed just how important a biological process might be for the origins and development of psychological characteristics. It also emphasised the nature side of the debate, by suggesting that these traits might be inherited from previous generations rather than being learnt through experience.

👁 The contributions of Galton and James

Darwin's ideas and work influenced a number of psychologists, but I'm now going to focus on two key individuals, neither of whom would be considered strictly to be part of the biological approach, but nevertheless both men introduced and developed key elements that were hugely important for this approach and for the nature side of the debate.

I've already mentioned the importance of Sir Francis Galton, and he had crucial roles to play in bridging the gap between Darwin's theory of natural selection and how it might apply to psychology, and also in introducing the nature and nurture debate to psychology. It's somewhat ironic then that Galton could not technically be described as a psychologist, but rather he was an extremely gifted and intelligent polymath who spent only 15 years of his life considering psychological issues.

The other key individual, William James, was a psychologist, but again only for part of his life. James is particularly famous for the range of his contributions to psychology, but also for his reluctance to stick to any one approach or to commit himself to any single of school of psychology (Robinson, 1993). Nevertheless, we will be focusing here on his ideas about instinctive behaviours, another important part of the nature side of the debate, and also **habits**, which made an important contribution to the nurture side.

It seems that Galton's work on mental inheritance was driven in part by the prevailing trend of the time to attribute success, greatness and genius solely to environmental factors (Schultz & Schultz, 2004). This trend may have reflected the need of the time for people to believe that they could achieve great things even if they came from less successful backgrounds and families. But Galton's book *Hereditary Genius* (1869) was based around biographical data that suggested that successful people tend to have successful parents and successful children. In Galton's sample they mainly consisted of influential scientists, judges and doctors and, because of the limited opportunities available to women at the time, all of them were male. Through the then groundbreaking use of statistics, Galton was able to show that the number of successful people that run in families is far greater than would be expected due to chance alone.

It could be argued that success runs in families not just because mental characteristics that underlie success are inherited, but also because people born to successful fathers are likely to be born into a better environment, will receive a better standard of education and will generally have more opportunities and privileges than the rest of the population. Galton was seemingly unconvinced by this argument but nevertheless accepted the limitations of his methods – he was unable to control for the impact of environment on success.

Driven by the need to find a better method Galton (1883) came up with a means of establishing the relative contributions of heredity and environment that is still used widely today, namely the twin study. This method makes use of the fact that there are two different types of twins: fraternal or dizygotic twins, and identical or monozygotic twins. Because of the ways these two different types of twins develop they also differ in how genetically similar they are.

Fraternal or dizygotic twins occur when two ova are separately fertilised by two sperm and then develop in the same womb. Such twins are as genetically similar to each other as are any brothers or sisters who share the same biological parents but not any more so. In contrast, identical or monozygotic twins develop when a single fertilised ovum splits and forms two separate embryos. In this second case the twins are genetically identical.

For psychological traits that are due to innate factors there should be greater similarities between identical twins than fraternal twins. In addition Galton was interested to see if twins who were similar on traits initially became less so when they separated and went into different environments, and also if twins who were initially dissimilar for particular traits became more similar when raised in the same environment.

Galton's ideas were impressive and, as we'll see later, his twin study method would become a vital tool for studying the influences of nature and nurture on a huge range of psychological traits. It's arguable, however, that the results he himself reported were not strong enough to support his conclusion that nature was a far more significant influence on human psychology than nurture.

Nevertheless Galton believed so strongly that nature had the more dominant role to play that he proposed a way of improving the human condition through the control of genetics. He coined the term **eugenics**, which he envisaged as an applied science that would study and seek to improve aspects of human nature that are determined by genetics (a kind of 'artificial selection', in contrast to Darwin's natural selection). Given that Galton believed he had already shown that nature was more important than nurture and that people with positive and socially desirable traits such as intelligence could pass those traits on to their children, he believed that people with those positive traits should be identified, encouraged through the use of incentives (such as money) to marry and to marry as early as possible, so to hopefully increase the number of children they might have, and that those couples should be further supported, so as to give them the best conditions in which to raise their children (Hothersall, 2004).

Eugenics was initially a very popular idea and was perceived, at least by some quarters of society, and by many governments around the world, to represent a path towards a superior human race by greatly improving its genetic stock. Unfortunately eugenics has a much darker side and it became a way for powerful people and groups to target other groups that were considered undesirable or a drain on society's resources. Discrimination, segregation and even sterilisation (sometimes voluntary, sometimes compulsory) of certain groups, based on whatever trait or grouping was considered undesirable (class, race, mental retardation, psychiatric disorders, criminality, sexuality and so on) became justified within different countries as part of the science of eugenics. Such practices were taken to their most severe and frightening extent in Nazi Germany where compulsory sterilisation, deportation and eventually systematic murder were applied to millions of people on the basis that they were considered genetically undesirable.

Clearly Galton is not responsible for the terrible things that were carried out under the name of eugenics, and he never condoned the idea that people should be coerced into taking part in eugenics programmes. However, his focus on certain traits being essential for the betterment of society, and his insistence that these traits are primarily determined by hereditary factors, always had the potential to be problematic and abused. It is entirely possible for a majority group in a society to identify the importance of a particular heritable trait (such as intelligence), and to identify that certain minority groups appear to commonly display below average levels of that trait in the same society (i.e., particular racial groups might be targeted for seemingly being less intelligent).

However, with the focus on nature it's possible to downplay or simply ignore the fact that people from those particular groups might also, because of history, social structures and prejudice, be much more likely to belong to the poorer classes of society, and therefore also have fewer educational and occupational opportunities, poorer diets and living conditions. By encouraging a focus solely on apparently inherited traits this often meant that the importance of environment and nurturing was often ignored by governments and other powerful groups (whether intentionally or not), sometimes with disastrous consequences. It's perhaps because the eugenics movement led, or at least was connected to, such negative outcomes in the twentieth century that there was something of a backlash against the nature side of the debate in that century.

If Galton could be accused of dogmatism and overstating his position with regard to the nature and nurture debate, then the American philosopher and psychologist William James can be argued to have been much more open-minded and balanced in his views. He was hugely influential in the early development of the new science of psychology, particularly in America, but we'll focus on two particular contributions that are relevant to this debate and to the behaviourist and biological approaches to psychology.

James, like Galton, was inspired and strongly influenced by Darwin's work on evolution. Within his landmark textbook, *The Principles of Psychology*, published in 1890, James first used the term evolutionary psychology, convinced that evolutionary theory would have a huge part to play in the development of psychology as a subject (Schultz & Schultz, 2004). Although James disliked committing himself to one particular position or approach we might argue that he took much more of an interactionist view of the nature and nurture debate than had Galton. He identified two key concepts that related to human behaviour – **instincts** and habits. As noted before, the former would be hugely important for developments in the nature side, whilst the latter would be equally important for the nurture side.

Following Darwin and Galton, James proposed that some aspects of human behaviour are present from birth due to genetic predispositions. These instinctive behaviours are likely to have evolved via natural selection because they represent behavioural adaptations to specific situations and problems related to reproduction and/or survival that humans would have faced throughout their evolutionary histories.

Amongst the instinctive behaviours James identified were parenting skills, love, sympathy, sociability, the tendency to fight or defend oneself and one's young, and fears of specific objects (such as heights and strange animals), all of which can be seen to have some clear value for either our survival, the survival of our kin or our ability to reproduce. Although James stressed that instincts initially emerge without instruction, experience or learning (reflecting the nature side), he didn't deny they could later be modified by such things (suggesting interaction between nature and nurture).

This point is further developed in James' description of habits: repetitive or established actions or patterns of behaviour that reflect the plasticity of the nervous system. Whilst instincts are present at birth, habits are developed through experience, many of them early on in life. New habits can be acquired and developed throughout life, though as we get older the existing habits may block the acquisition of some or facilitate others.

◉ The emergence of the behaviourist approach

It's interesting to note, then, that within *The Principles of Psychology* James identified these two key concepts of instincts and habits, both of which would be hugely influential in the development of the nature and nurture debate throughout much of the next century.

Both instincts and habits were initially addressed by John Watson when he started the behaviourist approach. You may recall in Chapter 4 that Watson had identified three unlearned emotional response patterns in children (fear, rage and love). Indeed during the earlier stages of behaviourism, Watson (1914) described the term instinct as 'short, useful, and convenient' (p. 106), identified instincts as important influences on animal behaviour, and even suggested that a considerable proportion of animal behaviour could be best described as instinctive.

But the behaviourist approach is not traditionally associated with the nature side of the debate and over time Watson's position gradually shifted – by 1919 he described how a wide range of human behaviours, including some that James had identified as instincts (such as fighting and maternal care), were 'really consolidations of instincts and habit' (Watson, 1919, p. 282) and, as indicated by his work looking at emotions in infants, including Albert B, it's clear that by 1920 he thought very few emotional behaviours were innate. By 1924, in his book *Behaviorism*, Watson asks the fundamental question 'Are There Any Instincts?', to which his concluding answer, simply put, is no. Behaviours may often appear to be instinctual but in all cases they are in fact habits: if a child displays anger, fear or affection at an early age, then this is because s/he has learnt to do so.

And so it was that psychology, particularly in America, moved from being a study of instincts and habits, as suggested by James, highlighting the importance of both nature and nurture, and some degree of interaction between the two, to being described in Watson's later form of behaviourism as effectively the study of habit formation, where nurture and the environment are the only determinants of behaviour. Any terminology or concepts suggesting innate contributions to behaviour, including instincts and inherited talents and abilities, are dismissed or entirely absent from Watson's behaviourism after 1924. This returned psychology, or at least behaviourist-dominated American psychology, back to the blank slate of Aristotle and Locke, suggesting absolute psychological equality at birth and that all future developments in a person are entirely the result of environment, experience and social conditioning.

Why did Watson move from an apparently interactionist position, reminiscent of James, to the extreme environmentalist one which characterised his later work and much of the behaviourist position and American psychology in general for the next few decades? Hothersall (2004) suggests there were a number of reasons, including important research on animals and humans between 1914 and 1924 (some of it by Watson himself and some by other psychologists) that suggested that many of the behaviours once thought to be instinctual could be explained partially or entirely as acquired habits.

Another problem with instincts was the apparent circularity of some of the arguments for their existence and impact on human behaviour. For example, why is there so much aggression and conflict in the world and throughout history? Because these are instinctive traits present in all humans. But how do we know this? Well, because there's so much aggression and conflict in the world and throughout history.

A final complication rested on Watson's insistence that psychology should be a subject that carried out direct study of observable phenomena. The processes involved in habit formation were observable, could be manipulated experimentally, and the results of these manipulations could be studied and recorded. Instincts, on the other hand, were a product of an animal's genetic inheritance and therefore it was unclear how they might be observed, manipulated or studied directly.

As Watson became less and less convinced of the existence, measurability and impact of instincts he moved further away from the nature and interactionist positions, instead believing that habit formation was the key to understanding human behaviour and solving society's ills. Therefore both Watson and behaviourism adopted an extreme environmentalist/nurture position.

As we noted in Chapter 4, following scandals in his private life Watson moved out of academia, but continued to write books and articles on psychology aimed at the general public and gave many public lectures and radio addresses (effectively making him the first 'pop psychologist' – Buckley, 1982). Behaviourism continued to thrive within academic psychology in America, thanks to a number of neobehaviourists – psychologists inspired by Watson's ideas of the 'science of behaviour', the collection of objective data and an extreme environmentalist position. But the environmentalist message that Watson presented was popular with the American people too, partly because Watson was a charming and charismatic public speaker and had a clear style of writing, but also because what he said resonated with them. Even before the full dangers of the eugenics movement became apparent via its use in Nazi Germany, it's arguable that the nature position proposed by Galton *et al.* was never likely to appeal to the masses. Eugenics suggested it was possible to change and improve society but only by encouraging those people who were already successful, powerful and intelligent (all thought by Galton to result from inherited traits) to have more children. Theories that focused on instincts and innate talents stressed that some people were born more likely to succeed, whilst others would always struggle or have limited options available to them. None of these messages would have been particularly encouraging or inspiring for those people who didn't appear to have the necessary innate talents or inherited traits – they and their children were seemingly being condemned to the same lives they had always lived, with no hope of change or improvement.

Contrast this then with Watson's message of hope and change: there are no limits imposed by genetic factors, problematic patterns of behaviour are not set in stone and can be changed through a new environment or via means of appropriate counter-conditioning, and change is always a possibility. Watson's message was that people were not trapped by class, birthright or genetics, children could grow up to be whatever one wanted them to be, and the right nurturing from parents and social environments could solve all problems. Watson promised the potential improvement of the individual, the individual's children and of society as a whole, but in a way that didn't reward only those who were already privileged and successful. The following paragraph from *Behaviorism* is often quoted to show just what Watson thought his approach to psychology was capable of in terms of its impact on individuals and society:

> Give me a dozen healthy infants, well formed, and my own specified world to bring them up in, and I'll guarantee to take any one at random and train him to become any type of specialist I might select – doctor, lawyer, artist, merchant-chief, and, yes, even beggarman and thief, regardless of his talents, penchants, tendencies, abilities, vocations, and race of his ancestors.
>
> (Watson, 1924/1930, pp. 103–104).

Watson would later admit that this claim was not something he was ever able to test and that he rather exaggerated the point beyond the available facts (Schultz & Schultz, 2004), but it neatly demonstrates his position, and that of the extreme nurture movement generally. Hopefully it's also easy to understand why such an approach would have been so enthusiastically received by so many people. Behaviourism and the nurture approach continued to be popular amongst many psychologists and the general public, particularly in the US, for several decades, but what of instincts and the nature approach?

⬖ Developments in the nurture approach

Some psychologists continued to support the opposite side of the debate, both within the US and outside, but work on instincts and the nature side in the early twentieth century tended to develop most successfully outside of America and even outside of psychology itself.

The scientific study of ethology arose in Europe, as part of the discipline of biology (Passer *et al.*, 2009), and focused on the behaviour of animals within their natural environment. Driven by concepts derived from the theory of evolution via natural selection, ethologists argued against the blank slate idea of behaviourism, stressing instead that every animal species (including humans) comes into the world with certain predispositions to act and behave in certain ways.

Ethologists noted that some behaviours in animals appeared from birth and were instinctive, not learnt and were triggered automatically by certain stimuli. Such behaviours were described by ethologists as **fixed action patterns** and were always important for the animal's survival.

One commonly reported example is shown by newly hatched gull chicks. They will peck at a red spot on their parents' bills, which stimulates the parent bird's regurgitation reflex, and the hatchlings then ingest the parent bird's regurgitated food. So the presentation of a particular stimulus, in this case the presence of a red spot on a bill-shaped object, automatically initiates a particular behaviour, in this case the chick's pecking behaviour. Young chicks can be 'fooled' into pecking at other objects just as automatically if they are similarly shaped to a parent bird's bill and they are marked with a red spot. Generally speaking, the more similar another object is to the natural object, the more likely it is to stimulate the fixed action pattern.

However, as ethologists continued with their research on different species and different stimuli they learnt that some fixed action patterns could be modified through experience. For example, Passer *et al.* (2009) report the research of Hailman (1967) – which showed that although gull hatchlings can be fooled by inanimate objects made to look like an adult gull's beak, older chicks seem able to learn what the whole head of an adult gull looks like, and therefore will only peck at the inanimate object if it appears to be connected to something made to resemble the head of an adult gull.

In addition, ethologists also found, as psychologists had, that some apparently instinctive behaviours actually involve learning and are not innate at all. However, whilst Watson had argued that such evidence implied that all apparently instinctive behaviours are really learnt, ethologists used this as an impetus to carefully research and establish exactly which behaviours were genuinely instinctive, which were learnt and which showed evidence of interactions between innate species adaptations and learnt adaptations acquired by individual animals through interaction with their environment.

Such work by ethologists was highly important for the biological approach to psychology, and although ethologists are biologists they have frequently worked together with comparative psychologists, and continue to do so, to share knowledge about animal behaviour. One of the traditional differences between ethology and comparative psychology, other than the former being rooted more firmly in biology and the latter being a specific branch of psychology, is that ethologists were usually more likely to study animal behaviour in the natural environment whereas comparative psychologists were more likely to study animals in laboratories.

It has sometimes been argued that a lot of the research on animal behaviour carried out by comparative psychologists lacked **ecological validity,** that is, the research failed to approximate the real conditions under which animal behaviour naturally occurs. It may be that a lack of ecological validity may account for some of the results of animal experiments carried out by behaviourists that suggested that certain behaviours were learnt rather than instinctual. Certainly the work carried out by ethologists frequently enabled experiments that had been carried out on animals by psychologists under controlled but artificial laboratory conditions to be replicated under more naturalistic conditions, which helpfully addresses issues of ecological validity.

The decline of the behaviourist and extreme nurture positions

Just as ethologists, who had originally focused on instinctive behaviours and fixed action patterns, were discovering that sometimes learning interacted with or could modify innate patterns of behaviour, psychologists were also coming to terms with the fact that the extreme nurture position proposed by behaviourism was equally incomplete.

Several neobehaviourists had followed Watson and had further developed and modified his ideas, though had also remained true to most of his fundamental principles, including extreme environmentalism. Burrhus Frederic Skinner was one of the later neobehaviourists and also one of the most radical, strongly supporting Watson's vision of a potentially utopian future guided by behaviourist principles and the importance of nurture over nature. However, although Skinner would remain a dominant figure in behaviourism and psychology until his death in 1990, arguably the dominance of behaviourism and the nurture position within psychology waned during this period.

A key reason for behaviourism's decline was its continued denial of the contribution of innate and inherited capacities in human psychology. Skinner argued that all behaviours are entirely learnt and in 1957, in his book *Verbal Behaviour*, he tried to use behaviourist principles to put forward the case that the one behaviour unique to humans (spoken language) was no exception to this. He pointed out that all behaviours can either be reinforced (rewarded), not reinforced (ignored), or punished by others. As part of Skinner's ideas on operant conditioning he had consistently shown that behaviours that are in some way rewarded are more likely to be repeated, whilst behaviours not reinforced or actively punished would be less likely to be repeated. Skinner had shown that even quite complex and elaborate behaviours could be conditioned in this way over time and he sought to argue that even the apparent complexity of human language could be accounted for in this way.

Whenever children make utterances these, like all other forms of behaviour, are either reinforced, not reinforced, or punished, most commonly by parents or caregivers, but also by older siblings and other family members and later by teachers. If a child says a word, or even something resembling a word, and it leads to a smile or attention from parents, then this strongly increases the likelihood that the child will say that word again. On the other hand, if the listener frowns or otherwise expresses disappointment, then the child may avoid that word, or the precise pronunciation of that word in future. Over time, Skinner argued, the child learns to speak, purely via regular correction, support, praise and criticism from others in the environment, and based on that feedback puts sounds together as words and words together as sentences.

However, despite Skinner's brave attempt to try and explain the whole process of language acquisition purely in terms of conditioning, it seems far too simplistic. As critics have correctly noted, there is more to learning language than simply acquiring it one word at a time and receiving rein-forcement or punishment about the usage and pronunciation of each word. Language is as much about the complex rules of grammar that underlie the way in which words are combined and sentences are constructed. Although Skinner argued that the rules of grammar could be learnt in just the same way as the words, by imitating the usage of adults and by being rewarded or punished based on the accuracy of their imitation, it seems unlikely that such processes could explain the rapid mastery of grammar shown by children in the first few years of life.

Skinner's most famous critic with regard to his approach to language acquisition was the linguist Noam Chomsky, who argued that the biggest problem of Skinner's approach was its failure to explain the almost endless creativity, originality and flexibility of human language (Chomsky, 1959).

Children have a highly impressive capacity to produce and understand an almost unlimited number of sentences, many of which they may never have heard before and some of which will never have been spoken before. Chomsky argues that such flexibility and creativity is only possible at such a young age if, instead of having to learn everything about language from others, the child already has some innate ability to understand the rules of language. So, given the degree of flexibility shown even early on in life, and the limited range of opportunities a child has to learn the rules that underlie language, it seems more likely that such rules are inherited, part of a genetic endowment that nearly all humans possess. Based on these rules, and with interaction with the environment, language 'grows in the mind-brain of the child' (Maher & Groves, 1998, p. 47).

Although Chomsky (1959) specifically attacked Skinner's attempt at a behaviourist explanation of language, it's arguable he was more broadly questioning all attempts by behaviourists to reduce and simplify psychological phenomena so that they could be explained solely within an extreme environmentalist framework.

Chomsky has never denied that a child requires appropriate social interaction and environmental stimuli to trigger the innate hypothetical **language acquisition device** that he thinks underlies and guides language development, and it would also be surprising if operant conditioning and parental reinforcement played no part in this process at all. The problem with Skinner's explanation is not that it cannot successfully account for some aspects of language acquisition, but rather that by denying that a child is born with any innate grasp of the structure of language it seems to be woefully incomplete.

The cognitive revolution

Chomsky's attack on Skinner and behaviourism and the proposal of his own more innate/interactionist theory of language was also part of a more general move away from the dominance of behaviourism in American psychology, and the formation of a new approach to psychology, namely cognitive psychology.

Ideas about the mind/brain being involved in the acquisition, storage, and retrieval of information, and carrying out information-processing, had arguably been considered outside of America and behaviourism for some time earlier in the twentieth century, but there hadn't been a specific approach that brought these ideas together under a common banner. However, the so-called 'cognitive revolution' refers to an intellectual movement that largely occurred in America in the 1950s and 1960s as behaviourism became a less dominant approach and psychologists returned to focusing on internal mental processes and even concepts such as consciousness.

It's probably fair to say that the move in American psychology from behaviourism to the cognitive approach was more evolutionary than revolutionary (it wasn't really a scientific revolution in the sense that Kuhn, 1962/1970, described them; see also Leahey, 1997). Cognitive psychologists continued to use experimental methods, they continued to measure behaviour and they continued to stress the importance of learning and environment on psychological processes. But not surprisingly there are also important differences between the behaviourist and cognitive approaches. 'In focus box 7' explores these differences.

In focus box 7

As you may recall from Chapter 2, one key difference between the cognitive and behaviourist approaches is that the former focuses more on the study of humans than it does on animals.

Behaviourism had assumed that the rules underlying learning – classical and operant conditioning and imitation – were effectively the same for all species, so results of experiments carried out on rats and pigeons could be directly applied to humans. Given that it was ethically more appropriate to carry out tightly controlled learning experiments on, for example, rats and pigeons than humans, experiments on certain types of animals tended to become the norm in behaviourism and then the results were generalised to all other species, including humans.

Whilst behaviourism focused on the idea of universal laws that applied to all species and aimed to show that the environment impacted on all animals in much the same way, cognitive psychology had taken note of the work in ethology, which suggested that each species of animal had its own different specialist traits that aided their survival.

Cognitive psychologists noted that humans seem to possess a range of specific cognitive abilities that are either unique to them (such as language) or that are qualitatively and/or quantitatively different from those displayed by other species (e.g., although other species may display evidence of reasoning, problem-solving, memory and perception, humans use these abilities in extremely flexible and complex ways). Therefore cognitive psychologists argue that if you want to understand the psychological abilities of humans, then you need to carry out appropriate experiments on humans.

A second important distinction is that the subject matter of the two approaches is quite different. Behaviourism had focused on how the external environment impacts on human behaviour, but cognitive psychology is far more interested in the kind of internal mental processes that Watson had attempted to discard from his vision of the subject.

Behaviourists had tended to argue either that such abilities didn't really exist, or that they couldn't be studied scientifically, or that they could be explained solely in terms of the basic learning principles that are present in all animals (hence Skinner's attempts to explain human language entirely in terms of conditioning and reinforcement).

Cognitive psychologists, spurred on by Chomsky's (1959) critique, argued that such abilities were real, could be studied, could not be reduced to behaviourist principles, and that to understand these abilities it's important to know what is happening internally, within the mind of the person, in between stimulus and response (behaviourists had largely restricted their attention to the stimulus and the response, and not on intermediary internal responses).

A third key difference, and the one most relevant to this chapter, was again driven by Chomsky; the suggestion that cognitive abilities are inherent from birth, that a healthy human infant brain has a number of innate rule-based systems that underlie pretty much everything that humans do. These innate rule-based cognitive systems underlie mental activities such as memory, attention, perception, reasoning and problem-solving, as well as language.

Perhaps mindful of the criticisms that have been aimed at behaviourists – that they adopt an extreme and inflexible position on the nature and nurture debate, which downplays, dismisses or ignores innate contributions to psychology – cognitive psychologists are generally more interactionist. Although they stress that the basic cognitive systems are innate, they are by no means argued to be fully formed; instead they require a certain amount of environmental stimulation and interaction to operate.

As we also noted back in Chapter 2, human cognitive systems have commonly been modelled metaphorically on computers (see Crowther-Heyck, 1999; Schultz & Schultz, 2004): humans are seen to possess numerous innate programmes with which they are hard-wired, but these programmes still require input from external sources to be able to perform their functions.

Just as every computer is slightly different, because it may have slightly different programmes and because it will have different data inputs, much the same can be said of humans. Human cognitive systems are likely to be broadly similar at birth (e.g., all humans will be born with some form of memory system), though there may be some differences due to genetic inheritance (some aspects of cognition may be inherited so some people have a better memory than others and pass the genes underlying their better memory onto their offspring). Also, cognitive systems will change and develop over the course of a lifetime due to training, experience, practice, regular or irregular usage, diet and nutrition, and numerous other variables.

So in this manner, the cognitive psychology approach postulates a much more interactionist vision of psychology than its behaviourist predecessor. It takes certain ideas from ethology (innate abilities and predispositions that are helpful for survival) but also acknowledges elements of the behaviourist position (that environment and experience make a considerable impact on and can shape, impair or improve these abilities), and combines the two by suggesting that the brain is a complex biological computer with multiple interactive cognitive systems that perform the mental operations that enable us to think, perceive and communicate. Crucially, though, cognitive psychology rejects the blank slate idea because, as Pinker (2003) convincingly puts it, a truly blank slate cannot *do* anything.

The end of the extreme nurture position

It's worth stating that the supposed 'fall' of behaviourism was a complex affair. Some behaviourists, such as Skinner, stuck to their extreme and radical views, others whole-heartedly embraced cognitive psychology because they had never fully dismissed the ideas of mind and consciousness or innate abilities in the first place, whilst others simply carried on with their work as they had before but made attempts to embrace the new language of cognition. But it's not simply that cognitive psychology became more compelling and successful throughout the 1950s, 1960s and beyond (though it did). In addition, behaviourism's extreme environmentalism became harder to defend even for psychologists working in the field of animal learning.

For example, the blank slate idea stresses that animals have no instincts or innate predispositions, which means that it should be entirely possible through conditioning techniques to teach any animal any behaviour. Schultz and Schultz (2004) report the work of Marian and Keller Breland, two former students of Skinner who took operant conditioning from psychology laboratories and applied it to training animals for shows and entertainment.

They trained over 6000 animals from more than 150 species to perform all kinds of behaviours that they would never naturally carry out in the wild, apparently supporting Skinner's position. However, the Brelands' methods were hampered by something that was displayed by many of the animals they attempted to train from various different species. Despite being rewarded to behave in particular ways the animals would often revert to innate behaviours, even when this meant delaying their reward. This tendency of organisms to revert to instinctive behaviours over conditioned responses, called **instinctive drift**, suggests that instincts not only exist but that they can also override behaviourist principles of learning.

A related challenge comes from research on humans. Behaviourism argues that because there are no innate instincts or tendencies it should be equally easy to condition a person to fear anything they are not already frightened of. Yet Seligman (1971) found that it was easy to condition people to fear some things, such as snakes, spiders, dogs and heights, but much harder to condition them to be frightened of others, such as cars or screwdrivers.

What are the important differences between the two types of thing? It's not their actual danger level as potentially all of them could be dangerous or harmful under the right circumstances. Seligman's suggestion is that the former category consists of things that have been encountered throughout our evolutionary history and throughout that time have been considered dangerous, so therefore we have developed a genetic predisposition to be frightened or at least wary of those things.

The latter category, on the other hand, consists of things that have not been encountered throughout our evolutionary history and, although they can be dangerous, having a fear of them has not provided any survival value so such fears are not passed on over generations.

Seligman called this phenomenon **biological preparedness**, which is based on evolutionary ideas that organisms able to identify and learn to fear genuine threats in their environment would have survival and reproductive advantages. Over time such innate predispositions to fear genuine environmental threats would become widespread adaptive traits for most humans and their primate relatives (Öhman & Mineka, 2003). Biological preparedness is related to instinctual drift: both show that an instinctual tendency towards an emotion for a particular object makes it easier to condition.

Therefore, even outside of the cognitive movement, psychologists from biological and behaviourist approaches were starting to recognise the value of the interactionist perspective. Clearly classical and operant conditioning can explain how various associations are learnt but not why some behaviours and emotions can be more easily conditioned than others, and not why certain specific behaviour patterns continue to re-emerge despite successful conditioning of alternatives. By positing the existence of certain predispositions and innate tendencies that can interact or interfere with behaviourist principles a much clearer picture of the nature and nurture relationship emerges.

Other approaches

So far this chapter has discussed how the behaviourist approach tradition-ally adopts an extreme nurture position, and how biological and cognitive approaches tend to defend the nature side of the argument and argue against the blank slate, but also often consider how innate aspects of psy-chology interact with learning and environment. Therefore, to varying extents, biological and cognitive psychologists could be argued to adopt an interactionist position.

Before I discuss whether this general trend towards interactionism in psychology means that the nature and nurture debate is effectively over, I should very briefly explain where the psychodynamic and humanist approaches stand in relation to the debate. It's worth stating that I'll be addressing both approaches in more detail later in the book, and it's also worth reminding you of what I hope was obvious from Chapter 2 – that both adopt generally very different approaches to psychology than the ones discussed in this chapter so far. Nevertheless, both could be argued to have some position on the debate.

The psychodynamic approach

As you may recall from Chapter 2, this approach stresses the role of unconscious processes on thinking, emotion, personality and behaviour. Sigmund Freud is perhaps the most famous and influential psychodynamic theorist, and his view of the mind was that it consists of three separate but interactive components. Although all three compo-nents contribute to who and what we are, we have only varying degrees of conscious awareness of them and their interactions. It is this dynamic, largely unconscious and often disharmonious relationship that underlies this approach and that also makes it so distinct from other approaches in psychology.

Freud was to some extent influenced by the evolutionary theory of Darwin and adopted the idea of instincts, which we've already discussed throughout this chapter. However, Freud had a specific take on instincts, viewing them as predominantly selfish and animalistic drives, often with a socially unacceptable component to them; either the nature or type of behaviour itself (e.g., we might wish to attack someone physically but this is rarely socially acceptable, except in certain sports or in warfare) or the timing of it (we might desire to have sex with someone, which is not in itself socially unacceptable, but it would be if we did so on a packed train). Instincts in psychodynamic terms then are biological drives (such as eating, drinking, aggression, sex, removal of waste products) that need to be satisfied and gratified immediately and unconditionally, and are driven by a need for pleasure or, at the very least, the release of tension or the end of pain or frustration.

Freud named the element of personality that acts as the source of all these basic impulses and drives the **id**. It is the most primitive and instinctual component of human nature, it is present from birth and it is also the part of the mind that we have the least conscious awareness of. Freud (1933) argued that humans could not operate at the sophisticated and social level that they do driven by their id alone, for the id has no consideration of reality, values, morality or good and evil.

The growing child interacts with parents and others and comes to realise that meeting the urges of the id, or at least doing so immediately, is unrealistic and not always possible. This leads to the development of the second component, the ego, very early on in childhood, as the child learns that although most of its urges will be met, this will only happen under certain conditions or within certain limits. We are largely conscious of the ego, which tries to perform rationally and realistically, using strategies and habits, memories of past experience and perception of the environment to get the id what it wants, but within the aforementioned limits (Hothersall, 2004).

As the child gets older Freud proposed that s/he faces certain moral challenges and is exposed to various standards of morality and ethics, set down by parents, teachers, religious organisations, the state, the law and society in general. These moral standards are internalised and represented by the third component, the **superego**, which provides all the absolute rules of what should and ought to be done in various situations, and what ideals the child should aspire to, plus it condemns and seeks to deny and restrain the demands of the id through anxiety and guilt. As with the ego, we have some conscious awareness of the superego but it's not total.

Via this brief description of Freud's three components of mind or levels of personality (which should be thought of more as metaphorical ideas rather than as real entities existing within the brain), it should hopefully be clear that, whilst the psychodynamic approach is very different from the biological and cognitive stances, it is still very much interaction-ist. Human beings within this psychological view are born with certain innate drives and instincts, represented by the id, which continue to man-ifest themselves throughout the person's life and behaviour, even if the person doesn't realise this. However, the importance of parental upbring-ing, learning, the environment and society are clearly pointed to by the later emergence of both the ego, representing the practical realities of the world, and the superego, which represents assorted acquired moral codes and prohibitions.

Whilst both the ego and superego are internalised, they result from interactions with the environment and what the child learns from them, though this learning may not always be accessible to conscious aware-ness. The id's demands will never greatly change or go away but what can change with experience is the way in which the three compo-nents interact and work together, and ultimately how successfully the id can be appeased in socially acceptable ways, without being exces-sively restrained, which Freud thought could lead to problems with mental health. So although Freud thought that the fundamental nature of the id could not be changed, the rationality of the ego and the morality of the superego are shaped and changed through experience, and these factors in turn interact with and determine how the id is satisfied.

Although Freud argued that a child's personality was fairly well settled by the age of five years, the fact that it can be shaped by external parental and societal factors before then stresses how this approach is genuinely interactionist. In addition, the fact that Freud proposed psychoanaly-sis as a method of treatment for psychological problems displayed in adulthood but rooted in childhood again implies that elements from the environment (in this case, the patient–therapist relationship) can interact with the innate elements represented by the id. We will return later to Freud's ideas and the psychodynamic approach, particularly in Chapter 8.

The humanist approach

Whilst the psychodynamic approach sees the nature and nurture debate from quite a different angle, by focusing on the impact of conscious and unconscious forces and their impact on mental health and morality, it nevertheless still addresses the roles of innate and learnt factors and their impact on a person. The humanist approach, on the other hand, is quite different in how it responds to the debate.

In many ways it acts as a challenge or a protest against the debate, specifically the dehumanising aspects of it. It acknowledges that it is an important debate and is not critical of behaviourist, biological, cognitive or psychodynamic approaches for taking up positions or trying to objectively study it, but also warns of the dangers of adopting too narrow or too polarised an approach, because this is both artificial and reductionistic (there will be more about reductionism in Chapter 9).

Because the humanist approach to psychology favours an idiographic stance and was grounded in a positive and client-centred approach to psychotherapy and mental health, by therapists and founders Carl Rogers and Abraham Maslow, it focuses as much on the needs of individuals as it does on generalised ideas and theories, and as much on subjective knowledge as objective knowledge. In these two senses the humanist approach is extremely different from the positions adopted by behaviourists, and biological and cognitive psychologists.

It's not so much that humanistic psychologists consider these approaches to be wrong, but rather they suggest that they fail to fully understand and explain what it means to be human. One of the problems with many psychological studies and theories, they argue, is that they focus on how a particular variable or set of variables (some innate within the person, some environmental) appear to affect a particular trait or behaviour. But the humanist approach stresses that an individual needs to be looked at holistically, as a whole person within the context of their past, present and future. Such an approach is not really conducive for laboratory-based experimental work.

It's difficult to sum up exactly where humanistic psychology stands on the nature and nurture debate because it doesn't really stand anywhere. One of its specific aims when it was founded in America in the mid-twentieth century was to challenge the dominant position in psychology of the time – behaviourism – and it was particularly critical of that approach's extreme environmentalism and its attempts to explain the influences of nature and nature on humans primarily by studying rats and pigeons in laboratories. But as you'll have seen in this chapter, since the mid-twentieth century the dominance of behaviourism has been challenged as much by the successes of the biological and cognitive approaches as by the humanist approach, so psychology is not as one-sided or as narrow as it was when humanistic psychology first emerged.

Humanistic psychologists still largely consider themselves to be in a position where they can offer a critical voice in various areas of psychology, including the nature and nurture debate. This involves them questioning whether the traditional nomothetic methods of science are always the best or only way to study this debate, encouraging the use of various alternative methodologies if these are appropriate (using qualitative methodologies to record people's experiences of how they feel the different factors of nature and nurture impact on their lives), and acknowledging that the debate often focuses on how factors in the past created the present whereas it is equally important to focus on how individuals can initiate constructive change for the future. Overall then, humanistic psychology ultimately seeks to question and supplement what is provided by the other approaches in this debate.

Is the debate still relevant?

It used to be the case that this debate was described as nature versus nurture, as if it might be possible to choose a winner, to identify which component had the only or greater impact on psychology. The idea that all aspects of psychology might derive solely from either nature or nurture is now widely dismissed, sometimes being referred to as a **single cause fallacy**.

Behaviourism's attempt to try and explain psychology solely in terms of environmental factors and learning, although popular at the time and successful in terms of its exploration of the roles of classical and operant conditioning and imitation in many behaviours, is generally thought now to have ended in failure. Developments in behaviourism, ethology, cognitive psychology and even in psychodynamic and humanistic approaches throughout the twentieth century seemed to indicate that psychology was moving more towards an interactionist position, whereby genes and environment were both acknowledged to contribute to mental traits and behaviours. The questions that remained were about the relative contributions of genetics and environment to different traits and behaviours, and how the two might interact.

An important focus in psychology over the last few decades has been to address these questions. So in answer to the question, is the debate still relevant, well yes it is, though the debate has certainly evolved since the time of Plato and Aristotle, and even since behaviourism and ethology took it in such extremely different directions in the first half of the twentieth century.

A key development has been in a relatively new field of study, **behavioural genetics**, which specifically seeks to identify the roles that genes play in the behaviour of humans and other animals, to disentangle that from the contribution that environments make, and to find out in what ways the two interact. Although behavioural genetics is not exclusively a branch of psychology, because it involves contributions from geneticists, biologists and ethologists, psychologists nevertheless have made an important contribution to this exciting area.

Behavioural genetics

In two very important senses, Sir Francis Galton can be considered the father of the behavioural genetics movement. First, the statistics used in behavioural genetics were either initially developed by Galton or later derived from his pioneering work (Schultz & Schultz, 2004). Second, as we noted earlier in the chapter, the twin-study method that Galton devised has become a cornerstone for work in behavioural genetics.

Twin studies and variants on the twin-study methodology have been greatly extended since Galton's day. How closely related two people are in genetic terms can tell us something about possible genetic contributions to various psychological traits and behaviours. If we also have information about the extent to which the same two people share the same environments, then we can also learn something about the possible role of environment for these traits and behaviours. If two people are very closely related (identical twins are as genetically similar as it's possible for two people to be) and they share a particular trait or behaviour, then this might mean that the trait or behaviour has a genetic basis. As Galton noted, if the closely related people who share the same trait/behaviour have also been raised in different environments, then this further strengthens the possibility that genetics are involved.

So by looking at thousands and thousands of people, looking at whether traits do or do not run in families, comparing people who have been adopted with both their biological parents (with whom they should share 50 per cent of their genes) and their adopted parents (with whom they should share no genes), by comparing dizygotic (fraternal) twins and monozygotic (identical) twins, and also by looking at the rare cases of these two types of twins who have been adopted separately and raised in different environments by different families, it's possible to collect large amounts of data about the contributions of both genetics and environment.

A number of things have changed since Galton's day. The first is the number of people available to study: although it's rare to find cases of monozygotic twins who have been adopted and then raised in different environments (which is the ideal comparison to make because they are genetically identical, but their environments are different) psychologists now seek them out and when they are found they can provide very important data about the nature and nurture debate. Even when such cases are not available researchers are now better placed to carry out larger scale twin studies, of both types of twins, raised together and apart, than ever before. Such studies have also been carried out in many different countries, which means it's possible to establish if the effects of genes and environment are similar cross-culturally. So there is now more data available and it's also accumulating.

A second change is that it's now much easier to carry out longitudinal studies of twins and families, which means that it's possible to follow the same twins or families over a longer period of time and establish if the contributions of genetic and environmental factors change or stay the same over time.

A third factor is the quality and range of tests available to psychologists. In Galton's day psychometric tests of personality, intelligence and cognitive abilities were relatively new and not widely used. Contemporary tests are based on psychological research and theory, are carefully designed and tested for their validity and reliability, and are standardised so that everyone involved is tested in as similar a way as possible. This means that twins and family members involved in these studies will be given an extensive range of psychological and physiological assessments, which may include tests of reading, writing and spelling, intelligence tests, various measures of cognitive abilities such as memory, perception and attention, tests of personality and mental health, obtaining information about occupations, hobbies and social activities, and even gaining a full medical history, and measures of heart rate and blood pressure. It's therefore potentially possible to establish the heritability of a wide range of psychological and physiological traits – the extent to which genetic individual differences contribute to individual differences in the observed traits.

A final factor is increased consideration of issues that may confound research of this kind. So, for example, if monozygotic twins are more similar in their intelligence scores than are dizygotic twins, then this might be attributed to their greater genetic similarity, therefore suggesting that intelligence is primarily an inherited trait rather than one that is influenced by environment or upbringing. However, as Furnham (1996) notes, some psychologists point out that because identical twins look a lot more similar than fraternal twins it's possible that their parents and other people just treat them more similarly. So here a genetic factor (physical appearance) leads to environmental differences (the ways the twins are treated), and it may be these environmental differences rather than the genetic ones that actually affect intelligence in this case.

An ingenious way to test this possibility has been developed, which involves finding and comparing identical twins who were thought to be fraternal, and fraternal twins who were thought to be identical. Again, there aren't many of these cases but results from those that have been studied suggest that it is whether the twins are actually genetically identical rather than whether they and others thought that they were that leads to greater similarities in intelligence scores. So here at least the research suggests that greater similarities in intelligence can be put down more to genetic than environmental factors.

What conclusions can be reached from behavioural genetics studies?

As I acknowledged earlier, data from behavioural genetics studies are still being accumulated and analysed, but nevertheless some patterns do seem to be emerging. Already one key pattern is quite clear: nearly all psychological traits and behaviours (such as personality traits, mental illnesses and IQ scores) involve at least some contributions from both genes and environmental factors. There are variations for different traits and behaviours, as you might expect.

For example, based on IQ scores there is good evidence to suggest that genes play a very important role in intelligence, and that genes account for as much if not slightly more of the variation in IQ scores as environmental factors do (Plomin & Spinath, 2004). That said, environmental factors do still have a considerable impact on IQ scores as well, and it's worth stressing that the inheritance of certain genes cannot cause someone to have a set level of IQ. Instead it seems that genes simply provide a framework for certain possibilities, but the environments that a person is born into or experiences throughout life will determine more precisely their IQ scores at different points in time.

A very important example of the ways in which genes and environments can interact and influence potential psychological outcomes is the concept of the reaction range, 'the range of possibilities – the upper and lower limits – that the genetic code allows' (Passer et al., 2009). So to say that a psychological trait such as intelligence is genetically influenced is not to say that it is entirely fixed at birth or that it cannot be modified, but rather that a person inherits the potential to achieve a certain degree of intelligence that is likely to fall somewhere between two intellectual levels. Where exactly the person ends up within these two genetically determined levels will be affected by various environmental factors, such as a good or poor quality diet, the availability of books, computers and intellectually stimulating toys throughout childhood and the quality of schooling the child receives.

Just to stress how complicated these interactions can be, even if a child inherits the potential to achieve a high level of intelligence and also receives an enriched and intellectually stimulating environment whilst growing up, it's still possible for them to fail to reach their upper potential if other factors, such as their personality or motivation (which may also be affected by genetic and environmental factors) mean that they fail to make the most of their biological and environmental advantages.

A final thing to stress about estimates of heritability that are derived from behavioural genetics research is that they relate to the population the data were collected from. This is important for two reasons.

First, populations and groups vary so therefore the precise contributions of genetics and environment may vary for the same trait in different groups, places or countries.

Second, the data refer to the population and not individuals. So even if we find that within a particular population about 40 per cent of the variation in a particular trait, for example sociability, is due to genetic variation, this does not mean that a particular person's level of sociability is 40 per cent down to their genes and that the remaining 60 per cent is down to the environment. These estimates are based on the data taken from samples from a particular population, but there will still be variation for individuals.

Nevertheless, estimates of heritability are still extremely useful for identifying patterns in the contributions of genes, environment and the interactions between them for various psychological traits and behaviours.

That the results from studies of behavioural genetics suggest that most psychological traits are the result of a complex interplay of genetics and environment has led some researchers to try to identify which genes specifically contribute to these traits. The bulk of the research so far suggests that there aren't single genes that account for human intelligence or the complex patterns of thoughts and behaviours that we see in mental illnesses such as schizophrenia. Other researchers have been more interested in trying to identify which features of the environment are most likely to affect our tendency to develop certain traits; for example, which is the most important environmental contributor to whether we reach our full intellectual potential, or whether a genetic predisposition to depression actually manifests itself.

This kind of research is important because it can identify risk factors for mental illnesses or possible ways of giving children the best start in life, but it's also important to emphasise that we now understand that genetics and environment are not really separate determinants of behaviour but operate together as an integrated system. Genes may provide us with dispositions towards a behaviour or trait, but that behaviour or trait may only occur under the right conditions or in the optimal environment. A particularly good example of this is reported in 'In focus box 8'.

In focus box 8

A very clear and useful example of the way that genetics and environment appear to operate together to influence behaviour is demonstrated by research on the monoamine oxidase A gene (MAO-A gene).

Low activity of this gene had been linked with violent, aggressive or anti-social behaviour, but two important studies, one of men in New Zealand (Caspi et al., 2002) and another on boys in America (Foley et al., 2004), suggest that simply having low MAO-A activity does not itself correlate with violent or anti-social activity.

However, low MAO-A activity when coupled with abuse in childhood or parental neglect was found to lead to anti-social behaviour later in life. Caspi *et al.*, for example, found that the men in their study who'd had bad childhood experiences and low MAO-A activity were four times more likely to have been convicted of a violent crime before they reached the age of twenty-four.

This represents a particularly clear example of a particular gene and a particular type of environment jointly affecting behaviour, but it may hint at the much bigger picture: that it is the interaction of genes and environment that is essential when studying psychology.

Conclusions

Overall, then, I think it's safe to say that the nature and nurture debate itself is still relevant, but we can conclusively dismiss the idea of nature versus nurture, because this creates a false dichotomy. Most approaches in psychology now accept some form of interactionist position, even though the different approaches may focus on very different elements.

Important developments, particularly within behavioural genetics, have created new research paradigms that in turn have enabled psychologists to have a much clearer idea about the contributions of nature and nurture to a wide range of psychological traits and behaviours. There is now a general acceptance and understanding that it is not really about which is more important, nature or nurture, but rather that the debate can be better defined as 'nature via nurture' (Ridley, 2003), so a key focus for psychology, particularly within the biological approach, is to identify how environments affect the ways that genes express themselves.

However, it's worth remembering the warning of the humanist approach: we may need to consider whether the traditional methods of science are sufficient to fully understand this debate or whether there might be more to it. From the brief history of the debate I've presented here, I've tried to show that decisions about the contributions of nature and nurture are not always based solely on scientific evidence.

The popularity of eugenics and of Watson's behaviourism in different places and points in history shows how political ideology, public opinion and views on the importance of freedom and equality can contribute to this debate. Therefore psychology should not just consider the contributions and interactions of nature and nurture, it should also explore further how attitudes, beliefs and political persuasions, at both an individual and societal level, can shape or contribute to developments within this debate. In Chapters 6 and 7, we'll consider specifically how biases in psychology towards gender and culture respectively have impacted on the subject.

Further reading

Pinker, S. (2003). *The blank slate: The modern denial of human nature.* London: Penguin.

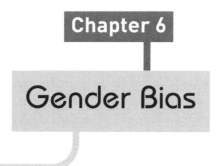

Chapter 6

Gender Bias

Men and women clearly differ biologically and anatomically in certain ways, there's no real debate to be had about that. But often we are led to believe that men and women also differ psychologically in various ways too, for example in terms of cognitive abilities, personality and emotions. Whilst many psychologists and members of the general public accept and even promote the idea that the sexes differ on numerous psychological traits and abilities, others argue that these differences might not really exist or that they might be exaggerated, or if they do exist that the differences are more a result of cultural categories and stereotypes than a result of biology. In this chapter we'll try to address what gender bias is, what it can do, how it has affected psychology and what we can perhaps learn from this.

◉ What is gender bias?

To understand what gender bias is it is initially necessary to identify what we mean by gender. The term generally relates to the characteristics that distinguish males from females. Gender is usually distinguished from the term sex, which relates very specifically to the biological or actual physical state or category that a person anatomically or functionally belongs to. So when categorising someone as a man or woman based on the presence or absence of particular sexual/genital organs, or by whether they produce sperm or ova, we are technically describing their sex.

Defining gender is much more difficult as many different definitions of the term are used. A crucial distinction was made by the psychologist John Money who argued that whilst it was appropriate to use the word sex to describe the aforementioned biological or physical differences there should also be a word that refers to the psychological, cultural and behavioural differences that commonly relate to males and females, that is gender (Money & Ehrhardt, 1972). This distinction between sex and gender is still commonly used today, though there is some confusion about the precise relationship between the two terms.

Clearly the terms are closely related – most people who display a male gender role are also biologically categorised as men, and the female gender role is similarly connected to the biological category of women. However, this is not always the case; for example, transsexuals are individuals who identify with a gender that is inconsistent with their biological sex. And at a more mundane level, although various traits, behaviours and physical characteristics may commonly be ascribed to men *or* women, the fact is that very often they can be used just as appropriately to describe the traits, behaviours and physical characteristics of the other sex (Crawford & Unger, 1995).

In addition, whilst some psychologists argue that gender 'is what culture makes out of the "raw material" of biological sex' (Crawford & Unger, 1995, p. 39), gender is also commonly just used as a synonym for biological sex, which makes things rather more confusing. However, for the purposes of this chapter the word gender will primarily be used to describe the way that males and females are characterised psychologically rather than biologically.

Having defined gender, what then is meant by gender bias? It can refer to many things but predominantly in this chapter we'll be focusing on the idea that although psychology has long sought to understand gender – to identify the differences between males and females in terms of their psychology, exactly what those differences are, and to measure how considerable they are – it may have made a fundamental mistake. That mistake is that psychologists have commonly failed to recognise that their own discipline may be fundamentally biased.

Feminist psychology, which focuses very specifically on trying to understand gender both within psychology and outside in the wider world, broadly argues that throughout much of its history the discipline of psychology has been dominated by males and has been carried out from a largely 'male perspective'. Such dominance and perspective is argued to inevitably direct research and theory in some directions at the expense of others, and may potentially reinforce or even seek to justify existing inequalities in the name of science.

It's important to stress that feminist psychology is not a straightforward category either – there are different forms of feminist psychology and not all feminist psychologists think or argue exactly the same things. But what nearly all feminist psychologists can be said to have in common is that they are interested in the concept of gender and how women are affected by it.

Similarly, gender bias is not a straightforward term either. In fact sometimes gender bias is argued to take one of two different forms, **alpha bias** and **beta bias** (Hare-Mustin & Marecek, 1988). The distinction is that some theories or approaches in psychology are said to exaggerate the differences between males and females and these are said to be examples of alpha bias. In cases of beta bias, on the other hand, there is an attempt to minimise or downplay the differences between males and females. A key issue with beta bias is that such theories or explanations tend to be based around research on men, and these results are then erroneously applied to women.

You might be wondering, if some theories are guilty of alpha bias and others of beta bias then where does the truth lie? That question is not an easy one to answer, though it might be argued that simply by being aware of such biases, why they happen and what impact they can have some sort of progress is already being made.

◉ Is psychology dominated by men?

One of the arguments used as evidence for gender bias in psychology is that women have often been neglected or discriminated against in the history of the subject. This neglect and discrimination has taken various forms, but I'll be discussing three of them here: the lack of access to and support within psychology for women; the neglect of contributions by women in the history of psychology; and biases in who is studied, in what contexts they are studied and how they are studied.

It's worth stressing that these three forms of neglect and discrimination towards women are hardly unique to psychology. They partly reflect broader cultural trends from particular times and places and therefore apply just as much (and as we'll see, possibly more so) to other sciences and many other academic disciplines. What makes psychology so important in this regard, and distinguishes it from many other sciences and disciplines, is that it specifically aims to study and tries to explain gender.

It is interested in the effects of culture on individual men and women and their masculinity and femininity, but inevitably it is also part of the very culture that it seeks to investigate. Therefore, to understand gender psychologists must be particularly mindful of the risks and potential consequences of gender bias.

Lack of access and support for women

There is no question that women have made a hugely significant contribution to the history and development of psychology. However, when psychology first started in the late nineteenth-century cultural trends and societal prescriptions did not make it easy for women to be involved.

As noted before, such restrictions and assumptions were not unique to psychology: it was widely accepted in America and Europe that women should not be pursuing independent careers but should instead be focusing on marriage, having a family and tending the home. Although in the twenty-first century women may be encouraged to 'have it all' – relationships, a family and a career – this was certainly not the case in the late nineteenth and early twentieth century.

During this period Valentine (2010) notes that there were many barriers and obstacles to women wanting to forge a career in psychology, or even simply study it in the first place. Although Valentine is specifically referring to women in Britain one of the most famous early cases of a woman struggling to find a place within psychology was American.

In the late nineteenth century Mary Whiton Calkins had difficulties even being accepted officially onto a graduate programme in psychology at Harvard University (Hothersall, 2004; Schultz & Schultz, 2004). William James welcomed her to the programme, despite the protestations of the university and its president, but although she was allowed to attend classes she was never officially registered as a student, nor was this the final impediment she would face in her pursuit of a career within psychology.

Despite meeting all the requirements of the award of a Ph.D. at Harvard and gaining glowing recommendations from James and his colleagues, Calkins was denied her doctoral degree. Although she went on to have a successful career in psychology, which included her becoming the first woman president of the APA in 1905, she never received her Ph.D. from Harvard. In fact, Hothersall (2004) points out that Harvard didn't award a doctoral degree to a woman until as late as 1963.

If Calkins is perhaps the most famous case she is certainly not the only one. Historians of psychology have noted that many women psychologists, in both America (Hothersall, 2004; Schultz & Schultz, 2004) and Britain (Valentine, 2010), faced 'discrimination, subordination and segregation' (Valentine, 2010, p. 972) despite showing just as much ability and, considering all the barriers they faced, probably much greater determination and commitment than their male counterparts.

This widespread sexism and bias took numerous forms and persisted throughout much of the twentieth century, and arguably can still be said to exist in some form or another even today. The difference in modern times is that such problems are more likely to be implicit rather than explicit. In the past, prejudice towards women was easier to detect given that it was expressed publicly and not considered unacceptable, whereas now it is socially censured and illegal. Although this clearly represents progress it does mean that prejudiced attitudes are now much more likely to be hidden from public view, or discussed only amongst like-minded people, and therefore any effects are likely to be much more subtle.

In the past, however, examples of discrimination ranged from women being denied access to university education altogether (only a few decades earlier Calkins would not have been admitted to Harvard at all), to being excluded from certain jobs and positions within universities, to being paid less and having fewer opportunities for promotion than men in the same roles. Valentine (2010) notes that women were frequently denied access to common rooms and were excluded from professional society dinners.

However, on the more positive side it has been noted that, despite such clear and explicit examples of discrimination against women, psychology was actually much more enlightened and forward-thinking than other sciences of the time.

For example, Schultz and Schultz (2004) note that by the early twentieth century, twenty women had earned doctoral degrees in psychology from American universities, and in the 1906 edition of *American Men of Science*, 12 per cent of the psychologists listed are women, both of which are impressive statistics given the restrictions and barriers that women faced at the time.

Women were also accepted into the BPS from the time it was founded in 1901 (Valentine, 2010), and although the APA was founded solely by a group of men in 1892 this again reflects the limited number of women who were at that point working within psychology. As female psychologists emerged they were actively encouraged to join the ranks of the APA (Schultz & Schultz, 2004).

By contrast, female doctors were not permitted membership of the American Medical Association until 1915 (Walsh, 1977, cited in Schultz & Schultz, 2004) and the Royal Society, perhaps the oldest scientific society in the world, did not accept women until 1948. It's also worth remembering that Calkins became the APA's first female president as early as 1905, and that her progress at Harvard was stunted not by her fellow male psychologists but by the administration of the university.

Psychology then seems slightly unusual compared to other sciences of the time; although women faced numerous obstacles to their advancement in the field, they still seem to have been given more encouragement and support to participate than women in other fields. There is unlikely to be one single reason to account for this, though Valentine (2010) summarises two likely possibilities, both related to the youth of psychology as a subject: psychology needed all the support it could get so perhaps women were accepted merely to swell the numbers; and possibly because psychology was such a new area the male dominance so apparent in other sciences had not been so firmly established, allowing women to get a foot in the door.

However, given that psychology seems to have been more supportive of women being involved in its development and progress than other sciences of the time, and that the women who were involved, despite their small numbers and the difficulties they faced, were clearly dedicated, highly talented and hard working, we might ask why women are not more recognised for their contributions to the history of the subject. We'll address that point next.

The neglect of contributions by women in the history of psychology

So women have undoubtedly made numerous contributions to the history of the subject, but when members of the general public are asked to name a famous figure in the history of psychology I suspect that very few of them would come up with the names Mary Calkins or Beatrice Edgell, for example.

Of course, this is somewhat unfair as the layperson is probably most likely to come up with the name Sigmund Freud (who was not truly a psychologist at all in the strict definition of the word) over the likes of John Watson or Stanley Milgram, for example. That Freud's name comes up more than Calkins or Edgell is not really to do with gender bias but probably has much more to do with the way that psychology generally, and the psychodynamic approach more specifically, has been promoted and represented over the last century or so.

Perhaps a better test would be to ask distinguished psychologists to give and rank the ten most important psychologists of all time. This is pretty much what Korn, Davis and Davis (1991) did: they asked twenty-nine leading historians of the subject to come up with their lists and then compared these to a list that had previously been obtained and compiled by asking ninety-three graduate department of psychology chairpersons to do the same thing. The full details of the results themselves don't matter too much for this chapter (though if you're interested, the top choice for historians was Wilhelm Wundt, followed by William James and Sigmund Freud, whilst for chairpersons the top choice was Burrhus Skinner, followed by Freud and James, and overall the two groups had seven names in common in their rankings) but what is important is that all those listed were white males. So when key figures in contemporary psychology are given an opportunity to choose the most important figures in the history of their subject women psychologists are notable by their absence.

If women psychologists have made notable contributions to psychology, and I don't think there can be any doubt at all that they have (we have discussed the work of a few influential women psychologists in this book and far more are identified by Greenwood, 2009; Hothersall, 2004; Schultz & Schultz, 2004; Valentine, 2010), then what can account for the fact that their contributions rarely seem to be recognised as being as important as many of their male counterparts? It certainly can no longer be said to be because of the ratio of male to female psychologists – whilst psychology in the early part of the twentieth century was certainly dominated by men and there were very few women, this trend has slowly reversed. Hothersall (2004) reports that the percentage of Ph.D. degrees in psychology awarded by American universities to women has risen from 25 per cent in the 1920s to 42 per cent in the 1990s, and such trends may mean that well over half of the psychology doctorate degrees currently being awarded are going to women.

So why has the gender bias persisted? One argument often put forward is based on the idea that the subject of psychology, particularly its history and practice, is largely embedded in an androcentric (male dominated) culture. Some feminist critics point out that psychology was started by men, that most historians of psychology are men and that fundamentally the history of psychology is a social construct that seeks to maintain the male dominance of the discipline (O'Connell & Russo, 1991).

These critics argue that, whether consciously or not, many of psychology's historians have, in the past, misattributed and devalued the contributions of women, whilst highlighting and exaggerating the contributions of men. They also argue that there is circular relationship between a male-dominated psychology and a male-dominated world, with some psychological theories and research findings reflecting androcentric values and assumptions from wider society, which then in turn go on to justify further stereotyping and discrimination against women. We'll discuss this point further in the Section 'Biases in who is studied, how and in what contexts'.

But is this position hopeless? According to feminist psychologists the answer is very clearly no. For example, O'Connell & Russo (1991) identify a number of ways in which they believe that women in psychology can seek to counter the neglect and gender bias that has arguably dominated the discipline since its beginnings. For example, they stress that there is a need for women to be more aware of the problems; for them to actively participate more within psychology, both its present and future directions and the study of its history, and be mindful of the barriers to such participation; to focus specifically on identifying and countering examples of gender bias; and by seeking to increase the number of women who hold powerful leadership roles in psychology.

Around two decades have passed since the publication of the O'Connell and Russo article (itself part of a special issue of the journal *Psychology of Women Quarterly*, one of a new group of journals that specifically focuses on psychological issues related to women, gender and feminism) and in that time some progress can already be seen to have been made.

For example, most recent books on the history of psychology devote sections to the neglect of women and highlight the contributions of female psychologists, whilst introductory psychology textbooks now routinely highlight and criticise androcentric theories. It seems that increasing numbers of women in psychology, a greater awareness of the problems that they have faced in the past and the emergence of journals such as *Psychology of Women Quarterly* mean at least that female psychologists are no longer being neglected to the extent that they once were. This at least is an important step in the right direction.

◉ Biases in who is studied, how and in what contexts

So far we've discussed how psychology has not always been as accessible or supportive to women as it might have been and how women's achievements and contributions to the discipline may have been downplayed or neglected throughout much of its history. But there is a third aspect of psychology that has faced criticism, namely its methodologies.

Crucially, feminist critics have noted that psychological research can be biased in many different ways, for example by not recording or reporting the sex of the participants involved, by studying men more than women, and by researching one sex more than the other in particular contexts or research areas, for example by studying affiliation among women but rarely among men, and the opposite pattern for aggression (Crawford & Unger, 1995).

Similarly, in the past a lot of research was carried out that looked specifically at whether mothers who worked outside of the home endangered the psychological well-being of their children. Such research emphasised the norm that women should be at home looking after their children and stressed the dangers that could arise if women chose to deviate from that norm. Although this may indeed be a valid area for research, it is also research that reflects a particular value system, one that puts forward a specific societal norm and seeks to maintain it by concentrating on the negative consequences of what happens when women reject that norm.

Such research might be acceptable if it were balanced by other studies that investigate the impact that fathers' work commitments have on the mental health of their children, or if there were more studies that considered and investigated the possible benefits of mothers who work. Both would represent examples of research that challenge the norm, plus they would provide a more complete picture of the impact of parental working practices on child mental health and well-being. However, for the most part there have been fewer examples of these two types of study than of those that focus on the negatives caused by mothers working (Crawford & Unger, 1995). This suggests an area of research that has been strongly affected by gender bias.

Sex differences

A final and particularly controversial area that I'll address within this section is work on sex differences. Psychology has long had an interest in this area, but the research tends to be controversial in several ways. One area for concern is the impact that reporting differences between the sexes can have on members of both sexes.

For example, any research that reports findings that one sex is better than the other at a particular ability shoulders a huge weight of responsibility because it may create a stereotype or reinforce an existing one. Whilst some psychologists argue that it is their scientific duty to study and report such differences, and that there should be no problems as long as the research is carried out and reported in an entirely objective, impartial and neutral way, other psychologists, particularly those from a feminist perspective, doubt whether true impartiality is possible given the way that both psychology and notions of gender are so firmly entrenched in culture.

As noted earlier, gender bias is argued to take two possible forms: alpha bias, in which differences between males and females are said to be exaggerated, and beta bias, where differences are minimised or downplayed. The latter may particularly reflect the earlier criticism that in some areas of research men have been studied more than women. The idea here then is that men are widely studied, but important experiences or circumstances that are unique to women are ignored so an assumption is simply made that women are the same as men, without research being carried out to confirm this.

But there are other problems with research into sex differences that are both separate from but may nevertheless interact with the two forms of gender bias. Over the last century there have been numerous studies carried out on sex differences on a number of psychological traits, including a range of social behaviours and cognitive abilities. One problem is that the results are far from consistent and straightforward, and are sometimes entirely contradictory.

Furnham (1996) notes that these contradictions and inconsistencies may result from a number of different factors. For example, they may be due to the different methods employed to measure the psychological concepts being looked at (e.g., some rely on observational studies, others on self-report questionnaires and some others on comparisons of males and females carrying out tests under laboratory conditions) or because of ambiguities to do with the concepts themselves.

They may also be due to the fact that different populations may be tested, so studies may look at sex differences in populations with different ages, in different cultures or at different levels of social class – all variables that may interact and/or correlate with sex/gender and therefore we may question the validity of any inferences based on sex differences alone.

Finally, sex differences may also vary according to even minor variations in the tasks used or the situations under which the data are collected. Although these problems in psychological research are not unique to sex differences by any means, feminist psychologists note that the impact and potential dangers are greater in this research area because they can contribute to stereotyping and discrimination.

To address many of the problems that seem apparent when individual studies into sex differences are compared it is possible to carry out **meta-analyses**, in which the results of several studies on a related research question are combined statistically, and **systematic reviews**, in which important research in the area is identified, synthesised and appraised collectively.

A review of more than 2000 studies by Maccoby and Jacklin (1974) suggested that although there was evidence for some differences (e.g., throughout childhood boys are more aggressive than girls; girls have greater verbal ability than boys and this continues into adolescence; males are superior at visual–spatial tasks in adolescence and adulthood; and males seem to have greater mathematical ability on average, though differences are not as great as those for spatial ability) there was no support for a number of popular myths about the two sexes, such as females being more social than males, or males being more analytic than females. In other areas the authors noted that the evidence was simply too ambiguous or inconclusive, such as whether one sex is more anxious, competitive or more compliant than the other. Overall, they found more evidence for similarities than differences between males and females.

More recently Hyde (2005) carried out an analysis of forty-six major meta-analyses to assess the impact of gender differences on a whole range of psychological traits and abilities, including cognitive abilities, verbal and nonverbal communication, aggression, leadership, self-esteem and moral reasoning. Her conclusions were that gender had either only a small effect or no effect at all on most of the variables studied, including those that had been previously been argued to show reliable differences, such as verbal behaviour and mathematical ability. The few exceptions were that men masturbated more than women, had more positive attitudes about sex in uncommitted relationships and, consistent with Maccoby and Jacklin (1974), were more physically aggressive than women.

Hyde was also interested in whether gender differences were affected by social context and the impact of gender roles. She therefore looked at meta-analyses of studies where participants knew that they were being observed (under these circumstances, expectations about appropriate gender roles are likely to be more influential on behaviour), or where they did not know they were being observed, or where they were told that they could not be identified as either male or female (under these latter circumstances people may feel more free to behave contrary to societal expectations based on gender).

The results suggest that some differences between men and women are greater when the person feels they are being observed and when others know their gender, but such differences can be less great or even disappear when the person feels less constrained by social expectation – that is, when they don't think they're being observed or when their gender status is hidden from others. Overall then, this suggests that at least some apparent differences between men and women are in some way a product of social context and therefore are not immutable.

It seems that who has been studied, how the research has been carried out and in what contexts may all raise questions about how successfully psychology has studied gender and so-called sex differences. Debate and interpretation of the data are still ongoing, but there are enough good reasons to suggest that biases in how data are collected and interpreted can impact on our understanding of the psychology of men, women and the differences between them. Such problems do not simply have consequences for psychology, they can also impact on opportunities for men and women, and addressing such problems may help to combat discrimination, prejudice and stereotyping.

Does gender bias matter and what can psychologists do about it?

How much does gender bias matter? This partly depends on who is being asked. Approaches to psychology that arise more from the positivist-realist or nomothetic traditions (those that adopt more of a 'natural science' perspective and assume that psychology can be an objective science through careful, standardised measurements and observations of 'real' things in the world), have tended to argue that gender bias is not that important. Traditionally this has applied particularly to psychologists from the biological and behaviourist approaches that might have argued in the past that biological contributions to psychology, and the stimuli and responses of behaviourism, are entirely the same whether they are studied and measured by male or female psychologists.

But following more recent developments in the past few decades within women-centred and feminist psychology, a greater awareness has arisen that psychology as a discipline can be and indeed has been affected by gender bias. The full extent of gender bias on psychology is unclear, debatable and arguably may never be known, but this growing awareness has nevertheless had some impact on all areas of the discipline.

One result of these developments is that no particular approach within psychology is to blame for gender bias, nor are any approaches immune from it. Whilst the aforementioned biological and behaviourist approaches may be argued to be more susceptible to gender bias if they assume the idea of an entirely impartial observer, such an idea is no longer as widely accepted as it once was.

The fact is that gender bias can occur within any approach to psychology. Freud's psychodynamic approach is arguably much more qualitative, idiographic and less in the natural science vein, and yet Freud has frequently been accused of anti-female bias (see Chodorow, 1991). However, despite Freud's ideas the psychodynamic approach as a whole cannot be considered to share this bias – there have been many successful women within this approach and the psychoanalyst Karen Horney was perhaps the first of many to challenge Freud's views on women and was one of the earliest examples of a psychologist with distinctly feminist concerns (Hothersall, 2004; O'Connell & Russo, 1991; Schultz & Schultz, 2004).

As for what can be done about gender bias, it requires that both men and women continue to identify and question purely androcentric concepts and methodologies within psychology, that they identify research areas of particular significance to women that have so far not been sufficiently addressed within the discipline, and that they consider and investigate the ways in which social trends, expectations and stereotypes continue to shape and maintain existing gender roles. Clearly much progress has been made in the history of psychology to combat gender bias, but most feminist psychologists would no doubt argue that there is still much more left to be done. Of course to varying extents concepts, trends, expectations and stereotypes may all be products of culture. Therefore in Chapter 7, it's highly appropriate to consider the impact of cultural bias on psychology.

Further reading

Crawford, M. & Unger, R. K. (1995). Gender issues in psychology. In A. M. Colman (Ed.), *Controversies in psychology* (pp. 37–57). London: Longman.

Hyde, J. S. (2005). The gender similarities hypothesis. *American Psychologist, 60*(6), 581–592.

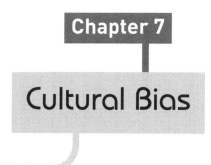

Chapter 7

Cultural Bias

The fundamental aim of psychology is to understand human nature as a whole but, as we saw in Chapter 6, this is a discipline that has tended to be dominated by western, white middle-class men who have often carried out their research on white middle-class male university students.

In Chapter 6 we focused on the issue of gender and showed that psychology has changed over time so that there are now far more women psychologists and much greater attention is paid to who participates in psychological research, both of which may help to lessen the potential for gender bias. But as mentioned at the end of Chapter 6, and as you might have guessed from the title of this chapter, gender is not the only area in which there is the potential for bias.

What is cultural bias?

Science, particularly the natural sciences and the nomothetic tradition, seems traditionally to have been rather good at discovering regularities and general principles that explain how particular forces or systems work in relatively predictable ways.

When psychology was first conceived it sought to follow in the footsteps of the older sciences by trying to find the regularities and general principles that explain mental processes and behaviour (Teigen, 2002). Such a pattern can be seen in Watson's attempts to make psychology a natural science using standardised objective experimental methods to identify laws of learning that were thought to apply equally well to all animals, including humans. However, it could be argued that as psychology sought generalisable laws applicable to all animal species, it focused less on considerations of variation. One particular form of variation we're going to consider here is that of cultural differences.

The assumption then is that culture – defined here as 'the enduring values, beliefs, behaviours, and traditions that are shared by a large group of people and passed on from one generation to the next' (Passer *et al.*, 2009, p. 18) – may shape and/or impact on mental processes and development, and on behaviour, in various ways, some subtle, some less so.

However, the majority of research and studies carried out in all major areas of psychology throughout the twentieth century tended to focus on people from western cultures, particularly Western Europe and America. The results from these studies formed the basis for theories about learning, cognitive processes, social and emotional development, mental illness and so on, and also for tests of personality and intelligence. The implicit assumption was that these results from western participants (also commonly white and from middle- or upper-class backgrounds) had **universality** – that is, they were independent of time and place and were in no way culture bound (Teigen, 2002).

Such an assumption was rarely backed up with evidence, however, or even explicitly tested. On the rare occasions where psychologists did consider the impact of culture on their results it's questionable whether the methodologies used were appropriate or valid. As we'll see later, psychologists face numerous difficulties when trying to carry out research that makes cross-cultural comparisons, but this partly explains why so many psychologists have failed to make these comparisons over the years, because of issues of convenience. Simply put, psychological studies that don't include cross-cultural comparisons tend to be much easier to carry out.

This trend towards assuming that research carried out on white participants from western countries can be generalisable to all humans in all parts of the world, which is almost certainly apparent in the majority of psychological research carried out in the history of the subject, represents a clear example of cultural bias in psychology: the failure to test for, consider or acknowledge the impact that culture or cultural differences might have on mental processes and behaviour. Of course just as theorists from western cultures may fail to investigate or consider critical differences in people from non-western cultures, the opposite could also be true and would also constitute cultural bias, though examples of this are arguably far less common in psychology.

It's worth stressing that despite this trend, there have been exceptions. For example, Passer *et al.* (2009) note the work of two behaviourists, Neil Miller and John Dollard, who in 1941 stressed that just as psychologists studying rats in a maze have to know a great deal about the maze to interpret the rat's behaviour, culture could be considered the equivalent of a human maze – both represent the structure of the individual's social environment and therefore there needs to be an understanding of this structure to fully understand the behaviour that takes place within it.

However, even when psychologists did acknowledge the importance of culture for their subject, very few made direct comparisons of different cultures, perhaps assuming that this was more the domain of anthropology. But in more recent times, just as psychologists came to realise the dangers of gender bias, they have also made a greater effort to address cultural bias and to study different ethnic and cultural groups.

This has culminated in a new field, cultural or cross-cultural psychology, which specifically considers how people from different cultures are psychologically similar and different, and what it is about these cultures that may lead to the differences. A key development in this new field was the creation, in 1972, of the International Association of Cross-Cultural Psychology (IACCP). This organisation, which is still going successfully in the twenty-first century, has a membership of around 800 psychologists in more than 65 countries and seeks to facilitate communication between psychologists who are interested in and are from different cultures plus it strives to take psychology beyond its traditional Euro-American focus (Lonner, 2000).

There has been some suggestion that, as the literature and theory in this area has grown, cultural psychology and cross-cultural psychology should actually be viewed as two separate approaches, with the former focusing more on what specific features of cultures may affect mental processes and behaviour in different ways and the latter assuming that certain psychological processes might be universal and using comparisons between different cultures to test this. However, because this distinction is relatively new and there is some overlap between the two different approaches I will use the terms synonymously throughout the rest of the chapter.

Different types of culture

An important distinction has been made between two different types of culture, based on an important source of cultural variation: individualism. This is considered to be a largely bi-polar construct, with individualism at one end of the scale and collectivism at the other (Kim, 1995). You can read more about individualism and collectivism in 'In focus box 9'.

In focus box 9

Here we'll be explaining a particular distinction made by some psychologists between two types of culture – individualism and collectivism. We'll also discuss some of the problems with making such distinctions.

Individualism emphasises personal goals (as opposed to the goals of groups or an entire society) and notions of self-identity, so that people tend to define themselves based on their own personal attributes, behaviours and achievements. Individual choice and responsibility are also encouraged and looser ties between people are the norm. Certain cultures seem to promote or embody individualism and these tend to be industrialised western societies, including Britain, most western European countries, Australia and North America.

Collectivism, on the other hand, focuses more on the importance of group loyalty, relations and ties between people and to social groups and extended families. Individual goals and achievements tend to reflect the goals and achievements of the larger group. Again certain cultures seem to embody collectivist values and attitudes, and these are often cultures in Asia, Africa, the Middle East and South America.

As noted before, it's important to stress that just as there are dangers in assuming that the mental processes and behaviours of people around the world are exactly the same as those reported by psychologists carrying out research on people in Britain, for example, there are also problems assuming that all collectivist and individualist cultures are exactly the same – as Fiske (2002) notes, there is not a singular type of either culture. Both India and China are considered to be examples of collectivist cultures, but clearly there are huge differences between the two.

There are also similar problems with making assumptions that all countries from a particular part of the world share exactly the same type of culture. So, for example, although Japan, North and South

Korea, China and Taiwan are all countries in East Asia, it would be wrong to assume that these are all collectivist cultures, or even if they are that they view notions of collectivism and individualism in exactly the same ways.

For example, Hendry (1987) argued that whilst the East Asian countries just referred to can all be seen as examples of highly collectivistic cultures, Japan is unusual in that it also considers individualism to be acceptable, as long as a person's individualistic behaviours do not get in the way of their obligations to others. This is just one example of a difference within a particular group of countries, but there are likely to be many others and therefore psychologists need to consider the possibility and impact of such differences.

Fiske (2002) also questions the assumption that any given country can be considered to have a single set culture at all. All countries and societies are extremely heterogeneous, so it can be difficult to apply strict labels of either collectivism or individualism to a particular country. However, it's also important to note that a failure to consider the lack of heterogeneity within countries has been an important criticism of more traditional approaches to psychology.

For example, as noted before, for a long time the participants in most experiments carried out on university undergraduates in America and Britain tended to be white because this reflected the fact that most university undergraduates at the time were white. The failure of psychologists in those countries to study black participants or those from other ethnic minority groups in various research areas was a considerable weakness and potentially limits the ability to generalise findings from such research.

Although we've noted that there are some significant concerns and caveats about the usefulness and accuracy of the individualism and collectivism distinction, it's arguably still a broadly helpful one given that it stresses that there may well be important cultural differences and provides a framework for studying them.

So we have now defined the distinction between individualism and collectivism and identified how this can be applied to different cultures. We have also noted that the distinction needs to be used cautiously, but as long as this is done it can be used to counter the tendency to assume that results acquired using American or European participants are automatically and entirely generalisable to people from other cultures. As with the work on gender it's important to at least consider the possibility of similarities and differences, rather than simply fail to consider them at all due to an inherently biased position.

For example, psychologists from western cultures might assume based on their own experiences in those cultures that all people take joy in their own achievements and that this is a universal process that occurs throughout the world. However, such an assumption may not be correct and in fact a study by Stipek (1998) comparing American and Chinese college students suggests just that. Whilst the American students did indeed reveal a preference for expressing pride in one's own achievements, Chinese students preferred to express pride in the achievements of others, such as a family member, a friend or a colleague.

Later in this chapter we'll identify further examples of how this distinction has been used to study differences in psychological processes that were once assumed to be entirely universal and unaffected by culture.

Ethnocentrism

Another crucial part of cultural bias is ethnocentrism. We haven't explicitly referred to it in the chapter so far but nevertheless it has been hinted at. Ethnocentrism can be defined as a belief or attitude that one ethnic group is superior to another or to all other ethnic groups. Usually the person who has the belief/attitude of superiority is a member of the group that they consider to be superior.

Ethnocentrism is sometimes thought of as an outright example of negativity towards other ethnic groups, but often it relates to something a little more subtle than that: an assumption than one's own ethnic group is the norm or 'natural' and that others are by comparison in some way strange, different, unsophisticated or even primitive. Either way, ethnocentrism can be dangerous because it can lead to stereotyping of and discrimination against members of particular ethnic groups.

Psychologists have studied ethnocentrism and the psychological processes behind it, and have considered ways that it might be combated or reduced. However, as we've noted before, psychologists do not simply study phenomena – often they can also be affected by it and/or display it themselves. In fact ethnocentrism can be viewed as being potentially even more dangerous when it is perpetrated by psychologists because what are subjective beliefs and value judgements may be mistaken for scientific truths.

Along with the cases of discrimination against women noted in the previous chapter, Schultz and Schultz (2004) have noted how Jewish psychologists often became victims of anti-Semitism and how African Americans also faced prejudice, both in terms of earning doctoral degrees and finding academic jobs.

Problems with ethnocentrism and potential solutions

The potential problems with ethnocentrism for psychology's understanding of the impact of culture on mental processes and behaviour are hopefully obvious. Just as feminist psychologists questioned whether male-dominated psychology could be trusted not to discriminate against women, cross-cultural psychologists have warned that ethnocentric attitudes could affect how white psychologists from western industrialised cultures classify and categorise people of different cultures.

For example, if a psychologist studying cultural differences in intelligence already has any ethnocentric tendencies and then goes on to develop intelligence tests that are biased (whether intentionally or not) in favour of the cultural group that s/he belongs to then other groups taking those tests are likely to perform systematically less well, which not only reinforces the psychologist's beliefs about their own culture but also propagates this idea to other psychologists and the general public.

This example is indicative of one of the greatest controversies in the history of psychology: whether people from white middle-class backgrounds in western countries perform better on intelligence tests than do other groups, and if they do, what are the reasons for such differences? Discussing this controversy is rather like opening the proverbial can of worms, but it is generally argued that although people from white middle-class backgrounds in western countries do tend to perform better, at least one of the reasons for this is that many intelligence tests are in some way culturally biased. You can read more about this controversy in 'In focus box 10'.

In focus box 10

Psychologists have considered two ways in which traditional tests may be problematic when it comes to assessing intelligence in non-western cultures.

First, many traditional intelligence tests are based on linguistic content and require knowledge that is likely to have been learnt and acquired within certain cultural contexts, such as the western education system. So because these tests are at least partially built around products of particular cultures they are to some extent culturally bound and therefore give advantages to people from those cultures.

Second, Sternberg (2004) argues that traditional intelligence tests are based around academically orientated problem-solving skills that people from western cultures need to succeed at school, university and for many jobs. Although this is how success is defined in these cultures, and intelligence is therefore related to success in these sorts of environments, Sternberg argues that other cultures may have very different measures of success because people will have to meet the adaptive demands of very different environments. Therefore, if intelligence is defined by successfully adapting to the environments of one's culture, then intelligence will take very different forms in different cultures.

In western culture traditional intelligence tests are an appropriate way of measuring the analytical and academic skills and knowledge needed to succeed. People in other cultures, Sternberg argues, need the same universal mental functions and processes to succeed and be considered intelligent (e.g., they need to recognise and define a problem, mentally represent it, formulate a strategy, allocate mental resources, monitor the solution and evaluate their success or otherwise) but the mental contents (the types of knowledge used) are likely to be quite different.

Based upon these two different problems, psychologists have developed different ways to look at intelligence from a cross-cultural perspective. To deal with the problem of intelligence tests traditionally being connected to language and cultural experience efforts have been made to identify culture-free or culture-fair tests. Such tests are usually non-verbal and are not tied to a specific culturally acquired knowledge base but instead require the person being tested to look for and identify relations between objects or patterns.

The most famous example of this kind of test is probably the Raven Progressive Matrices (Raven, 1962), which tests a person's ability to identify the pattern in a series of drawings by getting them to choose the missing item that completes that pattern. Performance on the Raven correlates positively with measures of intelligence derived from more traditional intelligence tests, suggesting that it is to some extent testing the same underlying ability, but with the added advantage that it is not culturally bound (Passer *et al.*, 2009).

Sternberg (2004) proposes an alternative route, which is that psychologists seek to develop tests or measures of skills and knowledge that are contextually important – adaptive and valued within the particular culture being researched. Unlike the Raven, these tests may not correlate at all with more traditional intelligence tests, or they may even correlate negatively so that children who perform well on the contextually important skills may score lower, on average, on more conventional western intelligence tests.

Although this might seem counter-intuitive, Sternberg argues that western-style education may not seem to have much relevance or value in many cultures and therefore many children in these cultures will be likely to be taught indigenous knowledge and skills by their parents that are perceived to have more direct and adaptive value (such as learning about natural herbal medicines used to treat parasitic illnesses), at the expense of their school work. So the more time and effort they spend learning the indigenous knowledge and skills, the less experience they have with the kind of academic analytical skills tested by western intelligence tests.

Overall, Sternberg's work emphasises an intriguing possibility that intelligence, defined in very particular ways within western psychology and culture, may be conceived very differently in different cultures. This doesn't mean that no comparisons between cultures are possible with regard to intelligence, but to interpret these comparisons successfully psychologists need to be less ethnocentric and instead develop a greater understanding of the specific cultural context in which they are seeking to study adaptive behaviours and possibly culturally specific forms of intelligence.

The challenges of cultural bias and cross-cultural psychology

Hopefully two things have been obvious from reading this chapter so far: first, psychologists have a responsibility to address cultural bias, and second, psychologists have found this to be quite a challenge. What reasons can be identified that explain the difficulties with studying psychology cross-culturally? One important issue relates to two concepts originally adapted from anthropology: **emics** and **etics**.

Emics are psychological constructs that are particular to a specific culture and can be contrasted with etics, which are constructs that are believed to be universal and therefore apply to all humans regardless of culture. A key problem in cross-cultural research is that it may not always be clear which constructs are emics and which are etics.

As we've discussed before, psychologists are influenced by the culture they have spent most of their life in and may believe that a particular psychological construct that exists in their culture is actually an etic – that it occurs universally in all cultures. When they go to another culture to investigate this it potentially leads to a problem: a specific form of cultural bias called imposed etics where the supposed etic (really an emic) the psychologist believes to exist universally is inappropriately applied to this new culture. In a worse case scenario, the psychologist identifies an emic in this new culture but mistakes it for the etic they were looking for, in effect finding the particular psychological construct they were expecting to find. A better result occurs if the psychologist becomes submerged within the new culture and comes to realise that the two constructs found in the two cultures are actually subtly different. Under these circumstances the psychologist is now able to identify two emics and study the similarities and differences between them across the two different cultures.

A related difficulty with cross-cultural research involves language. If the psychologist comes from one culture and doesn't understand the language of the other culture that is being studied, there are always likely to be problems caused by failures in communication, problems with interpreters or with translation of materials.

In English there are numerous subtleties of language and regional variations, particularly in relation to psychological concepts, and the same is likely to be true of other languages too. Even very minor problems with communication or translation could have important implications when trying to identify whether the exact same psychological concept exists in two different cultures.

When psychologists are attempting to use a particular scale, questionnaire or measure for two different cultural groups who speak different languages a particular technique has been identified as useful, namely **back translation** (Coolican, 1999). This involves the scale in its original language being translated into the language of the second culture before then being translated back again into the original language. If the meaning of the scale is still as intended after these two translations, then it can be said to have 'translation equivalence', which obviously improves the validity of the research.

Even if the scales or measures used are said to be equivalent in content another problem may relate to issues with their administration, referred to as **method bias** (Lin, Chen & Chiu, 2005).

There may be all kinds of differences between two cultural groups, which may arise due to the way the measure is administered. For example, different cultural groups may display different levels of social desirability – the tendency of participants to want to give socially acceptable answers (Coolican, 1999). Social desirability may vary across cultural groups anyway, but may be particularly heightened in some cultural groups in some situations more than others.

Also, respondents in some cultures may be more familiar with the means of measurement, the style of administration and the conditions in which measurement is carried out. For example, people in western cultures may be very familiar with standard 'exam conditions' or the way in which intelligence and aptitude tests are traditionally carried out, but this may not be the case for people in all cultures.

If method bias exists in a particular study, then there is a danger that differences are put down to intrinsic psychological traits or abilities of the group rather than the bias resulting from the administration procedures. Again, there are ways of measuring social desirability and of familiarising participants with procedures and tests, both of which may need to be considered when comparing groups from different cultures.

Another more general issue is that cross-cultural psychology is not just about selecting a particular psychological trait, sticking pins into a map of the world, and testing and comparing that trait in random places. Although cross-cultural research is a key way of addressing cultural bias, carrying it out requires much thought and preparation and a clear rationale (Lonner, 2000).

So which cultures should be studied, and why? What is it about these cultures that makes studying or comparing them so interesting and beneficial, and what particular cultural elements are of interest? How will communities, populations and samples be selected, and what is the rationale for choosing them? And exactly which mental processes and behaviours will be looked at, and again what is the rationale behind choosing them? Each of these questions may be difficult to answer but ideally they should all be considered before a psychologist embarks on carrying out cross-cultural research.

All of the difficulties so far discussed in this section contribute to perhaps the most obvious problem with cross-cultural research, which we alluded to earlier: arguably it is just that much more difficult, time-consuming and complicated to carry out than research within a single culture, just as it's more difficult to study cultures other than one's own. In addition, on the occasions where cross-cultural or cultural work involves travelling to other countries and potentially having to spend long periods of time immersing oneself within the culture there are practical issues related to acquiring the necessary funding for the research and finding the time required to carry it out.

However, although Fiske (2002) acknowledges these difficulties, he points out that not studying culture in psychology because it's considered difficult would be analogous to developmental psychologists not studying children because they take too long to grow up, or biological psychologists not studying neurons because they are too small and there are too many of them. Essentially he argues that if psychologists think that culture does contribute to or interact with mental processes and behaviour, then it is their responsibility to study it, regardless of how difficult or inconvenient this might be.

There may be many obstacles to studying culture in psychology, but as we've noted throughout this book, there are obstacles to studying all areas of the discipline. If culture is considered to be genuinely important, then psychologists need to continue to seek ways around these obstacles, based on the impressive – albeit sometimes flawed – work that has already been done.

How have considerations of culture affected the different approaches to psychology?

As was noted at the start of this chapter, psychologists in the early history of the subject tended to assume that the principles and concepts they studied in Europe and America occurred universally for all humans and were unaffected by cultural differences. Following the consideration of cultural bias and the rise of cross-cultural psychology, how has this affected the five different approaches to psychology discussed in this book? As you might imagine, the impact has been extremely variable but we'll consider each approach in turn.

The behaviourist approach

Of all the approaches, this is perhaps the one that, in some ways at least, is naturally most inclined towards cross-cultural psychology. This approach stresses the impact of different environments and learning on behaviour, which relates very closely to some of the ways that culture is assumed to affect behaviour.

The enduring values, beliefs, behaviours and traditions that are shared by cultural groups and passed on from one generation to the next (to refer back to the definition presented at the start of the chapter) are very likely to be acquired through behaviourist principles of classical and operant conditioning, and the observational and imitation learning of Bandura's social cognitive theory (1989; as we noted back in Chapter 2, Bandura's position represents a form of neobehaviourism but one that is far less extreme than that of Skinner's and incorporates cognitive aspects such as beliefs and expectations).

You may also remember from the start of the chapter that behaviourists as far back as 1941 were noting that it was essential for psychologists to study culture so that they could fully understand the context in which behaviours take place.

However, it's also worth remembering that one of the grounds on which the behaviourist approach was commonly criticised was its tendency to study rats and pigeons in laboratories and then generalise those results to humans. So it's not just that behaviourists didn't tend to study the principles of learning across different cultures, they often didn't always study those principles in humans as much as they should have done either. Nevertheless, it does seem that the basic principles underlying human learning do apply universally across cultures.

The biological approach

You might think, given that the human brain is assumed to be pretty much the same across people of all cultures, that the biological approach wouldn't have much interest in cross-cultural differences. However, as was explained in Chapter 4, the biological approach acknowledges that the brain and nervous system, which underlie, create, influence and interact with our psychological states, develop throughout the lifespan due to a complex interaction of genes and environmental factors. The biological approach, therefore, acknowledges that cultural factors may affect brain development.

One such example relates to hemispheric lateralisation in the human brain, the idea that certain cognitive functions are dominated by one hemisphere or the other. Considerable research suggests that in most humans linguistic abilities are based in the left hemisphere of the brain, whilst pictorial stimuli are most commonly processed by the right hemisphere. However, the Chinese language is very different from the written alphabet-based languages found in western cultures because instead of words it uses pictorial images to represent objects and concepts.

Passer et al. (2009) suggest that, because of this, left hemispheric lateralisation for language may be less common amongst Chinese speakers than speakers of English and other alphabet-based languages, and indeed they report findings from Tzeng et al. (1979) that suggest this might be the case for the areas of the brain involved in reading and writing. Although this is only one example, a greater focus on cultural factors in brain development may reveal that there are many others.

The cognitive approach

As we have noted before, cognitive psychology adopts an interactionist perspective regarding the relationship between mental processes and the environment. This means that researchers and theorists within this approach seem quite open-minded about the idea that internal processes involved in thinking, problem-solving, memory, perception and so on might be affected by cultural factors. Earlier in the chapter we discussed Sternberg's views on intelligence, which definitely reflect this idea, and there has been an accumulation of evidence within cognitive psychology over the past decade or so that provides evidence of cross-cultural differences in cognition.

For example, Qi Wang, a leading expert in this growing field, found evidence from American and Chinese college students that when asked to report their earliest childhood memory participants from the two groups show differences in both the type of events recalled and how far back they could recall (Wang, 2001).

Chinese students tended to provide brief accounts that were more likely to relate to collective activities (i.e., they involved others) and general routines, plus the events were more likely to be emotionally neutral. American students, on the other hand, were far more likely to report lengthier memories of specific events that were emotionally significant and that focused on them as individuals. Such findings are consistent with the collectivist/individualist cultural distinction discussed earlier.

However, what is particularly interesting is that culture seemed to not just affect the content or subject matter of the memory: the average age of the earliest memory reported by Americans was almost six months earlier than that of Chinese students. It's possible that cultural differences in the way that events are experienced, or the way the person views themselves in relation to the events, can impact on how they are stored in memory and affect their memorability.

The humanist approach

As noted before, this approach expresses dissatisfaction with various dehumanising aspects of traditional western psychology and stresses the importance instead of personal growth and fulfilment. But the key figures behind humanistic psychology were American and the approach was very much a product of an individualistic culture, focusing as it does on the importance of the individual defining their own values, rather than basing them on cultural traditions.

Perhaps not surprisingly, this approach has traditionally not considered cross-cultural comparisons as much as it might have done. Nevertheless, as with other approaches, humanistic psychology has recently started to consider the merits of cross-cultural comparisons and interactions.

For example, Montuori and Fahim (2004) take a very different approach to the one we've discussed elsewhere by stressing that a very good reason for experiencing other cultures is that this might provide an important opportunity for learning and personal growth. They suggest that via cross-cultural encounters people can become more keenly aware of their own values and cultural predispositions, and in turn this may make the consideration and exploration of other cultures easier in the future.

Here the focus is much more on the idea of individuals having cross-cultural encounters, and the psychological benefits they may experience through this, rather than how psychology should attempt to study different cultures, but the two are by no means mutually exclusive, plus this focus reflects the idiographic stance traditionally taken by the humanist approach. Montuori and Fahim argue that such a process may lead to less ethnocentrism and greater tolerance for cultural difference, so a humanistic consideration of culture could potentially have benefits for all psychologists.

The psychodynamic approach

Freud argued that the processes of unconscious conflict that under-lie human behaviour and personality are universal, and therefore we might expect the psychological conflicts that he argued children go through would appear in all cultures. Therefore an important part of the psychodynamic approach is that it should be tested cross-culturally.

However, even in Freud's time it was noted that his theories were based on a very limited sample – a combination of his own personal introspections and those of his patients, who primarily consisted of a small number of Viennese, Jewish women suffering from neuroses and hysteria. This is an extremely limited sample on which to base a theory that is supposed to explain all human behaviour.

The universality of Freud's theories was challenged and tested cross-culturally very early on, by the Polish anthropologist Bronislaw Malinowski. Malinowski (1929) studied the Trobriand Islanders of the South Pacific and discovered a family dynamic quite unlike the one that Freud described and argued was essential to a child's develop-ment of its superego. Therefore this was a rare early example of a psychological theory being tested cross-culturally, though it was per-haps in part a response to Freud's own interest in culture, displayed in a series of works sometimes referred to as his 'cultural books' (Paul, 1991).

Freud's cultural work is often criticised because he did very lit-tle work 'in the field' and was largely reliant on secondary accounts from others. Since Malinowski's work there have been numerous fur-ther attempts to test assorted aspects of Freud's ideas cross-culturally, so the psychodynamic approach is unusual in that its ideas have already been well tested in this regard. However, as with so many aspects of this approach, there is considerable debate about how exactly the find-ings from these various cross-cultural studies should be interpreted. The idiographic and unconscious aspects of the psychodynamic approach make hypotheses difficult to test and interpret even when focusing on just one culture, so not surprisingly cross-cultural comparisons tend to be even more problematic.

Conclusions

As with gender bias it's clear that psychology has gone through some major changes with regard to its considerations of cultural bias. Throughout much of the twentieth century very few psychologists seemed to consider that their tests might be culturally biased, that their results might be different if carried out in different cultures or with different participants, or that it might not be possible to generalise theories universally without first making cross-cultural comparisons. However, in more recent times psychologists have started to consider that various psychological processes may be shaped by culture in all kinds of ways.

Although cultural bias and ethnocentrism continue to represent potential dangers in contemporary psychology, more psychologists than ever before are now aware of these dangers and are considering possible solutions. Hopefully awareness and understanding of, and sensitivity to, culture will continue to flourish, creating a richer and broader conceptualisation of psychology in the process.

In this and Chapter 6, we have been focusing on a couple of ways that psychology may exhibit a somewhat distorted view of reality, and we have identified ways that psychologists have attempted to address this by questioning and tackling gender and cultural bias. In Chapter 8, we consider a very different question indeed: the question of whether human beings can be said to have free will.

Further reading

Lonner, W. J. (2000). On the growth and continuing importance of cross-cultural psychology. *Eye on Psi Chi, 4*(3), 22–26.

Sternberg, R. J. (2004). Culture and intelligence. *American Psychologist, 59*(5), 325–338.

Chapter 8

Determinism and Free Will

Do you have free will? Ask most people and they will probably say they do, or at least that they feel they do. In this chapter we will be addressing one of the trickiest and most long-lasting debates of all: whether humans are free to choose how they think and behave, or whether their thoughts and behaviours are determined by things beyond their control.

This is a tricky debate, partly because it threatens something that nearly all of us experientially believe to be true – that our personal will determines the choices we make and the actions we perform. Many psychologists have questioned this notion and in this chapter we'll address the basis for their arguments. But first we need to define some terminology.

👁 Definition of the problem – are we really free?

We'll start off by attempting to define free will, which is perhaps not as easy as it sounds. Free will is essentially the notion that humans respond freely, voluntarily and actively to events around them, that when they encounter or are presented with stimuli, choices or options they have the freedom to choose which to select, or in fact may choose not to select any of them at all. Ultimately it assumes that we're free to select our own course of action, behave in unconstrained ways, make our own decisions and determine our own lives.

One of the potential problems with this notion of pure free will is related to science. Science fundamentally looks for causes and as psychology attempts to promote itself as a science it needs to be able to identify causes for thoughts and behaviours. So what causes a person's thoughts and behaviours? You might want to answer, 'obviously the person causes them', but that doesn't help much because psychology acknowledges that people are complicated, so what aspect of the person actually does the choosing and what causes them to make a particular choice? Different psychologists tend to highlight different factors, as you might expect, and we'll identify where the five main approaches covered in this book stand on this issue throughout the rest of the chapter.

Of the five approaches only one tends to strongly defend some notion of true free will, and that is the humanist approach. Humanistic psychologists, such as Carl Rogers and Abraham Maslow, emphasise that people have the power to direct their own lives – a key part of the concept of free will. This approach doesn't deny that there are other forces in the world that may contribute to or frustrate our free choices, but nevertheless it stands firm on the idea that humans are fundamentally free to make their own choices.

Another key emphasis for humanistic psychologists is the notion of subjective experience and humans subjectively experience that they have free will. Humanistic psychologists note that subjective experience may not always be accurate and may actually run contrary to what objective methods of science tell us, but this approach stresses that nevertheless personal/private experience is important and human beings should acknowledge it because sometimes it is the only information they have available to them.

Rogers acknowledged that free will could be problematic when viewed from the objective perspective of science. As Leahey (1997) notes, Rogers saw himself as both a scientist and a therapist. In his role as the former he was well aware of the arguments for accepting determinism as the more likely position, but as a therapist he saw the inherent value of freedom, of people being thought of and treated as moral agents who have freedom of choice. It's interesting to note that even Rogers could see how compelling the notion of determinism is from a purely scientific position, but what exactly do we mean by the term?

Determinism

Determinism refers to the process whereby certain thoughts or behaviours cannot be said to result entirely from free will but instead are determined by external or internal factors or forces of some kind or other. Determinism should not just be thought of as a single position within this debate because there are in fact various different kinds of determinism, which are distinguished by the particular nature of the external/internal factors thought to be involved. Not surprisingly, different approaches to psychology are associated with different forms of determinism.

For example, back in Chapter 5 we introduced the term genetic determinism, which can be defined as 'the idea that genes have invariant and unavoidable effects that cannot be altered' (Passer *et al.*, 2009, p. 119). To put it another way, it assumes that genes determine human traits and behaviour. Ideas of genetic determinism are most likely to come from psychologists who adopt the biological approach, though it's worth remembering from Chapter 5 that although psychologists accept that genes do seem to play a major role in determining traits and behaviour, environments also play their part.

However, it's worth noting that this current position in the biological approach, which stresses the importance of an interaction between nature (genes) and nurture (environment), isn't necessarily any less deterministic. It could be argued that although it denies pure genetic determinism, it still proposes the idea that our thoughts and behaviours may be determined by factors beyond our control, but rather than those factors being solely genetic they are instead a mixture of genes, environment and the interaction between the two. Depending on one's interpretation there is not necessarily a greater place for free will within an interactionist biological psychology approach to thoughts and behaviour than one that puts all the emphasis on genetics.

In fact, genetic determinism is just one of many forms of **biological determinism**. Biological determinism can be said to refer to any theory or approach in which biological concepts or processes are said to determine our thoughts and behaviours. There are numerous examples in psychology, for example instincts: the inborn and unlearnt tendencies that William James and the ethologists argued predispose animals (including humans) to behave in certain ways.

Similarly, evolutionary psychology argues that many of our thoughts and behaviours may be shaped and determined, at least to some extent, by natural selection. For example, apparently free choices, such as what characteristics we find attractive in someone of the opposite sex and who we choose to marry, may in fact be partially determined by evolutionary strategies, designed to increase the chances of spreading our genes and producing healthy offspring (Buss, 1989).

Another more specific example is the flight or fight response, a sequence of activity that is initiated when sensory organs communicate to the nervous system the need for sudden activity, either for fighting or fleeing. Hormones are released that facilitate certain physical reactions, therefore strongly priming the person towards certain behaviours. This process is automatic, is not one that we usually choose to initiate, and therefore provides evidence of how biological processes can determine behaviour without a conscious choice on our part. We may not even ever become consciously aware of the stimulus that originally triggered the physiological response and caused us to feel anxious and on edge in the first place.

Very different kinds of unconscious processes are said to be involved in a second form of determinism we're going to consider here, namely **psychic determinism**. Psychic determinism is best associated with the psychodynamic approach because it looks for the causes and determinants of conscious thoughts and behaviours in the unconscious influences of the id, ego and superego (which we discussed back in Chapter 5) and the interactions between them.

For Freud, everything in the person's conscious mind and everything the person does has a cause. That cause is often unconscious, to some extent or other, and so may not be easily accessible or identifiable to the person who is having the thoughts or carrying out the behaviour. Nevertheless, Freud thought that the causes could be identified through psychoanalysis, the theory and method of therapy he developed specifically for this purpose.

Freud encouraged patients to reveal details of their everyday lives, things that might be considered trivial by the patient and which in isolation could be viewed as such by a therapist. However, Freud (1914) believed it was the analyst's job to seek themes in a patient's reminiscences – were there patterns to the things the patient forgot to do or the objects they mislaid? Other important examples were slips of the tongue; apparently minor verbal errors that Freud believed could reveal the struggle between different mental forces, those representing some underlying and unconscious need or wish, and those trying to keep such needs and wishes hidden (Reason, 2000).

So, for example, the case of someone crying out the name of a previous long-term partner whilst having sex with their current one could be explained away as just an error, but might also be reasonably argued to indicate that the person still has passionate feelings for their ex-partner (Passer *et al.*, 2009). If the person was genuinely not consciously aware of this fact, then Freud would claim that these feelings had been repressed into the subconscious mind because of their unacceptable nature (societal moral standards suggest it is unacceptable to be harbouring passionate feelings for ex-partners whilst having sexual relations with the current one). However, during the amorous encounter conscious control lapsed and the person's true feelings were expressed.

The collective technical term for apparently minor errors that could be argued to indicate a repressed motive or be a result of conflict between different unconscious forces, or even between unconscious and conscious forces, is **parapraxes**. Critics have often pointed out that many parapraxes can be accounted for in much more mundane ways that don't require the existence and influence of unconscious forces. Reason (2000) suggests, however, that parapraxes can genuinely occur, but just not as commonly as Freud might have suggested – many of the examples that Freud identified could easily be explained by more mundane behaviourist or cognitive concepts.

Parapraxes are just one everyday example of psychic determinism in action, but the psychodynamic approach argues that instinctual drives and unconscious forces can play deterministic roles in various aspects of human thought, personality, decision-making and behaviour. Freud tended to emphasise the importance of sexual instincts in particular and stressed that the events of early childhood were more important for determining adult personality and behaviour than other stages of the lifespan.

Later psychodynamic theorists have tended to focus less on infantile sexuality, considering the contributions of a much broader range of instincts and social and cultural factors to human psychology, and they have also tended to argue that personality continues to develop throughout the lifespan as people encounter new challenges.

However, although the precise focus of different psychodynamic theories varies, the psychodynamic approach as a whole still broadly agrees that biological drives and past experiences interact and lead to internal conflicts and personality styles that can influence thoughts and behaviours, often without the person being consciously aware of this. Therefore even post-Freudians and neoanalytic theorists (those who adopt a psychodynamic perspective but disagree with certain aspects of Freud's theory) could be said to agree with psychic determinism to some extent.

The final form of determinism that I am going to cover in this section is **environmental determinism**. This is most clearly associated with the behaviourist approach. As we've noted before, behaviourism, particularly in the form conceived and developed by Watson, adopted an extreme environmentalist position, which stressed that human beings and their behaviour are largely, if not entirely, shaped and determined by the environments they are raised in or exposed to. Behaviourism was promoted by Watson as a means of behavioural and social control, and humans were argued to be passive and malleable, so it's quite clear that there is little room for the idea of free will, at least not within the more traditional forms of behaviourism (though later we'll consider a very different version of behaviourism that offers a less deterministic perspective).

The traditional behaviourist approach, then, offers a very clear example of environmental determinism: the behaviours that humans (and animals) display are determined by the past and current environments they have interacted with and been shaped by. Humans may acquire new patterns of behaviour when they act within new environments and receive new patterns of reward and punishment, but the apparent flexibility, creativity and freedom of behaviour is actually negligible and illusory – humans are merely products of their environments. This might seem to be quite an extreme view but B. F. Skinner, the natural heir to Watson's radical vision of behaviourism, actually sought to take behaviourism in an even more radically deterministic direction.

Radical determinism

Skinner specifically questioned whether humans have free will in his 1971 book *Beyond Freedom and Dignity*. His central argument was that human freedom is an illusion and a superstition, one that prevents the methods of science from being used to achieve their full potential – the precise prediction and control of human behaviour.

Like Watson before him, Skinner argued that humans and all other animals live according to quite basic rules that shape their behaviour. Fundamentally, we seek to avoid bad things (punishment) and act in ways that will increase the number of good things (rewards or positive reinforcement) or end the bad things that happen to us. So, for Skinner, all behaviour is controlled by the contingencies of reinforcement in our environment, the pattern of rewards and punishments we receive. The causes of human behaviour, then, lie not within us but solely within the environment.

Skinner believed that the illusion of behaving freely emerges whenever we feel we are free of punishment or the threat of punishment. But even then Skinner argues that our behaviour is being driven not by genuine free will but by the pursuit of things that have made us feel good in the past. So behaviour perceived to be 'free' either involves us doing things that have given us pleasure in the past (such as when we were given chocolate to eat in the past this gave us pleasure so this reinforces the idea that eating chocolate leads to pleasure leading to an increased tendency to do this again in the future), or involves us doing things that in the past helped us to achieve things that we think will give us pleasure (saving money is not pleasurable in itself but in the past saving money may have resulted in us later being able to buy something we really wanted, so delaying reward enables us to achieve greater rewards at some point in the future). In both cases we are pursuing pleasure based on past experience, in more or less direct ways, and that is what is determining our 'choices' and behaviours rather than genuine free will.

Of course we don't just feel that our own behaviour is free, we also view other people as behaving freely too. However, Skinner again argues that this is illusory; we are simply unaware of the patterns of reinforcement they have acquired throughout their lives and other such environmental factors that dictate their behaviour. So if both our own freedom and that of the people around us likely to be illusory then, Skinner argues, what is the basis for thinking that humanity is in any way autonomous?

Perhaps this sounds a little bleak, but Skinner argued that realising all of this is actually a good thing. Once we realise that we're not free then as a society we can seek the best ways to encourage positive behaviours in others. Skinner had noted, following numerous experiments carried out on rats and pigeons, that behaviour can be most efficiently controlled via the use of positive reinforcement (giving people pleasant things) or even negative reinforcement (taking away negative things). Both of these are preferable to punishing undesirable behaviours, largely because punishment only teaches people what not to do, but doesn't tell them what they should be doing instead, nor does it encourage them to do it. In addition, punishment can breed resentment and bitterness towards the teacher, parent or authority figure.

So instead of the current system of society, where everyone is assumed to be an autonomous agent, Skinner advocates that we abandon our illusory beliefs in behavioural freedom, accept that environmental control and determinism are unavoidable, and instead seek to design a world in which socially acceptable and desirable behaviours are encouraged and directed by behaviourist principles – that is, primarily through positive and negative reinforcement.

This is the basic idea underlying Skinner's utopian novel *Walden Two* (published in 1948), a fictional exploration of the application of his psychological principles of behavioural control and conditioning to solving human problems and building a harmonious, successful and happy society (Hothersall, 2004). In the novel Skinner describes a rural, utopian community consisting of a thousand people who live according to principles of collective ownership and positive reinforcement. Children are raised collectively and biological family ties are minimised so that the children develop positive feelings about many or all adults within the community. The culture exhibits a range of positive features: consumption is minimal, the community members are happy, they are satisfied with their work, have ample leisure time and the community emphasises cooperation over competition. It sounds idyllic, but then it is a utopia. Specifically it's Skinner's utopia, a chance for him in the 1940s to write and promote the ideas, potential and techniques of behavioural control in fiction, at a time when he was not entirely comfortable saying the same things himself as an academic (Hothersall, 2004; Schultz & Schultz, 2004).

What's wrong with Skinner's radical determinism?

Obviously Skinner's denial of free will seems to oppose our own individual sense that we have it, and in this sense we're adopting the humanistic approach, arguing that what Skinner puts down to an illusion is actually an integral part of an important subjective inner world. But there are other arguments against Skinner's ideas that do not rely solely on an appeal for psychology to value the subjective knowledge and experience of personal freedom.

First, Skinner believes that everything we do is the product of reinforcement, but arguably such a position is not falsifiable. The philosopher of science, Karl Popper, argued that scientific theories should risk falsification (Popper, 1963) – that is, their predictions should be stated in such a way that they can be shown to be false. In fact Popper argued that it was far more important for a supposedly scientific theory to be in principle falsifiable than it was for it to be shown to be true. Popper used this argument to suggest that many of the ideas in the psychodynamic approach are unfalsifiable, because any example or evidence can be used to fit or confirm them (as demonstrated by our earlier discussion of parapraxes where various examples of behaviour were identified by Freud to show the effects of psychic determinism, but it's difficult to falsify Freud's claims).

But Popper's argument can also be applied to Skinner's **radical determinism** because Skinner effectively argues that everything we do is the product of reinforcement, even if we cannot find evidence of what that reinforcement might actually be. The danger here is that even if we do find some behaviour that is apparently not caused by prior reinforcement, by Skinner's argument the prior reinforcement could still be said to exist, we just don't currently know what it is. Therefore Skinner's hypothesis, that all behaviour is due to some form of prior reinforcement, can never be proven false.

A second important issue is Skinner's belief that all our actions are carried out solely on the basis of past personal experience and learning, and our expectation of future reward or punishment. This might very well account for some of our behaviour, but it fails to consider the possibility that as conscious agents we are not just passive receivers of environmental stimuli that trigger automatic behavioural responses, we are also often consciously aware of the stimuli and the responses, both in our own case and when witnessing the behaviour of others. It's been noted that we retain and may later use this information to act on the environment in different ways, something that I'll expand upon in the Section 'Soft determinism'.

It's also been suggested that human beings sometimes act spontaneously or creatively, doing things that they've never done before (arguably without knowing what the consequences of their actions will be). This may not be acting on the basis of genuine 'free will', but it is more than simply replaying what we've done before on the basis of past reward and punishment. On the other hand, it can be quite difficult to define what exactly we mean by truly spontaneous or creative behaviours.

Overall, Skinner's version of radical determinism is generally not supported in psychology, because of the combination of reasons we've discussed: it ignores our everyday subjective experience that we have free will, it is not falsifiable, and it denies that we have consciousness and cognitive abilities that allow us to interact with the environment and not just passively respond to it. So what are the alternatives?

Soft determinism

Psychology faces a difficulty: on the one hand, it has to explain the subjective experiences of most humans who feel that they have free will. On the other hand, psychologists are aware that there are numerous factors to do with biology, environment and possibly unconscious forces that may act on humans, possibly limiting or even entirely denying their personal sense of free will.

In addition, psychologists are aware that if their subject is to be thought of as scientific they need to understand why thoughts and behaviours occur – they cannot just be left unexplained or be thought of as occurring randomly. Faced with radical notions of determinism, such as those just ascribed to Skinner, many psychologists have attempted to come up with a compromise, sometimes referred to as **soft determinism**.

This form of determinism covers a broad range of different ideas and approaches, and there is no one single version of soft determinism. What all versions agree on is the idea of accepting some form of free will whilst also trying to explain this within the framework of a scientific psychology. The aim is to be able to show that our behaviour is determined, which fits in within the scientific framework, but to still somehow allow some space for notions of unpredictability and free will. Because of soft determinism's attempts to show that freedom can be compatible with notions of causation it is sometimes also called **compatibilism**. This form of determinism is probably the one accepted by most members of the general public and by most contemporary psychologists within the various approaches. Various psychologists have attempted to devise particular versions of soft determinism, including William James, who has popped up a few times within this book so far.

Soft determinists argue for what they see as a very important distinction, between causation, on the one hand, and coercion and compulsion on the other hand. They further argue that hard or radical determinists tend to mistakenly confuse these terms, so they assume that if thoughts and behaviour are caused then this means the person has been forced, coerced or compelled to think or behave in this way, and therefore this denies them free will. By contrast, soft determinists believe that this distinction is crucial because it allows for a thought or act to be both caused and free – a purely free act occurs without coercion or compulsion, but even a free act must still be determined by something. So soft determinism allows for some or even much of human thought and behaviour to be caused or determined by different factors or forces, but that doesn't mean we have to write off free will in the process.

Often when psychological approaches adopt hard or radical determinism it's because they're arguing from an extreme position in the first place. The versions of behaviourism put forward by Watson and Skinner were extreme in that they denied the contribution of any internal factors to human psychology at all, as well as adopting extreme positions on determinism. Arguably with the development of cognitive psychology a more complex and interactionist picture of human psychology emerged.

Although we noted before that an interactionist approach can still be just as deterministic as either an extreme nature or nurture position, cognitive psychology at least seems to have chosen to focus on active, adaptive and creative aspects of human beings. So the cognitive approach stresses that humans are actively involved in the processes of acquiring and applying knowledge; they decide to attend to some stimuli rather than others in the environment, and they often choose which things they want or feel they need to commit to memory (Schultz & Schultz, 2004). So in contrast to the radical behaviourist position the cognitive approach seems much more open minded about the idea of human free will.

Bandura's reciprocal determinism

In Chapter 7, you may recall that we introduced the social cognitive theory (Bandura, 1989). Bandura proposes a form of soft determinism that takes into account the importance of reinforcement, as suggested by behaviourism, but also recognises how internal cognitive processes and thoughts are both shaped and impact on environments. This is called reciprocal determinism and it stresses that just as thoughts and behaviours have causes, so do environments. Some of the things that can shape environments include how people reflect and regulate their thoughts, how they identify and refine their skills and what actions they choose to perform. Just as environments can determine thoughts and behaviours, self-generated thoughts can also determine behaviours and behaviours can then have various and varying effects and consequences on different environments.

Bandura also argues that spontaneous and creative thoughts and behaviours are possible within this version of determinism. Interaction with various environments and the capacity of the human cognitive system to store, reflect on and manipulate data means that it's possible for people to come up with novel ideas and if novel ideas can be carried out (which will of course depend on the person's capabilities and how much freedom is allowed within the particular environment they find themselves in), then this can lead to innovative actions.

Whilst the behaviourism of Watson and Skinner assumed that people were greatly limited by their past actions and the environments they were exposed to, Bandura's model – which sees a number of causal links between the person's attitudes, personality and cognitive skills, their behaviour and their environments – allows humans much greater freedom to potentially transcend their past experiences. This doesn't mean that everyone will be able to do this all the time, but nevertheless it does allow for greater human agency and free will than some of the more inflexible and radical forms of determinism discussed earlier.

Bandura's ideas are much more rooted in scientific ideas and well-established psychological principles than those of the humanistic approach, but nevertheless they still allow for some of the ideas of free will, intentionality, autonomy and agency that the humanist psychologists consider to be so essential to any complete scientific picture of human psychology. It's possible that Bandura's particular form of soft determinism could give us a clearer idea about how exactly free will can be accounted for within a deterministic framework.

We'll finish this section of the chapter with a summary of where the different approaches stand with regard to the free will and determinism debate – see the 'In summary box 4'.

In summary box 4

Behaviourist approach:

- Traditionally argues much more for determinism than free will
- Because of the focus on behaviour being shaped and determined by environments, this approach is associated with environmental determinism
- Skinner argued for an extreme version of environmental determinism, called radical determinism, which completely denies the concept of free will
- Problems with radical determinism include: it ignores our everyday subjective experience that we have free will; it is not falsifiable; it implies that we just passively respond to environments
- Bandura's social cognitive theory proposes reciprocal determinism, which acknowledges behaviourist principles but allows for the possibility of free will through the way that people interact with and interpret environments

Biological approach:

- Tends to argue more for determinism than free will
- Proposes that behaviours are caused by a combination of genetics, environment and interaction between the two, plus acknowledges that certain behaviours can be caused or occur through biological processes, without conscious control or intention; therefore this approach is associated with genetic or, more broadly, biological determinism
- Even within biological approaches it may be possible to have a form of soft determinism – human thought and behaviour may be determined by biological factors, but this doesn't always rule out free will or choice

Cognitive approach:

- Tends to argue for some form of free will, though still acknowledges importance of determinism
- Although genetics, biology and environment all influence the cognitive system, this approach stresses how active involvement, choice and creativity are involved in much of human cognition
- Therefore proposes a form of soft determinism

Humanist approach:

- Strongly argues for the concept of free will, though doesn't deny that other things may contribute to or frustrate free choice
- Focuses on value of subjective human experience, which suggests we do have free will
- As a therapeutic approach it stresses that people are fundamentally free to make their own choices and they should always be viewed in this way

Psychodynamic approach:

- Traditionally argues much more for determinism than free will
- Because of the focus on instinctual drives and unconscious forces and conflicts influencing human thought, personality and behaviour, this approach is associated with psychic determinism
- Freud was particularly focused on determinism, stressing the influence of sexual instincts and key events in early childhood, though he did think psychoanalysis could help people to change
- Later psychodynamic theories focus less on infantile sexuality, considering the impact of other instincts and social and cultural factors throughout the lifespan, but still favour psychic determinism to some extent
- It is particularly difficult to falsify psychic determinism

Why is free will important?

For much of this chapter we've focused on the issue of whether free will really exists and, for the most part, the assumption has been that it's important to believe that humans do have such a capacity. Skinner, on the other hand, argued that free will is an illusion that we would be better off without. But this raises an interesting related question – we don't know for certain whether free will really exists, but does it matter if we believe in the concept or not? Recent research from Vohs and Schooler (2008) suggests that whether we believe in free will or determinism could actually affect our sense of moral responsibility. You can read about this research in 'In focus box 11'.

In focus box 11

Determinism, particularly the more radical forms of it, may imply that what we do doesn't really matter because everything is predetermined anyway, so perhaps if people lost their belief in free will this would lead to a decline in moral behaviours. Vohs and Schooler were interested to see if otherwise honest and moral people would lie and cheat if their beliefs about free will were manipulated.

They carried out two experiments, the first of which involved participants being randomly assigned to one of two conditions. In one condition participants read an excerpt of a book about consciousness that suggested that rational people, including most scientists, now realise that free will is merely an illusion that is produced by the brain's biochemistry. In the other condition participants read a neutral excerpt also about consciousness but where there was no mention of free will.

In this first experiment the participants were given a computer-based mental arithmetic task and were told about a glitch with the programme that meant that effectively they could cheat whilst performing the task. They were also told that the experimenters would not know if they had cheated but they were encouraged to be honest. In reality the computer programme actually recorded the number of times that they cheated. The group that had read the anti-free-will text were found to be more likely to cheat than those who had read the more neutral text. In addition, the weaker people's beliefs were that personal behaviour is determined by one's own free will, the more often they were likely to cheat. However, in this first experiment cheating occurred through the participants not doing anything (they knew that by not pressing a button the answer to the question would be revealed to them) so the researchers wanted to see if the same effects would be found when participants had to carry out an active behaviour, which meant there was less ambiguity that what they were doing was deliberately cheating.

In the second experiment another group of participants were randomly assigned to conditions where they were either presented with a series of neutral statements (containing content unrelated to the free will versus determinism debate), statements that suggested it was possible to exert free will, or statements that stressed determinism. All participants were then given a very difficult cognitive test, which they scored themselves, and were instructed to take a monetary reward, the value of which was supposed to reflect the number of questions they'd got right; in order to do this they had to walk across the room and take the appropriate amount of money out of an envelope. However, during the scoring and reward stage the experimenter was purposely not present and as the answer sheets were immediately shredded after the scoring it was quite possible for participants to take more money than they should have done based on their actual score. Participants who had read the deterministic statements took more money, on average, than those in the other groups, suggesting that they were more likely to deliberately take money dishonestly – to claim that they had answered more questions correctly than they really had and 'reward' themselves accordingly.

Overall, these two experiments suggest that merely reading material that heavily endorses a deterministic perspective can affect people's attitudes and their subsequent behaviour. It's possible that a belief in determinism can undermine certain aspects of moral behaviour, which might have consequences if psychology, or science more generally, communicates ideas about determinism to the general public. Vohs and Schooler note that they only studied two aspects of modestly immoral behaviour and that the adoption of a deterministic viewpoint may have any number of effects, and they may not all be negative. Nevertheless, if deterministic messages can have negative impacts of the kind described in this study, then psychologists definitely need to consider this as they continue to wrestle with issues of free will and determinism. It's possible that whether we have free will or not is actually less important than whether we think we do.

Conclusions

It's perhaps not surprising that most humans believe that they have free will because this matches with their subjective experiences, and it's also a rather comforting belief. Intuitively we believe that we're free to choose our own course of action, make our own decisions and determine our own lives. However, our scientific understanding of the world suggests that our supposed freedom can operate only within certain limits – we cannot deny the influences of biology, past learning or of our brain's unconscious functioning.

It seems that despite our desire to believe in freedom we must accept some form of determinism. The question perhaps is not whether our actions are entirely free or entirely determined by other factors, but rather what is the balance between the two, and do different aspects of who we are differ in the extent to which they are determined? Therefore, we don't have to follow Skinner's line of argument and deny notions of free will entirely – some form of soft or reciprocal determinism may still be possible, which would allow us to have our cake and (choose to) eat it, though the precise details are at present not fully clear.

Pinker (2003) acknowledges that determinism is not a popular idea for people, but he warns that just because we don't like an idea doesn't mean that the idea is incorrect: we may not like the idea that we have limited or no control over our lives but this in itself is not a reason for theories based on determinism to be dismissed. In addition, as Blackmore (2003) notes, the feeling that we have free will is not in itself convincing evidence that we really do. However, as noted before, notions of free will seem to be deeply ingrained within us. Skinner considered free will to be an illusion, but again as Blackmore notes, describing something as an illusion doesn't mean that it doesn't exist; after all illusions can still have very powerful effects on us. The research from Vohs and Schooler (2008) reported in the Section 'Why is free will important?' suggests that beliefs and information about free will and determinism could have important real-world implications and psychologists need to consider this.

With that in mind, I'll finish this chapter by leaving you with something to think about – a quote from the psychologist Daniel Wegner: 'The fact is, it seems to each of us that we have conscious will. It seems we have selves. It seems we have minds. It seems we are agents. It seems we cause what we do. Although it is sobering and ultimately accurate to call it an illusion, it is a mistake to conclude that the illusion is trivial.' (Wenger, 2002, quoted in Blackmore, 2003, p. 136)

◉ Further reading

Bandura, A. (1989). Human agency in social cognitive theory. *American Psychologist, 44*(9), 1175–1184.

Blackmore, S. (2003). *Consciousness: An introduction.* Oxford: Hodder & Stoughton. Chapter 9 specifically relates to issues of agency and free will, though actually free will is addressed throughout the book.

Chapter 9

Reductionism

One of the things that students seem rather prone to say when criticising certain theories or approaches within psychology is that they are reductionistic. In fact some may argue that what we discussed Chapter 8, how certain approaches try to explain away free will, could be one example of reductionism. But what exactly is reductionism and are students correct to use the term in such a disparaging way? In this chapter we will answer both those questions, in an attempt to establish both the merits of and the problems with reductionism when used within psychology.

What is reductionism?

Psychological phenomena are complex and involve different processes and stimuli. Think of something as relatively simple as a handshake: we can think of what happens at the cultural level, the social rules that underlie when we shake hands, under what circumstances and who with; we can look at the behavioural level, of the rewards that can be gained from shaking hands, or the negative things that can happen that might make us reluctant to shake hands with certain people or under certain circumstances; we can look at the cognitive processes, such as having our attention drawn to an outstretched hand, recognising the person's face and knowing that this is someone we want to shake hands with, and the form of memory that enables us to remember the physical actions that underlie the social ritual of handshaking; and we can consider what brain processes are involved in initiating the hand movement, guiding it towards the other person's hand and grasping it with just the appropriate amount of force. So even with this one single social act there are multiple levels of explanation, including some that haven't been specifically referred to (e.g., we could ask what is happening at the chemical level in the bodies of the two people who are shaking hands).

That there are so many different levels to even simple phenomena is one of the things that can make psychology so interesting. On the other hand, it can be difficult to know which of the levels are most important to help us understand the behaviour we are looking at, and which are largely irrelevant.

For example, if we want to know why two people might shake hands, there's probably not a lot of point studying the chemical processes that cause neurons to communicate to enable one person to move their hand to that of someone else. But similarly, if we're interested in what processes of the brain and nervous system are involved in voluntarily shaking someone's hand in contrast to what happens when we pull our hand away automatically from a hot object, then studying the activity of neurons might be helpful in a way that studying the cultural traditions of the two people involved would not be.

According to Luria (1987), the tradition of reductionism began in science in the nineteenth century, particularly within biology. It was noted by certain scientists that it was possible to study and explain complex phenomena, such as the laws of living organisms, by reducing their complexity to separate and simpler parts, such as the study of separate cells in the body. This is basically what reductionism is: taking a complex process or phenomenon, which may be hard to study because of the context it's found in (such as the social context of a behaviour), and instead reducing it to some 'lower' or more simple level. For example, we might try to study and explain a particular set of behaviours of an animal by looking at levels of activity of a particular hormone released into that animal's bloodstream.

You might wonder why scientists would want to use reductionism. The main reasons are to provide a degree of clarification and simplification to apparently complex processes. As we've already noted, there are many possible levels of explanation and some scientists and psychologists question whether we need all of them and whether some just lead to unnecessary confusion or over-complication.

Part of the problem with social science explanations, such as psychological or sociological explanations, is that they can seem quite vague, and/or there may be many competing theories with no obvious way of testing which one is correct. This can partly be explained by the fact that social sciences are less well established so there is often an assumption that sciences such as physiology, which have much longer histories and greater prestige, would provide better explanations of the same phenomena. Through reductionism it is often argued that it's possible to get to the heart of the specific problem by finding the single lower level explanation that accounts for the various higher level psychological or sociological explanations and which may also be easier to test, verify or falsify scientifically.

Because reductionism focuses on trying to find simpler explanations based on breaking down complex phenomena into component parts, it is often contrasted with the notion of **holism**. Holism focuses on whole phenomena and is not really interested in studying their isolated parts but instead stresses the need to understand the complex interactions that take place. You might be wondering whether either one of the two approaches is better. You might also be wondering which is the more appropriate for psychology. We'll address this within the Section 'Is reductionism appropriate for psychology'.

Is reductionism appropriate for psychology?

Because reductionism was seen to be a popular and successful approach to biological processes and phenomena in the nineteenth century it's perhaps not surprising that it was also influential for the recently developed science of psychology. It was particularly important for the behaviourist approach, which offered an early example of reductionism in psychology.

Pavlov, Watson and Skinner all attempted to reduce animal and human behaviour to the laws of conditioning. The behaviourists argued that reference to vague mentalistic terms such as consciousness, mind and thinking obscured the scientific truth that undoubtedly lay beneath human behaviour and instead they sought the patterns of stimulus–response units that could be described much more objectively. If all behaviour could be reduced to the same basic elements, then this meant that psychologists could conduct laboratory experiments on all human behaviours, no matter how complex they might seem to be within a wider social context. As Schultz and Schultz (2004) put it, the behaviourists wanted psychologists to be able to study behaviour in a similar way to how biologists were studying living organisms and how physicists were studying the universe: by the breaking down the complex into its component parts, whether that meant cells, atoms or stimulus–response units.

It has to be said that the behaviourists were relatively successful in reducing assorted behaviours to combinations of various lower level motor, reflex or glandular responses to environmental stimuli, and in identifying the general rules of classical and operant conditioning that could explain how many associations between stimuli and responses were formed. However, as we've noted elsewhere throughout this book, the behaviourist approach has its limitations. It's highly questionable to suggest that the entire wealth of human behaviour can be reduced meaningfully in this way.

For example, back in Chapter 5 we discussed how Skinner had argued that even the full flexibility and creativity of human language could be reduced to the level of three basic behaviourist principles: imitation, reward and punishment. We noted then, via Chomsky's critique of Skinner's ideas, that although such processes might contribute to the learning and shaping of language, to reduce the entirety of human language acquisition to those processes alone vastly oversimplifies and underrates the complexity of what is going on within a child's brain. We'll be expanding on the problems that can occur with reductionism later in the chapter.

It's worth noting that the behaviourist idea that all behaviour could be studied through laboratory experiments led to a form of reductionism that doesn't just apply to behaviourism but to much of psychology. This is **experimental reductionism**; a methodological assumption that argues it is acceptable to study psychological processes by selecting a particular variable that is thought to affect behaviour and to study that variable in isolation under controlled laboratory conditions.

Such an approach has enabled psychologists to focus on specific psychological concepts in some detail and to accurately measure or carefully observe them, by controlling for confounding variables and minimising the possibility of random error. However, as Coolican (1999) has noted, the level of control that is provided by reducing complex psychological phenomena to individual variables in a laboratory could be argued to come with a cost. It's debatable how much these studies, carried out in artificial settings, tell us about the behaviour when it is taken out of its original social context.

On the other hand, it's worth noting that psychological research carried out in laboratories is far from meaningless: such research tests very specific hypotheses in a controlled way, and if hypotheses are supported then they can be tested again in other laboratories, to see if they are replicable. If there are concerns about how well the results relate to 'real' behaviour outside of the laboratory, then further studies can be carried out that do focus on the same variables but within their broader social context, therefore taking a more holistic approach.

This may involve carrying out studies 'in the field', in more naturalistic settings, and may also involve gathering qualitative data, which as we noted back in Chapter 2, are not reduced to a numerical form but represent information that seeks to gain the perspective or experience of the person within their everyday life, for example via open-ended questionnaires or getting people to fill in a diary. Such research comes with its own risks and weak points, which inevitably stem from and contrast with the strengths of the laboratory experiments: there is less control of extraneous and confounding variables and results can be harder to replicate.

In this way, however, the two broad types of methodology can be seen as complementary: both have potential strengths and weaknesses but with an awareness of these it's possible to study the same psychological phenomena in multiple ways and then compare, contrast and, where possible, combine the results and achieve a more meaningful understanding. Clearly experimental reductionism has a valuable place in psychology but to be certain that the psychological phenomena being studied are relevant to what actually happens in real life the potential artificiality of lab experiments needs to be considered and such research should be supplemented by other more holistic methods.

Reductionism within the cognitive approach

The cognitive approach has also been accused of displaying aspects of reductionism, including experimental reductionism. A very large proportion of the research carried out within cognitive psychology uses experiments in which conditions and variables are carefully controlled, and where participants are often responding to stimuli on a computer screen and pressing buttons. The problems here are similar to those identified for the behaviourist approach and experimental reductionism.

When people use their cognitive skills in the real world they are operating within a particular social environment, usually with the intention of performing a particular task and knowing that their behaviour will impact on their environment. The real world is messy and complicated but cognitive psychology experiments usually simplify and control events so that the participant is presented with a limited array of choices all determined by the experimenter (Eysenck & Keane, 1995). By necessity this limits what we can learn from these experiments because we know little about what normal processes occur when a person is performing naturally in a complex social environment, where stimuli can appear entirely unexpectedly, can vary greatly in terms of their emotional impact and physical intensity, can have more or less relevance to short-term and long-term goals, and can vary in a number of other socially and cognitively significant ways.

In more recent years cognitive psychologists have spent more time designing experiments that better reflect real-world tasks and demands and everyday experiences, plus developments in virtual reality (computer simulated) environments mean that it's now possible for psychologists to put participants into more life-like, immersive and vivid situations where they can interact with other people (whether real or created as part of the simulation), but where the researchers still have control over most of the environmental features. In effect, psychologists can now follow their participants around a virtual environment in a way that they could never realistically do within the real world, and such techniques are being increasingly used in practical ways, such as cognitive rehabilitation following brain damage (Attree, Brooks & Rose, 2005). As the technology behind virtual reality improves, cognitive psychologists may be able to use it increasingly to study cognition in a more holistic manner but without losing the rigour and control of traditional experimental studies.

But the cognitive approach faces another issue related to reductionism, sometimes called the **'decoupling problem'** (Eysenck & Keane, 1995). The human cognitive systems work together, so that as I'm typing this sentence I am using several cognitive abilities at once – I'm producing the words that I'm trying to type, I'm also reading them back to make sure that I haven't made any mistakes and that what I'm writing makes sense, I'm using memory to recall the ideas that I want cover, and I'm also listening to music in the background so I'm trying to attend to both the music and the typing at the same time.

In addition, it's likely that our cognitive systems also interact with other psychological systems, such as systems involved in emotion and motivation. And yet when researchers want to study an aspect of a particular cognitive ability, for example memory, they usually try to focus just on the memory system, effectively attempting to decouple it from other cognitive systems, and also try to keep other psychological states, such as emotion, constant for all participants (Eysenck & Keane). The logic is that by focusing on individual parts of the cognitive system more is learnt about that specific system – an approach that has been somewhat successful. However, if cognitive systems work together with each other and with other psychological systems when performing everyday tasks, then the cognitive approach is not acquiring a complete or entirely valid understanding by focusing only on the individual components.

In fact some critics have even gone so far as to suggest that the cognitive approach is in danger of trying to reduce psychology to cognition in the same way that the behaviourists tried to reduce mental processes to the level of behaviour – both approaches are fixated on some aspects of psychology to the exclusion of others (Eysenck & Keane, 1995; Schultz & Schultz, 2004).

Reductionism within the biological approach

As noted before, reductionism appears to have started within biology and therefore it's probably not surprising to find that biological approaches within psychology have commonly been associated with reductionism. In fact, it's arguable that for some scientists the ultimate goal is to reject the mentalistic terminology of psychology and instead replace it entirely with biological or physiological concepts. In a sense, the behaviourist focus on trying to find the rules of learning that applied to all animals, combined with efforts made to explain all human behaviour by reducing it to what happens at the level of rats and pigeons, was an example of biological reductionism.

But logically enough it's more common to see biological or physiological reductionism within the biological approach to psychology. Any attempt to explain some aspect of human behaviour, personality or thinking, such as aggression or mental illness, entirely via reference to genetics or the activity of certain brain processes or functions of the body, is adopting a form of biological or physiological reductionism.

For a good example of this form of reductionism we can refer back to Chapter 5. Back then we referred to research that had linked low activity of the MAO-A gene with violent, aggressive or anti-social behaviour. But as we also noted in that chapter, later research shows why reductionism of this kind can be potentially problematic. The studies by

Caspi *et al.* (2002) and Foley *et al.* (2004) suggest that simply having low MAO-A activity does not itself correlate with violent or anti-social activity, but rather the two are only connected when the child has had a very poor quality upbringing. This shows the importance of not fixating on just one level when attempting to explain complex psychological behaviours. Similarly, we noted in the opening chapter how theories of mental illness have long focused on trying to identify the biological causes behind the disorders. You can read more about one example of this in 'In focus box 12'.

In focus box 12

An important discovery for understanding and treating depression is that neurotransmitter systems, which help to transfer messages between the billions of neurons in the human brain, do not seem to work properly in people with depression. This is supported by the fact that the most effective antidepressant drugs seem to work by changing or prolonging the activity of neurotransmitters. However, work from other approaches in psychology stresses that focusing just on the role of neurotransmitter function in depression is too narrow.

For example, Culbertson (1997) reviewed numerous major studies looking at the relationship between depression and gender in various western countries, such as America and Canada, and also in various developing countries. The review suggests that in the western countries women are twice as likely as men to report feeling depressed, whereas in the developing countries ratios vary but generally suggest no difference in rates of depression for men and women. The reasons for these gender and cross-cultural differences are still unclear but there's no particular reason to think that they can be explained in any straightforward way by the abnormal neurotransmitter functioning theory of depression.

Of course it may yet turn out that there is a very specific relationship between neurotransmitter functioning and the gender and cross-cultural differences that have been identified, but it's unlikely that focusing research just on depression at the level of neurotransmitter functioning will uncover it. It may be that psychologists need to look at both the biochemical and sociocultural levels, or it may be that they also need to address factors that occur at some other level, but either way a purely reductionistic approach doesn't appear to be appropriate in this case, or indeed in the case of most mental illnesses, which seem to involve an interaction between a number of levels and factors. As noted back in Chapter 1, the biopsychosocial model (Engel, 1977), which stresses that sociology, psychology and biology are all factors in illness (both physical and mental), seems to provide a more fruitful framework for the study of mental illness than does a reductionistic approach.

Reductionism within the other psychological approaches

As we've stressed throughout this book, the psychodynamic and humanist approaches are quite different from the other three and are certainly not so much a part of the traditional empirical/positivist nomothetic science approach to psychology. Because reductionism usually relates more to the traditional approaches to science it should not come as a surprise to find that neither the psychodynamic nor the humanist approach can be classified as reductionistic in the way that the other approaches are sometimes thought to be. Because both of these approaches basically started out as ways to view human mental health and personality neither really carries out experimental research and therefore neither could be described as displaying experimental reductionism.

The main difference between the two approaches on this particular issue is that whilst the humanist approach is perhaps the only one of the five that can be said to completely reject the notion of reductionism, it could be argued that there are some reductionistic elements to the psychodynamic approach.

For the humanistic approach, the emphasis is entirely on holism. Humanistic psychologists are entirely focused on studying the whole person within the context of their life and environment. They are totally against ideas that would be considered completely acceptable for other psychological approaches, for example they have no interest in reducing the person to the level of a participant in a carefully controlled experiment, or of considering a person to be just another animal comparable with a rat or a pigeon, or of viewing the person in terms of their brain processes, genes or hormones. It's worth remembering that this approach is not intended to be particularly scientific, rather it's an idiographic and therapeutic approach and a critical voice to what are viewed to be the dehumanising aspects of psychology. Therefore it resists reductionism because it doesn't want to break down human experience into smaller elements and potentially miss the bigger picture in the process.

Concepts within the humanistic approach are not considered reducible. Take, for example, Maslow's concept of self-actualisation, the idea that humans are motivated to realise their full potential. Humanistic psychologists argue that it's possible for a person to reach their potential if they are able to satisfy all their more basic physiological and safety needs, such as having enough to eat, having a roof over their head, being able to get sufficient sleep, being in a stable relationship and having their emotional needs met. Once those fundamental needs have been addressed the person is able to move onto 'higher' levels of functioning, at which point they become able to rise above daily pressures, accept themselves for who they are, including their shortcomings, and strive to be free and creative in all their endeavours (Cardwell, 2000).

But crucially, there is no self-actualised part of the brain that can be seen via neuroimaging – personal growth is not measurable purely in terms of neurotransmitter activity (perhaps people who achieve personal growth show changes in their neurotransmitter activity but this doesn't mean that the former is reducible or limited to the latter), and the success of humanistic therapies and achieving self-actualisation are not things that can be measured purely in terms of behavioural change: how the person feels is considered more important than how they behave. It's possible that humanistic concepts can be measured objectively, but Rogers stressed that there is one aspect that objectively focused scientific psychology cannot fully measure – the subjective feelings of the person. This is the most important part for humanistic psychologists and it cannot be broken down into measurable components.

The psychodynamic approach is somewhat different because although it considers humans beings to be complex psychological creatures dealing with unconscious conflicts based on drives and past experiences, and dynamic interactions between different aspects of the personality, it is the focus on basic animalistic drives that means that this approach can be interpreted as being somewhat reductionistic in nature.

However, this approach is not strongly inclined towards biological reductionism in the same way that biological and behaviourist approaches are. The psychodynamic components of personality – Freud's concepts of id, ego and superego – cannot be reduced to individual areas or specific parts of the brain. It may be possible to identify brain areas that are involved in primitive drives and very basic emotions, which could be associated with the id; areas that are involved in reasoning, which could be associated with the ego; and areas that are involved in guilt, remorse and social control (the ability to suppress urges that if acted upon could lead to socially unacceptable outcomes), which could be associated with the superego. In fact there is a movement that links neuroscience and psychoanalysis, imaginatively called **neuro-psychoanalysis**.

But most psychodynamic theorists would probably argue that trying to link actual brain areas to these personality components rather misses the point. What matters most is identifying the traumas or conflicts experienced in the past, which have been repressed and/or distorted by the interaction of the different components in an attempt to minimise anxiety in the short term. In the longer term, though, these repressed or distorted traumas and conflicts tend to lead to psychological distress, whether this be destructive behaviour patterns, mental health problems or **psychogenic/psychosomatic illness** (illnesses primarily caused or made worse by psychological factors). It is addressing these issues that is at the heart of the psychodynamic approach, not trying to find their biological basis.

On the other hand, however, Freud was strongly influenced by the work of Darwin (Schultz & Schultz, 2004), and it is partially Freud's focus on biological instincts and drives for food, sex and the release of frustration, which he derived from Darwin's work, that make this approach reductionistic. Although the psychodynamic approach views human beings as having multiple levels to their personalities, based on experiences throughout childhood (particularly emphasised by Freud) and the rest of the lifespan (also thought to be important by many later psychodynamic theorists), it also fundamentally argues that rather complex behaviours can be manifestations of the aforementioned primitive biological drives and of unresolved conflicts and traumas from the past. So overall, in this sense the psychodynamic approach can be considered reductionistic, particularly when contrasted with the humanistic approach, which doesn't dwell on specific repressed conflicts or biological drives, but more on the whole human being as a conscious and free agent.

👁 Problems with and alternatives to reductionism

Throughout this chapter we've stressed that reductionism became particularly popular within science during the nineteenth century and that the success of reductionism in biology meant that it has subsequently been applied to psychology, with only varying levels of success. This is an important point in itself because it shows that just because a particular method can be extremely successful in one science that doesn't automatically mean that it will be just as successful when used in another. It's also important to stress, however, that reductionism is not in itself a bad thing, though it can lead to problems, some of which we've already discussed, and we'll expand on some of these throughout the rest of the chapter.

The key thing is that reductionism is an important part of science and it can be a useful way to clarify certain scientific problems and explain them in clear and precise ways. Human beings are complicated, but nevertheless sometimes aspects of their complicated human behaviour can be explained at lower levels.

For example, there is nothing wrong with saying that some aspects of human behaviour are explainable in terms of classical and operant conditioning and that these same processes may also explain learning in other animals. Similarly, it seems likely that even a complex mental illness like depression might be partially explainable in terms of neurotransmitter activity or other biological processes. The problems tend to begin when all aspects of complex human behaviour (and indeed certain animal behaviours) are explained, or in some cases explained away, by reductionistic theories; for example, trying to explain language acquisition purely in terms of classical and operant conditioning, or trying to explain depression without considering psychological and sociocultural factors.

So reductionism can provide useful insights in psychology but it should not be thought of merely as a way of looking for explanations at lower levels (such as physiological or biological) whilst getting rid of higher levels (such as psychological and sociocultural) entirely. As Luria (1987) noted, to fully study and explain a given phenomenon or event one has to understand its rules and mechanisms but without losing any of its individual characteristics. Luria gives an example from a completely different area of science: it's possible to reduce H_2O to hydrogen and oxygen, but whereas hydrogen burns and oxygen is necessary for burning, water has neither of these properties, but it does have **emergent properties** of its own, such as liquidity, which are not present in either of its two component gases (Toates, 2004). So to understand water it's certainly not just a case of focusing on its elements separately.

Similarly, reducing complex psychological phenomena to behavioural, biological or physiological elements, and taking them out of their social context, can often be similarly unhelpful. To use a popular phrase, reductionism can lead to a case of not being able to see the wood for the trees: by studying psychological phenomena but focusing only on particular levels it's possible to lose sight of the features that are of interest in the first place, and which can only be observed at higher levels.

In addition there are many examples of emergent properties in psychology. For example, there are billions of neurons in the human brain, but human brains are intelligent whilst individual neurons are not, so it appears that intelligence is an emergent property and we may learn very little about it by looking at the activity of groups of neurons in the brain. Similarly, many psychological processes and phenomena have a social component to them, so just as we need to consider the combinations of two gasses to fully understand water, we also need to study what happens when two or more people interact – we need to consider the characteristics of the people involved, the environment they are in, and how individual characteristics and situations can interact and lead to complex social behaviours that may not be apparent when viewed in isolation.

We've discussed two extreme positions in this chapter: various forms of reductionism, displayed to some extent by the behavioural, biological, cognitive and psychodynamic approaches, and holism, argued to be the best way to view humans according to the humanist approach. It might be tempting to ask, which is the right approach, or at which level should we be looking at psychology? But of course there is no single right approach or level for every form of psychological phenomena, and indeed different levels may be appropriate for certain types of research question but not for others. It is possible for reductionism to be used unwisely, either by stretching the terms of a theory beyond the context they were originally intended for (such as Skinner's attempt to explain human language in the terms used to describe animal learning in laboratory experiments), or by focusing only on one level without considering others (by focusing on genes, hormones or neurotransmitters when talking about behaviours such as aggression, or psychological phenomena such as mental illnesses, without considering the psychological and environmental aspects which give these biological and physiological processes context and meaning).

Psychology then doesn't have to choose between the holism of the humanistic approach, which may be entirely appropriate within therapeutic environments or when looking at how human beings strive to reach their natural potential, or the various forms of reductionism offered by the other approaches, which can and have been extremely useful for studying various psychological phenomena in different ways. What seems to be most important is that psychologists use the right tools for the job; that they select the appropriate level for their particular research question, and that they avoid using reductionism excessively, bearing in mind that influences on thought and behaviour can occur at various different levels. What the discipline of psychology as a whole may need to focus on now is how it can improve the communication between psychologists working at the different levels, one of the many things we'll be referring to in the final concluding chapter of this book.

◁◉▷ Further reading

Coolican, H. (1999). *Research methods and statistics in psychology.* London: Hodder & Stoughton. This book discusses many of the issues associated with experimental reductionism, including its strengths and weaknesses plus methodological alternatives to it.

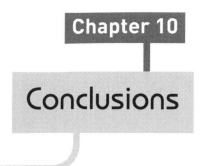

Chapter 10

Conclusions

This book has attempted what might be best considered as something of a whirlwind tour of psychology past and present. It has focused very specifically on six major issues/debates that have been around at least since the beginning of the discipline in the late nineteenth century, though in all cases the debates in some way pre-date the founding of psychology as a separate scientific discipline, and in some cases can be linked back to fundamental philosophical questions that have been discussed for thousands of years. In this sense the book has taken something of an historical approach to the issues/debates, how they have impacted on psychology and how psychologists have attempted to deal with, resolve and address them.

With each of the issues/debates there have been numerous twists, turns, developments, false dawns, new hopes and various proposed solutions in the last 150 years or so. Overall, I think the book has provided evidence that psychology has made real progress during that time, for each of the six issues/debates. Arguably there has been more progress in some areas than others, but this is only to be expected, particularly for a young proto science like psychology.

◉ Where does this leave psychology?

In the introductory chapter we noted that the philosopher of science, Thomas Kuhn, argued that what a proto science needs to develop into a fully-fledged science is a unifying paradigm. Having a paradigm, Kuhn argues, is helpful because it gives scientists a clear idea about what questions need to be asked and answered, what methods are appropriate when attempting to answer the questions and how the answers might be interpreted.

We don't necessarily have to accept all aspects of Kuhn's work on sciences to see that psychology in Kuhnian terms can still be considered to be a pre-paradigmatic science. It has many aspects of a science – most psychologists form hypotheses and collect data, some use quantitative statistics to analyse their data, others use robust qualitative methodologies to do so, theories are developed that attempt to account for and explain the patterns of data, and psychologists publish their findings and interpretations in journals that are often reviewed by their peers – but it still does not have a unified paradigm. Whether psychology will ever develop a unified paradigm, and for that matter whether it really needs one, are questions well beyond the scope of this book, but I think it's safe to say that what psychology does have instead are a number of fairly distinct approaches. We've discussed five of them in this book (it may be argued that there are more than this, but here we've focused on what are probably regarded to be the five most significant and long-lasting approaches from the last century) and where appropriate we've considered their stances on the six aforementioned issues/debates.

The merits and disadvantages of multiple approaches

At times having five distinct approaches has been an advantage for psychology and each of the approaches has made important contributions to the development of the subject. For example, the behaviourist approach brought increased scientific rigour, clearer definitions and greater objectivity to psychology and identified important methodologies and laws of learning that apply to humans and animals.

The biological approach has been a fruitful source of theories and has grounded psychology within important developments that have taken place in biology and medicine – our understanding of thought, emotion and behaviour has been greatly improved via developments in evolutionary theory, ethology, behavioural genetics and brain imaging, to name but a few examples.

Cognitive psychology incorporated numerous trends from within psychology itself and from areas as diverse as physics, linguistics and computer technology to create a new metaphor for the mind, which in turn allowed concepts such as consciousness, free will, thinking and imagination to be considered acceptable again as research topics following the period in which behaviourism had dismissed them as unscientific. The rise of cognitive psychology also saw a move away from the extreme environmentalism and radical determinism of the behaviourist approach.

Humanistic psychology has provided an important voice to argue for certain key notions and concepts that have sometimes been ignored or downgraded by other approaches – the fundamental rights for respect and dignity that have fed into ideas about research ethics, plus the importance of subjective experience, free will, personal growth and studying human beings holistically.

And psychodynamic theories have explored the murky depths of consciousness, considered the roles of traumatic events and unconscious and subconscious forces and components on our day-to-day lives, and speculated about how biological needs, societal rules and our attempts to balance and satisfy the two can shape our personalities or hinder our mental health in ways that we may not even realise.

Psychology then is an immensely diverse subject and having multiple approaches can sometimes open up debates, raise alternative possibilities, bring in new ideas, or enable a problem to be seen from a different and potentially very important perspective.

On the other hand, at times having five different approaches has perhaps hindered the development of psychology, like five people in a room all trying to solve the same problem but all speaking a different language and having a slightly different idea of what the problem is and how it might be solved. Under circumstances such as this you might expect progress to be slow and for there to be miscommunication, frustration and confusion, and this has often been the case with the history of psychology. When psychologists have compartmentalised and clearly defined themselves as being part of one approach or another it's sometimes led to inter-group conflict rather than Plato's notion of synthesis, and in some cases this has led to deeply entrenched and extreme views, which in turn has sometimes led to stagnation rather than progress.

It's impossible to say for certain whether psychology might, under different circumstances, have developed a unified Kuhnian paradigm at any point within the last 150 years and whether by doing so the subject might have made more progress with regard to the issues and debates covered in this book. Certainly Kuhn's ideas about science seem to imply that psychologists within a unified paradigm would have reached more of a consensus about the use and meaning of different terminology within the field (behaviourists, cognitive psychologists and psychodynamic thinkers all have very different conceptions of the meaning and value of the word consciousness) and about some of the fundamental points that feature in the different debates.

But on the other hand, it is also possible that some of the disagreements between the approaches might actually have been beneficial – through some psychologists clearly and strongly defining their positions it's enabled other psychologists to develop counter-arguments or alternative theories, and as we have seen over time in some areas of psychology there has been a move towards synthesis, compromise and interaction.

What progress has been made within the different issues and debates?

It's possible to see that there has been considerable progress and development in psychology since Wundt's founding of the discipline. In fact if Wundt were alive today to see contemporary psychology it's likely that he would barely recognise it.

1. Ethical issues in psychology

There were not really any major ethical issues in psychology in Wundt's day. Because consciousness was considered to be a uniquely human phenomenon and psychology was the science of consciousness this meant that animal ethics were not really an issue at first. As for the early experiments carried out on humans, these largely involved participants describing their sensations and internal experiences of the physical properties of various stimuli (such as reflecting on their size, intensity and duration), but also included measurements of reaction times, attention, emotional responses to stimuli, and word association (Hothersall, 2004; Schultz & Schultz, 2004). Such experiments were probably rather long-winded and repetitive, possibly even tiring and dull, but for the most part there would have been few ethical concerns.

However, as the scope of psychological research broadened, humans and animals were studied and experimented on in various ways. Animals were subjected to pain, deprivation, stress, and in some cases were killed as part of the research process. Humans were being interviewed and observed, and in certain experiments were sometimes deceived and placed under intense emotional distress. It became increasingly obvious that ethical standards were needed and professional psychological bodies responded by drawing up principles and codes of conduct.

Current ethical standards are extremely high, though debates and dilemmas still remain: animal rights activists still question the merits of animal experimentation, some psychologists argue that ethical restrictions and the bureaucracy associated with applying for ethical approval can greatly impede the progress of research, and new frontiers of research and advances in technology (e.g. research into virtual worlds and social networking sites) create new ethical issues that psychologists and ethical bodies are having to continually come to grips with. However, with research comes responsibility and psychology recognises this now more than ever.

2. The nature and nurture debate

Considerable progress has also been made in understanding the so-called nature versus nurture debate. At the start of the twentieth-century psychology was apparently dominated by controversial extremes – the dubious eugenics movement and the extreme environmentalism of the radical behaviourist school. Since then psychology has, for the most part, moved increasingly towards a much more interactionist position and it's no longer a case of adopting one side or the other: it's now widely acknowledged that both genes and environment are important determinants of behaviour, plus they interact in various and complex ways. The precise contributions of the two are still not entirely clear for the various different aspects of mind and behaviour, but behavioural genetics has provided psychologists with an excellent method that may give them every opportunity to find out. However, psychologists still need to remember that the roles of nature and nurture are not simply part of an abstract conundrum – there can be political and social ramifications of research in this area too.

3. Gender and cultural bias

Psychology has also come a long way from its origins as a science dominated by white male middle-class Europeans and Americans studying a combination of rats, pigeons and white male middle-class university students in laboratories. Progress has been slow in reducing bias, discrimination and stereotyping within psychology, and within education and science more generally, but it's probably fair to say that there are now far fewer obstacles to studying psychology and those that do exist are not directly related to sexual or racial discrimination. Two very important developments of the twentieth century – feminist and cross-cultural psychology – helped psychology as a whole to become more considerate of groups outside of the white male western middle-class norm that greatly dominated the early stages of the subject.

Feminist psychology has emphasised the roles and contributions of women to the discipline and has attempted to identify and reduce examples of gender bias in theories, and in terms of what research is carried out and who is studied. Women are no longer denied access to psychology and they no longer represent a small but barely tolerated minority. In fact, quite the opposite can be said to be the case – there are now large numbers of women within all branches and approaches within psychology, and many of them have achieved high levels of prominence and success. In addition, a study of psychology databases that was carried out by Hoffman and Quinton (1996) compared references to men and women authors for the period of 1974–1994 and found that there were almost twice as many references to women (66%) as there were to men (34%).

This is not to say that gender bias has been entirely removed from psychology, just as it hasn't been entirely removed from wider society either, and a lot of past research and theory that is still used within psychology today may show signs of gender bias. In addition, although many women have more power in psychology today it's still essential that all women are represented in and by the discipline – both who is doing the research and who is being researched. Therefore it may still be necessary to focus more on certain sub-groups of women who could still be neglected or underrepresented within psychology, such as women within certain cultures or women of lower socioeconomic status.

Psychology is also no longer as ethnocentric a discipline as it once was. In Wundt's time the general assumption was that psychology should be looking for the universal laws that explain the psychological processes of all people, and which apply equally in all parts of the world and across all time periods. But Wundt himself had recognised the importance of cultural and temporal differences, demonstrated by his ten-volume work *Völkerpsychologie*, which basically translates as cultural or ethnic psychology, published between 1900 and 1920 (Hothersall, 2004; Schultz & Schultz, 2004). Despite Wundt's significance as the founder of psychology this substantial body of work was largely dismissed and forgotten about by psychologists and historians of psychology, perhaps because it was not considered to be in keeping with the trends of the time – that is, to find the generalisable laws that were expected to apply equally to all animals and humans. As we showed in Chapter 7, it took a long time for psychology to reverse that trend, and even now most psychologists tend to carry out research within their own cultures for largely pragmatic reasons: cross-cultural research can be time-consuming and expensive plus it can create assorted methodological challenges. There is perhaps a justifiable concern amongst psychologists that although the current reliance on data from western cultures is not ideal it is better than a situation where cross-cultural research is carried out but is carried out badly and/or insensitively. But as with gender bias, progress in this area has occurred over the past few decades because psychologists are aware that cultural bias exists and that it can affect thoughts and behaviours in numerous and subtle ways. There is clearly much more important and critical work to be done in the cross-cultural field but arguably cultural variations are now at least considered within every major approach to psychology.

4. Determinism and free will

It's fascinating to look at the free will versus determinism debate in psychology because it's not really clear just how much progress has been made, in part because of the philosophical conundrum that still surrounds the notion of free will. Most humans would probably profess to have free will, or at least feel as though they do, and yet science seems uncertain as to whether true free will is even possible, which puts psychology in rather a difficult position.

There do seem to be genuine objections to notions of radical determinism, which go beyond the mere subjective feeling that it cannot be true, and so the current compromise position adopted by most contemporary psychologists seems to involve arguing for some variation on the idea of soft determinism, though the precise form that this might take still seems to be unclear.

One particularly interesting contribution to this debate is the Vohs and Schooler (2008) study reported in Chapter 8, which suggests that a person's belief in free will, or otherwise, is not arbitrary but may have real-world consequences. This is important because it suggests that whatever further progress is made by psychologists in understanding free will and determinism they have a responsibility to consider the impact of such progress on individuals and societies. You may recall that Freud (1917) suggested there had been three great shocks to the collective human ego – the Copernican discovery that humans are not at the centre of the universe, the Darwinian demonstration that humans are evolved from 'lower' animal species, and Freud's suggestion that our apparently rational selves are in fact strongly influenced by unconscious forces. Any suggestion that human beings genuinely have no free will would surely add a fourth equally intense shock to that list.

5. *Reductionism*

Reductionism has been considered to be a successful approach within various sciences, which has led some psychologists and psychological approaches to assume that the same principle is appropriate and should be applied to psychology. It's worth stressing that reductionism can be successfully used to focus on certain phenomena in great detail and to simplify our understanding of certain processes at certain levels of analysis. The problem is that sometimes this simplification and detail come at a cost, either because multiple levels of analysis are important and different details can emerge at different levels, or because the different levels can interact, again possibly leading to emergent psychological properties, or simply because thoughts and behaviours usually occur within a context and when they are studied in a different or supposedly 'neutral' context it's possible that the findings are not entirely valid.

This doesn't mean that reductionism is never useful or valid as part of psychology, nor does it mean that the holistic view taken by the humanistic approach is the only right way to view people or to study psychology, but rather that it's 'horses for courses': both reductionism and holism have their place within psychology but which is more appropriate is likely to depend on the specific phenomenon being studied and the specific research question that is being asked.

It certainly seems that at this point in the development of psychology reductionism should not be considered the overall end goal of the discipline and that for many psychological phenomena consideration of context, looking at how the phenomena can be explained at different levels and by different approaches, and also encouraging collaborative work between psychologists working at these different levels and within these different approaches, may represent fruitful directions for current and future work.

This idea is exemplified by the biopsychosocial model (Engel, 1977), which was referred to back in the very first chapter. As we noted then, this model has been criticised because it doesn't clearly specify exactly how these biological, psychological and sociological factors should be looked at and how exactly they are thought to interact. However, perhaps this simply reflects where psychology is in its development at the moment – without a unifying paradigm there are a large number of psychologists collecting and analysing a lot of data within a number of different approaches. How exactly these different approaches and levels fit together, and whether they even can, is still unclear, but if they are only ever considered separately, then these are questions we may never be able to answer.

The future

Predicting the future can be a dangerous business so I'm reluctant to say too much here. Given how much psychology has changed within the past 150 years, it would be difficult to envisage exactly how psychology might look in another similar period of time. But it is possible to consider recent trends in psychology that relate to the five approaches to psychology discussed in this book and these may indicate something about the near future of the subject.

The behaviourist approach

This approach was dominant in psychology, particularly in America, for much of the twentieth century, but its prominence has declined in recent decades, and this is particularly true for the more radical forms of behaviourism. This approach's extreme and inflexible position on several of the issues and debates covered in this book no doubt hastened its decline. The principles of classical and operant conditioning are accepted, have been studied widely and repeatedly and are still applied to practical fields such as animal training, education and clinical psychology.

But much of the recent progress in this approach has overlapped with developments within the cognitive approach, for example cognitive-behavioural therapy, which obviously incorporates principles from both approaches to treat anxiety and depression, and also Bandura's social cognitive theory, which emphasises internal mental concepts and the interaction between the individual and their environment, to give a more comprehensive and interactionist, and a less reductionistic and deterministic view of psychology than the one put forward by Watson and Skinner.

So the behaviourist approach has left behind an important legacy for later psychologists, which has helped us to understand how animals and humans learn, and many of the research findings of this approach are still widely accepted and form part of the knowledge base of contemporary psychology. However, interactions with cognitive psychology mean that radical behaviourist ideas are no longer favoured and are unlikely to resurface in psychology any time soon.

The cognitive approach

The apparent decline in the behaviourist approach is partly a result of the considerable progress of the cognitive approach, which has been psychology's real success story of the past few decades. It is probably the single most dominant approach in modern psychology and although it is far from being universally accepted by all contemporary psychologists it continues to have a far-reaching influence, not only within psychology (where for example it has been influential on social psychology and approaches to mental illness), but also beyond. A key development is cognitive science, an interdisciplinary study of how humans, animals and computers process information, which has seen cognitive psychologists collaborate with linguists, neuroscientists, philosophers, anthropologists and scientists working with artificial intelligence. This is a large and fast-growing field and cognitive psychologists have a huge role to play within it.

The biological approach

This is another approach that has also become much more prominent in the past few decades as psychology has been able to draw on advances within biology, such as an improved understanding of genetics and the functioning of the brain. As we noted in Chapter 9, psychology has long been associated with biology and there has sometimes been an assumption that at some stage our understanding of biology will become so great that we will be able reduce much of what we call 'psychology' to the level of biology. It is possible that psychology, or at least certain aspects of it, will become increasingly integrated with the biological sciences and this is already happening in areas such as behavioural genetics, evolutionary psychology and cognitive neuroscience (Simonton, 2004).

It's also interesting to note that members of the general public and non-experts seem to find psychological explanations that are supported by apparent evidence from neuroscience to be more satisfying and convincing than psychological explanations presented alone even when the neuroscientific evidence is irrelevant (Weisberg *et al.*, 2008), perhaps reflecting the idea that biological data are somehow viewed to be more properly 'scientific' than psychological data are. So perhaps there is some pressure on psychologists to integrate more with the biological sciences because of the greater prestige that they seem to have with the general public. Either way, it's likely that the relationship between the biological sciences and biological psychology will continue to make for an interesting courtship in the decades to come.

The humanist approach

However, as we've noted before, there is some resistance from within certain areas of psychology to the ideas of a total integration with or a reduction to biology. Traditionally much of this resistance has come from the humanist approach, which argues that its biological counterpart focuses predominantly on the importance of studying humans objectively, whilst ignoring the value of subjective elements. The humanistic approach was particularly prominent in America in the 1950s and 1960s, challenging both the behaviourist movement and dehumanising aspects of psychology and society more generally. Its impact since then has been relatively minor, partly because when radical behaviourism declined in popularity psychology moved away from extreme environmentalism, determinism and reductionism – all the things that the humanist approach had been particularly critical of.

Nevertheless, this approach has survived and has recently had something of a resurgence in the form of **positive psychology**, which was developed by Martin Seligman in the late 1990s. Whilst traditional psychology can perhaps be accused of dwelling on negative aspects of human nature (such as mental illness and aggression), positive psychology not surprisingly seeks to emphasise positive subjective experience and aims to develop a model that highlights the aspects of being human that make life worth living – hope, wisdom, creativity, humour, spirituality, courage and responsibility (Seligman & Csikszentmihalyi, 2000). Positive psychology has captured a lot of interest and enthusiasm in the last decade or so and, as Schultz and Schultz (2004) note, it may represent the most enduring legacy of the humanistic approach. However, it also seems mindful of the criticisms that had been applied to the humanistic movement and therefore stresses that the arguments and claims made by positive psychology are derived from rigorous experimental research. So positive psychology could represent a way that the legacy of the humanistic approach is maintained without compromising the scientific rigour and professionalism that are considered so important for many psychologists.

The psychodynamic approach

And what of the psychodynamic approach? It has grown and diversified greatly since Freud's time and there are now many types of psychodynamic theories, some with little in common with Freud's original ideas and work. Any theory that focuses on the human organism as dynamic or constantly changing or in conflict, with a particular emphasis on unconscious forces, internal representations and past experiences impacting on current thinking and behaviour can be considered psychodynamic.

It can be argued that this approach has had little direct impact on mainstream psychology (and vice versa), with the two representing very different systems based on very different traditions and assumptions. Nevertheless the two have interacted on occasion, particularly in areas involving mental health. In addition, as an interest in consciousness has steadily re-emerged within psychology in recent decades, there has been a renewed focus on the idea of unconscious and subconscious influences on thinking and behaviour. Although what cognitive and biological psychologists mean by 'unconscious' may be somewhat different from what psychodynamic theorists and therapists mean by the same term, there is now at least some communication and collaboration between these different approaches as between them they continue to try to understand the more elusive aspects of the human mind.

Final thoughts

Of course in addition to the developments and possible future direction of the five major approaches identified within this book, it's worth stressing again the continuing involvement of the feminist and cross-cultural psychologies, which should not necessarily be considered as separate approaches in their own right but nevertheless both interact with each other and continue to work with and challenge the five approaches.

All of this emphasises what a dynamic and eclectic subject psychology is. Arguably psychologists are no longer as tied to a particular school of thought or approach as maybe they once were and many draw inspiration from various sources and ideas inside and even outside of psychology. This means that the issues and debates we've discussed in this book will continue to evolve and be discussed by psychologists quite possibly for several decades or more, and there will no doubt be numerous further twists, turns and developments to come.

Further reading

Seligman, M. E. P., & Csikszentmihalyi, M. (2000). Positive psychology: An introduction. *American Psychologist, 55*(1), 5–14.

Simonton, D. K. (2004). Psychology's status as a scientific discipline: It's empirical placement within an implicit hierarchy of the sciences. *Review of General Psychology, 8*(1), 59–67.

Weisberg, D. S., Keil, F. C., Goodstein, J., Rawson, E., & Gray, J. (2008). The seductive allure of neuroscience explanations. *Journal of Cognitive Neuroscience, 20*(3), 470–477.

Glossary

alpha bias   A form of gender bias in which psychological differences between men and women are exaggerated.

animal-assisted therapy   A type of therapy where animals are used to aid or support the therapeutic process. In psychology this tends to involve helping people facing loneliness, bereavement, chronic pain, depression, etc., with the animal providing companionship, affection and a focal point in their lives.

anthropomorphism   The tendency to attribute human feelings or qualities to things that are not human.

anthrozoologist   Someone who studies human–animal interactions, focusing on all aspects of the human–animal bond

back translation   A technique used by psychologists attempting to use a particular scale, questionnaire or measure for two different cultural groups who speak different languages. The scale in its original language is translated into the language of the second culture before being translated back into the original language. If the meaning of the scale is still as intended after these two translations, then it can be said to have 'translation equivalence'.

behavioural genetics   A field of study that specifically seeks to identify the roles that genes play in the behaviour of humans and other animals, to disentangle that from the contribution that environments make, and to find out in what ways the two interact. It involves contributions from geneticists, biologists, ethologists and psychologists.

behaviourist approach A psychological approach that focuses specifically on the measurement, study and causes and effects of observable behaviour, which has traditionally been less interested in non-observable mental events, often either assuming that they do not really exist or aren't important for the science of psychology.

beta bias A form of gender bias in which psychological differences between men and women are downplayed.

biological approach A psychological approach that focuses on how the functions and structures of the brain and nervous system create, influence and interact with psychological states. It considers the roles of genetic, physiological and neurobiological factors and processes in behaviour, emotion, thinking and consciousness.

biological determinism Refers to any theory or approach in which biological concepts or processes are said to determine thoughts and behaviours.

biological preparedness A term developed by Seligman (1971) that describes an organism's innate tendency to learn certain associations more easily than others because such associations have survival and/or reproductive advantages.

biopsychosocial model A model or framework developed by Engel (1977) that stresses that sociology, psychology and biology are all factors in illness (both physical and mental), and considers the role of the three types of factors, both independently and the ways they interact.

classical conditioning A learning process that occurs when two stimuli are repeatedly paired together so that a response initially only elicited by one of the two stimuli is eventually elicited by the other stimulus alone.

cognitive approach A psychological approach that defines the human mind as a type of information processor, similar to a computer, and studies the internal processes involved in thinking, problem-solving, reasoning, memory, perception and attention.

cultural bias The phenomenon of interpreting and judging psychological phenomena by standards inherent to one's own culture, or the failure to test for, consider or acknowledge the impact that culture or cultural differences might have on mental processes and behaviour.

cultural or cross-cultural psychology A form of psychology that specifically considers how people from different cultures are psychologically similar and different, and what it is about these cultures that may lead to the differences. Cultural psychology and cross-cultural psychology may be viewed as two separate approaches, with the former focusing more on what specific features of cultures may affect mental processes and behaviour in different ways, and the latter assuming that certain psychological processes might be universal and using comparisons between different cultures to test this.

culture 'The enduring values, beliefs, behaviours, and traditions that are shared by a large group of people and passed on from one generation to the next' (Passer *et al.*, 2009, p. 18).

decoupling problem A problem in cognitive psychology whereby researchers tend to focus on an aspect of a particular cognitive ability, effectively attempting to decouple it from other cognitive systems and psychological states. But if cognitive systems work together with each other and with other psychological systems when performing everyday tasks, then focusing only on the individual components may not provide a complete or valid picture of their functioning.

defence mechanisms Unconscious strategies that are designed to help the conscious mind deal with unresolved conflicts. According to psychodynamic approaches, each individual has unique childhood experiences and will develop particular patterns of defence mechanisms in response to these.

determinism Refers to the process whereby certain thoughts or behaviours cannot be said to result entirely from free will but instead are determined by external or internal factors or forces of some kind or other.

dialectic method A method of argument introduced by the ancient Greek philosopher Plato whereby two or more people with different views seek the truth by ultimately aiming to agree with each other. This method requires both parties to consider the weaknesses of their extreme positions. The end result of such a process is most commonly to achieve a synthesis or combination of the two positions, or at least to encourage the two parties to consider each other's positions.

ecological validity A form of validity for a research study. For a study in psychology to be high in ecological validity, its methods, materials and setting must approximate the real-life situation that is under investigation. A study is said to be low in ecological validity if behaviour is not studied in conditions under which it normally occurs, or if such conditions are not realistically simulated.

ego   A part of the personality according to Freud's psychoanalytic theory. It develops very early on in childhood, as the child learns that although most of its urges will be met, this will only happen under certain conditions or within certain limits. The ego's role is to perform rationally and realistically, using strategies and habits, memories of past experience and perception of the environment to mediate the demands of the pleasure-seeking id and the moralistic superego.

emergent properties   Properties that a complex system has, but which individual members of the system do not have. For example, there are billions of neurons in the human brain, but human brains are intelligent whilst individual neurons are not, so intelligence is an emergent property in this case.

emics   Psychological constructs that are particular to a specific culture and can be contrasted with etics.

environmental determinism   Refers to the idea that human beings and their behaviour are largely, if not entirely, shaped and determined by the environments they are raised in or exposed to.

etics   Psychological constructs that are believed to be universal and therefore apply to all humans regardless of culture. Can be contrasted with emics.

eugenics   An applied but controversial science originally proposed by Francis Galton that seeks to improve aspects of human nature that are determined by genetics.

experimental reductionism   A methodological assumption that argues it is acceptable to study psychological processes by selecting a particular variable that is thought to affect behaviour and to study that variable in isolation under controlled laboratory conditions.

feminist psychology   A form of psychology that focuses on trying to understand gender both within psychology and outside in the wider world, whilst broadly arguing that throughout much of its history the discipline of psychology has been dominated by males and has been carried out from a largely 'male perspective'. There are different forms of feminist psychology but what nearly all feminist psychologists have in common is that they are interested in the concept of gender and how women are affected by it.

fixed action patterns   A term developed in the science of ethology to describe behaviours in animals that appear from birth and are instinctive, not learnt, are triggered automatically by certain stimuli and usually occur in a seemingly fixed and stereotypical fashion. Such behaviours are always important for the animal's survival and may be characteristic to a particular species. Similar to the concept of instinct as devised by William James.

free will   The notion that humans respond freely, voluntarily and actively to events around them, that when they encounter or are presented with stimuli, choices or options they have the freedom to choose which to select, or in fact may choose not to select any of them at all. It assumes that we're free to select our own course of action, behave in unconstrained ways, make our own decisions and determine our own lives.

gender   As distinguished from sex, this term generally relates to the characteristics that distinguish between males and females that are not based purely on biological or physical differences. As defined by Money and Ehrhardt (1972) it refers to the psychological, cultural and behavioural differences that commonly relate to males and females.

gender bias   Refers to the treatment of men and women in psychological research and theory such that psychological differences between the two are either exaggerated or downplayed. Gender bias is often argued to take one of two different forms: alpha bias and beta bias. Those theories or approaches in psychology that exaggerate the differences are said to be examples of alpha bias, whilst those that downplay the differences are said to be examples of beta bias.

generalisation   Within the behaviourist approach, the tendency to make the same behavioural response to two similar but different stimuli.

genetic determinism   The idea that our innate biological natures, acquired from the genes we inherit from our parents, can determine or restrict our choices and behaviours, producing unavoidable and unalterable effects in our lives.

habits   Aspects of human and animal behaviour that are said not to be present at birth but are developed through experience, many of them early on in life, though new habits can be acquired and developed throughout a lifetime. They are often repetitive or established actions or patterns of behaviour. Sometimes contrasted with instincts.

holism A method and approach to studying psychological phenomena that contrasts with reductionism. Holism focuses on whole phenomena and is not interested in studying their isolated parts but instead stresses the need to understand the complex interactions that take place.

humanist approach A psychological approach that reacted to seemingly pessimistic and dehumanising trends in psychology, stressing instead the innate goodness, uniqueness and potential of human beings. It stresses that mental health and social problems can arise when human beings are denied their fundamental rights to dignity, personal growth and freedom, and emphasises the importance of human subjective experience.

id A part of the personality according to Freud's psychoanalytic theory. It acts as the source of all basic impulses and biological drives (such as eating, drinking, aggression, sex, removal of waste products) that need to be satisfied and gratified immediately and unconditionally, and are driven by a need for pleasure or, at the very least, the release of tension or the end of pain or frustration. It is the most primitive and instinctual component of human nature, it is present from birth and it is also the part of the mind that we have the least conscious awareness of. The id has no consideration of reality, values, morality or good and evil.

idiographic A term that refers to approaches in psychology that are particularly concerned with the individual, that are more interested in private and internal mental experiences, or choose to focus on what makes animals and/or people unique. Such approaches are associated with and favour qualitative methodologies. Contrasts with nomothetic approaches.

instinctive drift A concept that refers to the tendency for organisms to revert to instinctive behaviours regardless of, or that may interfere with, behaviours they have learnt through conditioning.

instincts Aspects of human and animal behaviour that are said to be present from birth due to genetic predispositions. Instinctive behaviours are likely to have evolved via natural selection because they represent behavioural adaptations to specific situations and problems related to reproduction and/or survival. They appear to emerge without instruction, experience or learning, though may be modified by such things. Sometimes contrasted with habits. Instincts are also comparable with the concept of fixed action patterns.

language acquisition device A hypothetical brain mechanism first proposed by Chomsky to explain what underlies and guides a human child's language development. This device provides the rules that underlie language, so children are born with an innate capacity to acquire language, though appropriate social interaction and environmental stimuli are required to trigger the device.

learned helplessness A concept initially identified by Seligman and Maier (1967) that describes a tendency for an organism to give up trying to avoid an unpleasant stimulus because all past efforts to do so have been unsuccessful.

meta-analysis A statistical technique in which the results of several research studies on a related research question are combined statistically.

method bias A form of bias that is particularly problematic for researchers comparing two or more different cultures. The researchers may choose a method that respondents in one of the cultures may be more familiar or comfortable with than respondents in the other cultures being studied. Differences in performance may be put down to intrinsic psychological traits or abilities of the groups rather than the bias resulting from the procedures. This can be partially addressed by familiarising participants with all procedures and tests.

nociception A neural process which involves the detection of the occurrence of damage or the presence of a noxious stimulus, which then leads to a reflexive withdrawal response.

nomothetic A term that refers to any psychological approach or method that seeks to establish or identify general patterns or laws of mental activity or behaviour, which should apply equally well to all individuals. Such approaches are associated with and favour experimental and other quantitative methodologies. Contrasts with idiographic approaches.

neuro-psychoanalysis A movement that links neuroscience and psychoanalysis.

operant conditioning A learning process in which the likelihood of a specific behaviour occurring is increased or decreased through association with positive or negative outcomes.

parapraxes The collective term in Freudian theory for apparently minor errors in language or behaviour that could be argued to indicate a repressed motive or be a result of conflict between different unconscious forces, or even between unconscious and conscious forces.

partial replication A way to verify or reinterpret the results of ethically questionable research in psychology. The features of the original experiment are replicated as closely as possible, but the specific elements that are considered unethical are removed or modified.

positive psychology A branch of psychology with its roots in the humanist approach that seeks to emphasise positive subjective experience and aims to develop a model that highlights the aspects of being human that make life worth living.

positivist-realist position A view of or within science which suggests that truth or reality can be reached through the careful application of the objective methods of science, and anyone carrying out the same methods with the same degree of care should reach the same or very similar conclusions regardless of their background.

pre-science or pre-paradigmatic A stage of scientific development proposed by Kuhn (1962) to describe a science that has yet to develop a scientific paradigm and therefore consists of a loose collection of research, ideas, speculation and theories.

psychic determinism Looks for the causes and determinants of conscious thoughts and behaviours in the unconscious influences of personality components such as the id, ego and superego and the interactions between them.

psychoanalysis A method of treatment developed by Sigmund Freud for psychological problems displayed in adulthood but rooted in childhood experiences and unconscious conflicts.

psychodynamic approach A psychological approach that emphasises the role that drives and unconscious forces play in human thought, personality and behaviour, but also a therapeutic approach that seeks to help people with a variety of psychological disorders or personal problems. In this approach all individuals experience conflict and have their personalities shaped by the opposing demands of different unconscious forces. Freud's psychoanalysis is an example of the psychodynamic approach.

psychogenic/psychosomatic illness Physical illnesses caused primarily or made worse by psychological factors.

psychotoxic effects The negative effects of a drug on personality and/or behaviour.

qualitative methodologies/data   Methods that involve collecting and interpreting in-depth data, and where establishing the meaning and context of the data are particularly important. The data are not reduced or transformed into numbers but instead the focus is usually on the language and what it means to the person using it. Examples include interviews, case studies and textual analyses.

quantitative methodologies/data   Methods applied in traditional experimental psychology that involve collecting numerical data (or other data which can be transformed into numbers) and analysed using statistics.

radical determinism   An extreme form of determinism put forward by Skinner (1971) that not only assumes that the causes of human behaviour are to be found solely within the environment but also that free will is a complete illusion.

reductionism   Taking a complex psychological process or phenomenon, which may be hard to study because of the context it's found in, and instead reducing it to some 'lower' or simpler level. Contrasted with holism.

scientific paradigm   A term developed by Kuhn (1962) to describe a set of practices and rules that define a particular science at a particular time. Established sciences, according to Kuhn, have a single paradigm, which determines what sorts of questions are asked, what sorts of things are studied, how they are studied and how the results of scientific investigations are presented and interpreted.

sex   As distinguished from the term gender, sex relates very specifically to the biological or actual physical state or category that a person anatomically or functionally belongs to. So when categorising someone as a man or woman based on the presence or absence of particular sexual/genital organs, or by whether they produce sperm or ova, we are describing their sex.

single cause fallacy   A fallacy that occurs when it is assumed that there is a single, simple cause of an outcome when in reality it may have been caused by a number or combination of different things. It is often applied to the so-called nature versus nurture debate when it is assumed that something might derive solely from either nature or nurture when it's more likely to be some interaction of the two.

social cognitive theory   A theory developed by Bandura (1989), which acknowledges the importance of behaviourist principles such as reinforcement and the impact of environments, but also recognises how internal cognitive processes can be both shaped by and impact on environments. This theory also stresses that learning occurs not just through individual behaviour but also through observing the actions of others, the consequences of those actions, and internal reflections on both the actions and their consequences.

soft determinism (or compatibilism) Refers to any attempt within psychology to accept some form of free will whilst also trying to explain this within the framework of a scientific psychology. The aim is to show that freedom of choice can be compatible with notions of causation, hence compatibilism.

superego A part of the personality according to Freud's psychoanalytic theory. It is an internalised representation of various standards of morality and ethics, set down by parents, teachers, religious organisations, the state, the law and society in general. The superego provides all the absolute rules of what should and ought to be done in various situations, and what ideals the child should aspire to, plus it condemns and seeks to deny and restrain the demands of the id through anxiety and guilt.

systematic review A method of reviewing literature in which important research in a particular area is identified, synthesised and appraised collectively.

tabula rasa A Latin term, which loosely means blank slate, used by the seventeenth century philosopher John Locke to describe the state of a child's mind at birth, suggesting that it has no in-built mental content of any kind. It is the child's experiences that imprint on the mind, enabling the acquisition of knowledge about the world and shaping or causing the child's personality, behaviour and intelligence. Commonly associated with the behaviourist approach.

theory of recollection The explanation offered by the ancient Greek philosopher Plato for apparently innate dispositions and abilities. Plato suggested that the soul was immortal and reincarnated after death in a new body, and the apparent emergence of these innate characteristics and knowledge occurred as a child remembered the stored knowledge possessed by the immortal psyche.

twin studies A type of research design in which typically the similarity of monozygotic (identical) and dizygotic (fraternal) twins for various traits and behaviours is compared. Comparisons may also be made between twins raised in the same environment and those raised in different environments.

universality The idea that the results of a study are independent of the time and place in which the study was carried out and are in no way culture bound, so that if the study was repeated in another time, place or culture the results should be the same or at least very similar.

vertebrates Animals distinguished by the possession of a backbone or spinal column, including fishes, amphibians, reptiles, birds, mammals and therefore human beings.

Zeitgeist The spirit of the times – the general cultural, intellectual, ethical and/or political mood of a particular time and place.

References

Aronson, E. (2003). *The social animal.* (9th Edition). New York: Worth Publishers.

Attree, E. A., Brooks, B. M., & Rose, F. D. (2005). Virtual environments in rehabilitation and training: International perspectives. *Cyberpsychology and Behaviour, 8*(3), 187–188.

Bandura, A. (1989). Human agency in social cognitive theory. *American Psychologist, 44*(9), 1175–1184.

Beck, H. P., Levinson, S., & Irons, G. (2009). Finding little Albert: A journey to John B. Watson's infant laboratory. *American Psychologist, 64*(7), 605–614.

Bell, D., & Kennedy, B. M. (Eds) (1999). *The cybercultures reader.* London: Routledge.

Blackmore, S. (2003). *Consciousness: An introduction.* Oxford: Hodder & Stoughton.

Buckley, K. W. (1982). The selling of a psychologist: John Broadus Watson and the application of behavioral techniques to advertising. *Journal of the History of the Behavioral Sciences, 18*, 207–221.

Burger, J. M. (2009). Replicating Milgram: Would people still obey today? *American Psychologist, 64*(1), 1–11.

Buss, D. M. (1989). Sex differences in human mate preferences: Evolutionary hypotheses tested in 37 cultures. *Behavioral and Brain Sciences, 12*, 1–49.

Cardwell, M. (2000). *The complete A-Z psychology handbook.* (2nd Edition). London: Hodder & Stoughton.

Caspi, A., McClay, J., Moffitt, T. E., Mill, J., Martin, J., Craig, I. W., Taylor, A., & Poulton, R. (2002). Role of genotype in the cycle of violence in maltreated children. *Science, 297*, 851–853.

Chalmers, A. F. (1999). *What is this thing called science?* (3rd Edition). Buckingham: Open University Press.

Chodorow, N. J. (1991). Freud on women. In J. Neu (Ed.), *The Cambridge companion to Freud.* Cambridge: Cambridge University Press.

Chomsky, N. (1959). Review of verbal behavior by B.F. Skinner. *Language, 35,* 26–58.

Collins, H. M., & Pinch, T. (1998). *The Golem: What you should know about science.* (2nd Edition). Cambridge: Cambridge University Press.

Colman, A. M. (1988). *What is psychology?* London: Hutchinson Education.

Coolican, H. (1999). *Research methods and statistics in psychology.* London: Hodder & Stoughton.

Crawford, M., & Unger, R. K. (1995). Gender issues in psychology. In A. M. Colman (Ed.), *Controversies in psychology* (pp. 37–57). London: Longman.

Crowther-Heyck, H. (1999). George A. Miller, language, and the computer metaphor of mind. *History of Psychology, 2,* 37–64.

Culbertson, F. M. (1997). Depression and gender: an international review. *American Psychologist, 52*(1), 25–31.

Darwin, C. (1859). *On the origin of species by means of natural selection.* London: Murray.

Darwin, C. (1871). *The descent of man.* London: Murray.

Darwin, C. (1872). *The expression of the emotions in man and animals.* London: Murray.

Deneau, G., Yanagita, T., & Seevers, M. H. (1969). Self-administration of psychoactive substances by the monkey: A measure of psychological dependence. *Psychopharmacologia, 16*(1), 30–48.

Engel, G. L. (1977). The need for a new medical model: A challenge for biomedicine. *Science, 196,* 129–136.

Experimental Psychological Society. (n.d.). EPS and the use of animals in psychological research. Retrieved from http://www.eps.ac.uk/index.php/use-of-animals-in-psychological-research. Accessed date: 1 March 2011.

Eysenck, M. W., & Keane, M. T. (1995). *Cognitive psychology: A student's handbook.* (3rd Edition). Hove: Psychology Press.

Fiske, A. P. (2002). Using individualism and collectivism to compare cultures: A critique of the validity and measurement of the constructs: Comment on Oyserman *et al.* (2002). *Psychological Bulletin, 128,* 78–88.

Foley, D. L., Eaves, L. J., Wormley, B., Silberg, J. L., Maes, H. H., Kuhn, J., & Riley, B. (2004). Childhood adversity, monoamine oxidase A genotype, and risk for conduct disorder. *Archives of General Psychiatry, 61*(7), 738–744.

Freud, S. (1914). *The psychopathology of everyday life.* London: Ernest Benn.

Freud, S. (1917). A difficulty in the path of psychoanalysis. In *Standard edition* (Vol. 17, pp. 136–144). London: Hogarth Press.

Freud, S. (1933). New introductory lectures on psychoanalysis. In *Standard edition* (Vol. 22, pp. 3–182). London: Hogarth Press.

Furnham, A. (1996). *All in the mind: The essence of psychology.* London: Whurr Publishers Ltd.

Galton, F. (1869). *Hereditary genius.* London: Macmillan.

Galton, F. (1883). *Inquiries into human faculty and its development.* London: Macmillan.

Greenwood, J. D. (2009). *A conceptual history of psychology.* New York: McGraw Hill.

Haney, C., Banks, W. C., & Zimbardo, P. G. (1973). A study of prisoners and guards in a simulated prison. *Naval Research Reviews, 9,* 1–17.

Hare-Mustin, R. T., & Marecek, J. (1988). The meaning of difference: Gender theory, postmodernism, and psychology. *American Psychologist, 43*(6), 455–464.

Harlow, H. F. (1958). The nature of love. *The American Psychologist, 13,* 673–685.

Harlow, H. F., Dodsworth, R. O., & Harlow, M. K. (1965). Total social isolation in monkeys. *Proceedings of the National Academy of Sciences of the United States of America, 54*(1), 90–97.

Harris, B. (1979). Whatever happened to little Albert? *American Psychologist, 34,* 151–160.

Heider, F. (1958). *The psychology of interpersonal relationships.* New York: Wiley.

Hendry, J. (1987). *Understanding Japanese society.* New York: Croom Helm.

Herzog, H. (2010). *Some we love, some we hate, some we eat: Why it's so hard to think straight about animals.* London: HarperCollins.

Hoffman, C. D., & Quinton, W. J. (1996). References on women and on men in the literature: An archival CD-ROM search. *American Psychologist, 51*(12), 1336–1338.

Hothersall, D. (2004). *History of Psychology.* (4th Edition). New York: McGraw Hill.

Hyde, J. S. (2005). The gender similarities hypothesis. *American Psychologist, 60*(6), 581–592.

Kim, U. (1995). *Individualism and collectivism: A Psychological, Cultural and Ecological Analysis.* Copenhagen: Nordic Institute of Asian Studies.

Korn, J. H., Davis, R., & Davis, S. F. (1991). Historians' and chairpersons' judgements of eminence among psychologists. *American Psychologist, 46,* 789–792.

Kuhn, T. S. (1962). *The structure of scientific revolutions.* Chicago: University of Chicago Press.

Kuhn, T. S. (1970). *The structure of scientific revolutions.* (2nd Edition). Chicago: University of Chicago Press.

Lambie, J. (1991). The misuse of Kuhn in psychology. *The Psychologist, 4*(1), 6–11.

Lea, S. E. G. (2000). Towards an ethical use of animals. *The Psychologist, 13*(11), 556–557.

Leahey, T. H. (1997). *A history of psychology: Main currents in psychological thought.* (4th Edition). Upper Saddle River, N.J.: Prentice Hall.

Lin, Y.-H., Chen, C.-Y., & Chiu, P.-K. (2005). Cross-cultural research and back-translation. *The Sport Journal, 8*(4). Retrieved from http://www.thesportjournal.org/article/cross-cultural-research-and-back-translation. Accessed date: 20 March 2011.

Lonner, W. J. (2000). On the growth and continuing importance of cross-cultural psychology. *Eye on Psi Chi, 4*(3), 22–26.

Luria, A. R. (1987). Reductionism in psychology. In R. L. Gregory (Ed.), *The Oxford companion to the mind.* Oxford: Oxford University Press.

Maccoby, E. E., & Jacklin, C. N. (1974). *The psychology of sex differences.* Stanford, CA: Stanford University Press.

Maher, J., & Groves, J. (1998). *Chomsky for beginners.* Cambridge: Icon Books.

Malinowski, B. (1929). *The sexual life of savages.* New York: Harcourt, Brace and World.

McLaren, N. (1998). A critical review of the biopsychosocial model. *The Australian and New Zealand Journal of Psychiatry, 32* (1), 86–92.

McLaren, N. (2010). *Humanizing psychiatrists*. Ann Arbor, MI: Loving Healing Press.

Milgram, S. (1963). Behavioural study of obedience. *Journal of Abnormal and Social Psychology, 67,* 371–78.

Milgram, S. (1974). *Obedience to authority*. New York: Harper and Row.

Miller, W. R., & Seligman, M. E. P. (1975). Depression and learned helplessness in man. *Journal of Abnormal Psychology, 84,* 228–238.

Money, J., & Ehrhardt, A. A. (1972). *Man and woman, boy and girl: The differentiation and dimorphism of gender identity from conception to maturity*. Baltimore: Johns Hopkins University Press.

Montuori, A., & Fahim, U. (2004). Cross-cultural encounter as an opportunity for personal growth. *Journal of Humanistic Psychology, 44*(2), 243–263.

Morgan, C. L. (1903). *An introduction to comparative psychology*. (2nd edition). London: W. Scott.

Nagel, T. (1974). What is it like to be a bat? *Philosophical review, 83,* 435–450.

O'Connell, A. N., & Russo, N. F. (1991). Women's heritage in psychology: Past and Present. *Psychology of Women Quarterly, 15,* 495–504.

Öhman, A., & Mineka, S. (2003). The malicious serpent: snakes as a prototypical stimulus for an evolved module of fear. *Current Directions in Psychological Science, 12,* 5–9.

Orr, B. (2010). Dust and ruins – and hidden treasures. Why studying the history of psychology matters. *PsyPAG Quarterly, 75,* 30–33.

Passer, M., Smith, R., Holt, N., Bremner, A., & Sutherland, E. (2009). *Psychology: the Science of Mind and Behaviour*. Berkshire: McGraw-Hill.

Paul, R. A. (1991). Freud's anthropology: A reading of the 'cultural books'. In J. Neu (Ed.), *The Cambridge companion to Freud*. Cambridge: Cambridge University Press.

Pinker, S. (2003). *The blank slate: The modern denial of human nature*. London: Penguin.

Plomin, R., & Spinath, F. M. (2004). Intelligence: genetics, genes, and genomics. *Journal of Personality and Social Psychology, 86,* 112–129.

Popper, K. (1963). *Conjectures and refutations: The growth of scientific knowledge*. London: Routledge & Kegan Paul.

Raven, J. (1962). *Colored progressive matrices*. New York: Psychological Corp.

Reason, J. (2000). The Freudian slip revisited. *The Psychologist, 13* (12), 610-611.

Reicher, S. D., & Haslam, S. A. (2006). Rethinking the psychology of tyranny: The BBC Prison Study. *British Journal of Social Psychology, 45*, 1–40.

Ridley, M. (2003). *Nature via nurture: The origin of the individual*. London: Fourth Estate.

Robinson, D. N. (1993). Is there a Jamesian tradition in psychology? *American Psychologist, 48*(6), 638–643.

Rose, J. D. (2002). The neurobehavioral nature of fishes and the question of awareness and pain. *Reviews in Fisheries Science, 10*(1), 1–38.

Schultz, D. P., & Schultz, S. E. (2004). *A history of modern psychology*. (8th Edition). Belmont, CA: Wadsworth/ Thomson Learning.

Seligman, M. E. P. (1971). Phobias and preparedness. *Behavioural and Brain Sciences, 2*, 307–320.

Seligman, M. E. P. (1975). *Helplessness: On depression, development, and death*. San Francisco: W.H. Freeman.

Seligman, M. E. P., & Csikszentmihalyi, M. (2000). Positive psychology: An introduction. *American Psychologist, 55*(1), 5–14.

Seligman, M. E. P., & Maier, S. F. (1967). Failure to escape traumatic shock. *Journal of Experimental Psychology, 74*, 1–9.

Simon, C. (2007). *Neurology*. New York: Oxford University Press.

Simonton, D. K. (2004). Psychology's status as a scientific discipline: It's empirical placement within an implicit hierarchy of the sciences. *Review of General Psychology, 8*(1), 59–67.

Skinner, B. F. (1957). *Verbal behaviour*. New York: Appleton.

Skinner, B. F. (1971). *Beyond freedom and dignity*. New York: Knopf.

Slater, M., Antley, A., Davison, A., Swapp, D., Guger, C., Barker, C., Pistrang, N., & Sanchez-Vives, M. V. (2006). A virtual reprise of the Stanley Milgram obedience experiments. *Public Library of Science One, 1*(1), e39.

Sneddon, L. U. (n.d.) Can animals feel pain? *Pain: Science, Medicine, History, Culture*. Retrieved from http://www.wellcome.ac.uk/en/pain/microsite/culture2.html. Accessed date: 20 December 2010.

Sternberg, R. J. (2004). Culture and intelligence. *American Psychologist, 59*(5), 325–338.

Sternberg, R. J., & Grigorenko, E. L. (2001). Unified psychology. *American Psychologist, 56,* 1069–1079.

Stipek, D. (1998). Differences between American and Chinese in the circumstances evoking pride, shame and guilt. *Journal of Cross-Cultural Psychology, 29*(5), 616–629.

Teigen, K. H. (2002). One hundred years of laws in psychology. *The American Journal of Psychology, 115,* 103–118.

Toates, F. (2004). Introduction to brains, mind and consciousness. In G. Bearman, R. Graham, G. Riley & P. Wardell (Eds), *From cells to consciousness.* Milton Keynes: The Open University.

Valentine, E. (2010). Women in early 20th-century experimental psychology. *The Psychologist, 23*(12), 972–974.

Vohs, K. D., & Schooler, J. W. (2008). The value of believing in free will. *Psychological Science, 19*(1), 49–54.

Wang, Q. (2001). Culture effects on adults' earliest childhood recollection and self-description: Implications for the relation between memory and the self. *Journal of Personality and Social Psychology, 81*(2), 220–233.

Watson, J. B. (1909). A point of view in comparative psychology. *Psychological Bulletin, 6,* 57–58.

Watson, J. B. (1913). Psychology as the behaviorist views it. *Psychological Review, 20,* 158–177.

Watson, J. B. (1914). *Behavior: An introduction to comparative psychology.* New York: Holt.

Watson, J. B. (1919). *Psychology from the standpoint of a behaviorist.* Philadelphia: Lippincott.

Watson, J. B. (1930). *Behaviorism.* (2nd edition). New York: Norton. (Original work published 1924).

Watson, J. B., & Rayner, R. (1920). Conditioned emotional reactions. *Journal of Experimental Psychology, 3*(1), 1–14.

Weisberg, D. S., Keil, F. C., Goodstein, J., Rawson, E., & Gray, J. (2008). The seductive allure of neuroscience explanations. *Journal of Cognitive Neuroscience, 20*(3), 470–477.

Index

Reading Guide

This table identifies where in the book you'll find relevant information for those of you studying or teaching A-level. You should also, of course, refer to the Index and the Glossary, but navigating a book for a particular set of items can be awkward and we found this table a useful tool when editing the book and so include it here for your convenience.

TOPIC	AQA(A)	AQA(B)	OCR	EDEXCEL	WJEC	PAGE
Gender	x			x	x	121
Culture	x	x	x	x	x	135
animals in research	x		x		x	2, 30, 31, 32
ethics	x	x	x	x	x	29, 60
nature/nurture	x			x		84
free will and determinism	x		x		x	152
reductionism	x		x			169
Psychology as a science	x	x	x	x	x	4
Behaviourist approach	x	x	x	x	x	21
Biological approach	x	x	x	x	x	22
Cognitive approach	x	x	x	x	x	22
Humanist approach		x				23
Psychodynamic approach	x	x		x	x	24